Engl...
Romanian-English

Word to Word™
Bilingual Dictionary

Compiled by:
C. Sesma M.A.

Translated by:
Ana Cristina Dobrin

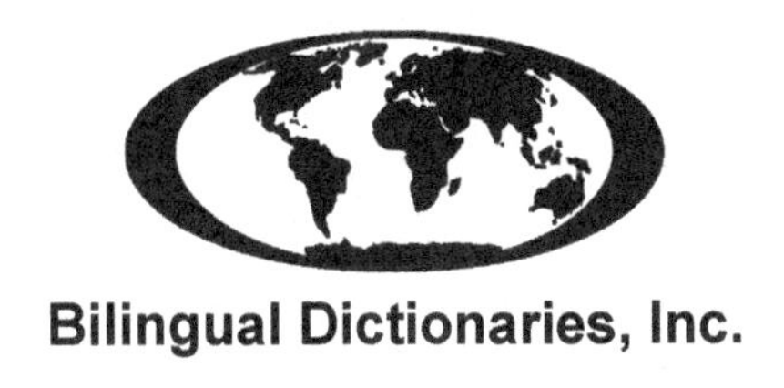

Bilingual Dictionaries, Inc.

Romanian Word to Word™ Bilingual Dictionary
1st Edition © Copyright 2008

Published in the United States by:

Bilingual Dictionaries, Inc.
PO Box 1154
Murrieta, CA 92562
T: (951) 461-6893 • F: (951) 461-3092
www.BilingualDictionaries.com

ISBN13: 978-0-933146-91-4
ISBN: 0-933146-91-4

Preface

Bilingual Dictionaries, Inc. is committed to providing schools, libraries and educators with a great selection of bilingual materials for students. Along with bilingual dictionaries we also provide ESL materials, children's bilingual stories and children's bilingual picture dictionaries.

Sesma's Romanian Word to Word Bilingual Dictionary was created specifically with students in mind to be used for reference and testing. This dictionary contains approximately 18,500 entries targeting common words used in the English language.

List of Irregular Verbs

present - past - past participle

arise - arose - arisen
awake - awoke - awoken, awaked
be - was - been
bear - bore - borne
beat - beat - beaten
become - became - become
begin - began - begun
behold - beheld - beheld
bend - bent - bent
beseech - besought - besought
bet - bet - betted
bid - bade (bid) - bidden (bid)
bind - bound - bound
bite - bit - bitten
bleed - bled - bled
blow - blew - blown
break - broke - broken
breed - bred - bred
bring - brought - brought
build - built - built
burn - burnt - burnt *
burst - burst - burst
buy - bought - bought
cast - cast - cast
catch - caught - caught
choose - chose - chosen
cling - clung - clung
come - came - come
cost - cost - cost
creep - crept - crept
cut - cut - cut
deal - dealt - dealt
dig - dug - dug
do - did - done
draw - drew - drawn
dream - dreamt - dreamed
drink - drank - drunk
drive - drove - driven
dwell - dwelt - dwelt
eat - ate - eaten
fall - fell - fallen
feed - fed - fed
feel - felt - felt
fight - fought - fought
find - found - found
flee - fled - fled
fling - flung - flung
fly - flew - flown
forebear - forbore - forborne
forbid - forbade - forbidden
forecast - forecast - forecast
forget - forgot - forgotten
forgive - forgave - forgiven
forego - forewent - foregone
foresee - foresaw - foreseen
foretell - foretold - foretold
forget - forgot - forgotten
forsake - forsook - forsaken
freeze - froze - frozen
get - got - gotten
give - gave - given
go - went - gone
grind - ground - ground
grow - grew - grown
hang - hung * - hung *
have - had - had

hear - heard - heard
hide - hid - hidden
hit - hit - hit
hold - held - held
hurt - hurt - hurt
hit - hit - hit
hold - held - held
keep - kept - kept
kneel - knelt * - knelt *
know - knew - known
lay - laid - laid
lead - led - led
lean - leant * - leant *
leap - lept * - lept *
learn - learnt * - learnt *
leave - left - left
lend - lent - lent
let - let - let
lie - lay - lain
light - lit * - lit *
lose - lost - lost
make - made - made
mean - meant - meant
meet - met - met
mistake - mistook - mistaken
must - had to - had to
pay - paid - paid
plead - pleaded - pled
prove - proved - proven
put - put - put
quit - quit * - quit *
read - read - read
rid - rid - rid
ride - rode - ridden
ring - rang - rung
rise - rose - risen
run - ran - run
saw - sawed - sawn
say - said - said
see - saw - seen
seek - sought - sought
sell - sold - sold
send - sent - sent
set - set - set
sew - sewed - sewn
shake - shook - shaken
shear - sheared - shorn
shed - shed - shed
shine - shone - shone
shoot - shot - shot
show - showed - shown
shrink - shrank - shrunk
shut - shut - shut
sing - sang - sung
sink - sank - sunk
sit - sat - sat
slay - slew - slain
sleep - sleep - slept
slide - slid - slid
sling - slung - slung
smell - smelt * - smelt *
sow - sowed - sown *
speak - spoke - spoken
speed - sped * - sped *
spell - spelt * - spelt *
spend - spent - spent
spill - spilt * - spilt *
spin - spun - spun

spit - spat - spat
split - split - split
spread - spread - spread
spring - sprang - sprung
stand - stood - stood
steal - stole - stolen
stick - stuck - stuck
sting - stung - stung
stink - stank - stunk
stride - strode - stridden
strike - struck - struck (stricken)
strive - strove - striven
swear - swore - sworn
sweep - swept - swept
swell - swelled - swollen *
swim - swam - swum
take - took - taken
teach - taught - taught
tear - tore - torn
tell - told - told
think - thought - thought
throw - threw - thrown
thrust - thrust - thrust
tread - trod - trodden
wake - woke - woken
wear - wore - worn
weave - wove * - woven *
wed - wed * - wed *
weep - wept - wept
win - won - won
wind - wound - wound
wring - wrung - wrung
write - wrote - written

Those tenses with an * also have regular forms.

English-Romanian

Bilingual Dictionaries, Inc.

Abbreviations

a - article
n - noun
e - exclamation
pro - pronoun
adj - adjective
adv - adverb
v - verb
iv - irregular verb
pre - preposition
c - conjunction

A

a *a* un, o
abandon *v* a abandona
abandonment *n* abandon
abbey *n* mănăstire
abbot *n* abate, stareț
abbreviate *v* a abrevia
abbreviation *n* abreviere
abdicate *v* a abdica
abdication *n* abdicare
abdomen *n* abdomen
abduct *v* a răpi
abduction *n* răpire
aberration *n* aberație
abhor *v* a urî, a detesta
abide by *v* a respecta
ability *n* abilitate
ablaze *adj* aprins
able *adj* capabil
abnormal *adj* anormal
abnormality *n* anormalitate
aboard *adv* la bord
abolish *v* a aboli
abort *v* a avorta
abortion *n* avort
abound *v* a abunda
about *pre* aproape de
about *adv* aproximativ
above *pre* deasupra, peste
abreast *adv* alături
abridge *v* a prescurta
abroad *adv* în străinătate
abrogate *v* a abroga
abruptly *adv* brusc
absence *n* absenţă
absent *adj* absent, distrat
absolute *adj* absolut
absolution *n* scutire, iertare
absolve *v* a scuti, a ierta
absorb *v* a absorbi
absorbent *adj* absorbant
abstain *v* a se abţine
abstinence *n* abstinenţă
abstract *adj* abstract
absurd *adj* absurd
abundance *n* abundenţă
abundant *adj* abundent
abuse *v* a abuza de
abuse *n* abuz, insultă
abusive *adj* abuziv
abysmal *adj* abisal
abyss *n* abis
academic *adj* academic
academy *n* academie

accelerate *v* a accelera
accelerator *n* accelerator
accent *n* accent
accept *v* a accepta
acceptable *adj* acceptabil
acceptance *n* acceptare
access *n* acces
accessible *adj* accesibil
accident *n* accident
accidental *adj* accidental
acclaim *v* a aclama
acclimatize *v* a aclimatiza
accommodate *v* a acomoda
accompany *v* a acompania
accomplice *n* complice
accomplish *v* a realiza
accord *n* acord
according to *pre* conform cu
accordion *n* acordeon
account *n* cont; relatare
accountable *adj* explicabil
accountant *n* contabil
accumulate *v* a acumula
accuracy *n* acurateţe
accurate *adj* precis
accusation *n* acuzaţie
accuse *v* a acuza
accustom *v* a se obişnui cu
ace *n* as
ache *n* durere
achieve *v* a îndeplini
achievement *n* îndeplinire
acid *n* acid
acidity *n* aciditate
acknowledge *v* a recunoaşte
acorn *n* ghindă
acoustic *adj* acustic
acquaintance *n* cunoştinţă
acquire *v* a căpăta
acquisition *n* achiziţie
acquit *v* a achita
acquittal *n* achitare
acre *n* acru, pogon
acrobat *n* acrobat
across *pre* peste
act *v* a acţiona
action *n* acţiune
activate *v* a activa
activation *n* activare
active *adj* activ
activity *n* activitate
actor *n* actor
actress *n* actriţă
actual *adj* actual, real
actually *adv* de fapt
acute *adj* ascuţit; acut

adamant *adj* diamantin
adapt *v* a adapta
adaptable *adj* adaptabil
adaptation *n* adaptare
adapter *n* adaptor
add *v* a adăuga
addicted *adj* stăpânit de
addictive *adj* nestăpânit
addition *n* adăugare
additional *adj* suplimentar
address *n* adresă
address *v* a adresa
addressee *n* adresant
adequate *adj* adecvat
adhere *v* a adera
adhesive *adj* adeziv
adjacent *adj* adiacent
adjective *n* adjectiv
adjoin *v* a se învecina
adjoining *adj* învecinat
adjourn *v* a amâna
adjust *v* a ajusta
adjustable *adj* ajustabil
adjustment *n* aranjare
administer *v* a administra
admirable *adj* admirabil
admiral *n* amiral
admiration *n* admiraţie
admire *v* a admira
admirer *n* admirator
admissible *adj* acceptabil
admission *n* admitere
admit *v* a accepta
admittance *n* intrare, admitere
admonish *v* a admonesta
admonition *n* admonestare
adolescence *n* adolescenţă
adolescent *n* adolescent
adopt *v* a adopta
adoption *n* adopţie
adoptive *adj* adoptiv
adorable *adj* adorabil
adoration *n* adoraţie
adore *v* a adora
adorn *v* a împodobi
adrift *adv* în derivă
adulation *n* adulaţie
adult *n* adult
adulterate *v* a falsifica
adultery *n* adulter
advance *v* a avansa
advance *n* avans
advantage *n* avantaj
adventure *n* aventură
adverb *n* adverb
adversary *n* adversar

adverse *adj* opus, contrar
adversity *n* nenorocire
advertise *v* a anunţa
advertising *n* publicitate
advice *n* sfat, părere
advisable *adj* recomandabil
advise *v* a sfătui
adviser *n* consilier
advocate *v* a sprijini
aeroplane *n* avion
aesthetic *adj* estetic
afar *adv* departe
affable *adj* afabil
affair *n* afacere; idilă
affect *v* a afecta
affection *n* afecţiune
affectionate *adj* afectuos
affiliate *v* a afilia
affiliation *n* afiliere
affinity *n* afinitate
affirm *v* a afirma
affirmative *adj* afirmativ
affix *v* a ataşa
afflict *v* a chinui
affliction *n* chin
affluence *n* afluenţă
affluent *adj* afluent
afford *v* a-şi permite
affordable *adj* posibil
affront *v* a insulta
affront *n* afront, insultă
afloat *adv* pe apă
afraid *adj* speriat
afresh *adv* iar, din nou
after *pre* după
afternoon *n* după amiază
afterwards *adv* după aceea
again *adv* iarăşi, din nou
against *pre* împotriva, contra
age *n* vârstă; epocă
agency *n* agenţie
agenda *n* agendă
agent *n* agent
agglomerate *v* a aglomera
aggravate *v* a agrava
aggravation *n* agravare
aggregate *v* a strânge
aggression *n* agresiune
aggressive *adj* agresiv
aggressor *n* agresor
aghast *adj* înspăimântat
agile *adj* agil
agitator *n* agitator
agnostic *n* agnostic
agonize *v* a se tortura
agonizing *adj* chinuitor

agony *n* agonie
agree *v* a fi de acord
agreeable *adj* plăcut
agreement *n* acord
agricultural *adj* agricol
agriculture *n* agricultură
ahead *pre* înainte
aid *n* ajutor
aid *v* a ajuta
aide *n* ajutor
ailing *adj* bolnav
ailment *n* boală
aim *v* a ţinti
aimless *adj* fără ţintă
air *n* aer
air *v* a aerisi
aircraft *n* aeronavă
airfield *n* aerodrom
airline *n* linie aeriană
airplane *n* avion
airport *n* aeroport
airspace *n* spaţiul aerian
airstrip *n* pistă
airtight *adj* etanş
aisle *n* culoar
ajar *adj* întredeschis
akin *adj* înrudit
alarm *n* alarmă
alarming *adj* alarmant
alcoholic *adj* alcoolic
alcoholism *n* alcoolism
alert *n* alertă
alert *v* a alarma
algebra *n* algebră
alien *n* străin
alight *adv* aprins
align *v* a alinia
alignment *n* aliniere
alike *adj* similar
alive *adj* viu, vioi
all *adj* tot, întreg
allegation *n* alegaţie
allege *v* a susţine
allegedly *adv* chipurile
allegiance *n* supunere
allegory *n* alegorie
allergic *adj* alergic
allergy *n* alergie
alleviate *v* a alina
alley *n* alee, cărare
alliance *n* alianţă
allied *adj* aliat
alligator *n* aligator
allocate *v* a aloca
allot *v* a distribui
allotment *n* repartizare

allow *v* a permite
allowance *n* permisiune
alloy *n* aliaj
allure *n* farmec
alluring *adj* fermecător
allusion *n* aluzie
ally *n* aliat
ally *v* a alia, a uni
almanac *n* almanah
almighty *adj* atotputernic
almond *n* migdală
almost *adv* aproape
alms *n* pomană
alone *adj* singur,
along *pre* de-a lungul
alongside *pre* de-a lungul
aloof *adj* mândru
aloud *adv* tare
alphabet *n* alfabet
already *adv* deja
alright *adv* în ordine, bine
also *adv* de asemenea
altar *n* altar
alter *v* a transforma
alteration *n* transformare
altercation *n* altercaţie
alternate *v* a alterna
alternate *adj* alternativ
alternative *n* alternativă
although *c* deşi, cu toate că
altitude *n* altitudine
altogether *adj* complet, cu totul
aluminum *n* aluminiu
always *adv* întotdeauna
amass *v* a aduna
amateur *adj* amator
amaze *v* a ului, a uimi
amazement *n* uluire, uimire
amazing *adj* uluitor, uimitor
ambassador *n* ambasador
ambiguous *adj* ambiguu
ambition *n* ambiţie
ambitious *adj* ambiţios
ambivalent *adj* ambivalent
ambulance *n* ambulanţă
amenable *adj* ascultător
amend *v* a amenda
amendment *n* amendament
amenities *n* comodităţi
American *adj* american
amiable *adj* amabil
amicable *adj* prietenos
amid *pre* în mijlocul
ammonia *n* amoniac
ammunition *n* muniţie
amnesia *n* amnezie

amnesty *n* amnistie
among *pre* printre, între
amoral *adj* amoral
amorphous *adj* amorf
amortize *v* a amortiza
amount *n* cantitate
amount to *v* a totaliza
amphibious *adj* amfibiu
amphitheater *n* amfiteatru
ample *adj* amplu
amplifier *n* amplificator
amplify *v* a amplifica
amputate *v* a amputa
amputation *n* amputare
amuse *v* a amuza
amusement *n* amuzament
amusing *adj* amuzant
an *a* un, o
analogy *n* analogie
analysis *n* analiză
analyze *v* a analiza
anarchist *n* anarhist
anarchy *n* anarhie
anatomy *n* anatomie
ancestor *n* strămoş
ancestry *n* neam, obârşie
anchor *n* ancoră
anchovy *n* anşoa
ancient *adj* antic, vechi
and *c* şi
anecdote *n* anecdotă
anemia *n* anemie
anemic *adj* anemic
anesthesia *n* anestezie
anew *adv* iarăşi, altfel
angel *n* înger
angelic *adj* angelic
anger *v* a înfuria
anger *n* furie
angina *n* anghină
angle *n* unghi
Anglican *adj* anglican
angry *adj* supărat
anguish *n* chin, durere
animal *n* animal
animate *v* a anima
animation *n* animaţie
animosity *n* duşmănie
ankle *n* gleznă
annex *n* anexă
annexation *n* anexiune
annihilate *v* a nimici
annihilation *n* nimicire
anniversary *n* aniversare
annotate *v* a adnota
annotation *n* adnotare

announce *v* a anunţa
announcement *n* anunţ
announcer *n* vestitor
annoy *v* a enerva
annoying *adj* enervant
annual *adj* anual
annul *v* a anula
annulment *n* anulare
anoint *v* a unge
anonymity *n* anonimat
anonymous *adj* anonim
another *adj* alt, înca un
answer *v* a răspunde
answer *n* răspuns
ant *n* furnică
antagonize *v* a opune
antecedent *n* antecedent
antecedents *n* trecut
antelope *n* antilopă
antenna *n* antenă
anthem *n* imn, odă
antibiotic *n* antibiotic
anticipate *v* a anticipa
anticipation *n* anticipare
antidote *n* antidot
antipathy *n* antipatie
antiquated *adj* demodat
antiquity *n* antichitate
anvil *n* nivovală
anxiety *n* anxietate
anxious *adj* neliniştit
any *adj* orice, oricare
anybody *pro* oricine
anyhow *pro* oricum
anyone *pro* oricine
anything *pro* orice
apart *adv* separat
apartment *n* apartament
apathy *n* apatie
ape *n* maimuţă
apex *n* vârf, culme
aphrodisiac *adj* afrodisiac
apiece *adv* de fiecare
apocalypse *n* apocalips
apologize *v* a se scuza
apology *n* scuză
apostle *n* apostol
apostolic *adj* apostolic
apostrophe *n* apostrof
appall *v* a îngrozi
appalling *adj* înfiorător
apparel *n* veşminte
apparent *adj* aparent
apparently *adv* în mod aparent
apparition *n* apariţie
appeal *n* apel; atracţie

appeal *v* a face apel
appealing *adj* rugător, atrăgător
appear *v* apărea; a părea
appearance *n* aparitiţie
appease *v* a linişti
appeasement *n* liniştire
appendicitis *n* apendicită
appendix *n* apendice
appetite *n* apetit
appetizer *n* aperitiv
applaud *v* a aplauda
applause *n* aplauze
apple *n* măr
appliance *n* dispozitiv
applicable *adj* aplicabil
applicant *n* aplicant
application *n* aplicaţie; petiţie
apply *v* a aplica
apply for *v* a solicita
appoint *v* a numi
appointment *n* numire; slujbă
appraisal *n* evaluare
appraise *v* a evalua
appreciate *v* a aprecia
appreciation *n* apreciere
apprehend *v* a aresta; a percepe
apprehensive *adj* inteligent; temător
apprentice *n* ucenic
approach *v* a se apropia de
approach *n* apropiere
approachable *adj* abordabil
approbation *n* aprobare
appropriate *adj* potrivit
approval *n* aprobare
approve *v* a aproba
approximate *adj* aproximativ
apricot *n* caisă
April *n* aprilie
apron *n* şorţ
aptitude *n* aptitudine
aquarium *n* acvariu
aquatic *adj* acvatic
aqueduct *n* apeduct
Arabic *adj* arab
arable *adj* arabil
arbiter *n* arbitru
arbitrary *adj* arbitrar
arbitrate *v* a arbitra
arbitration *n* arbitrare
arc *n* arc
arch *n* arcadă
archaeology *n* arheologie
archaic *adj* arhaic
archbishop *n* arhiepiscop
architect *n* arhitect

architecture *n* arhitectură
archive *n* arhivă
arctic *adj* arctic
ardent *adj* arzător
ardor *n* râvnă, ardoare
arduous *adj* dificil, aspru
area *n* suprafaţă
arena *n* arenă
argue *v* a se certa
argument *n* argument
arid *adj* arid, sterp
arise *iv* a apărea
aristocracy *n* aristocraţie
aristocrat *n* aristocrat
arithmetic *n* aritmetică
ark *n* arcă
arm *n* braţ
arm *v* a înarma
armaments *n* armament
armchair *n* fotoliu
armed *adj* înarmat; cu braţe
armistice *n* armistiţiu
armor *n* armură
armpit *n* axilă, subsuoară
army *n* armată
aromatic *adj* aromatic
around *pre* în jurul
arouse *v* a trezi; a stârni
arrange *v* a aranja
arrangement *n* aranjament
array *n* expoziţie; ordine
arrest *v* a aresta
arrest *n* arestare
arrival *n* sosire
arrive *v* a sosi, a veni
arrogance *n* aroganţă
arrogant *adj* arogant
arrow *n* săgeată
arsenal *n* arsenal
arsenic *n* arsenic
arson *n* incendiere
arsonist *n* incendiator
art *n* artă
artery *n* arteră
arthritis *n* artrită
artichoke *n* anghinare
article *n* articol
articulate *v* a articula
articulation *n* articulare
artificial *adj* artificial
artillery *n* artilerie
artisan *n* meşteşugar
artist *n* artist
artistic *adj* artistic
artwork *n* operă de artă
as *c* ca

as *adv* pe când
ascend *v* a urca
ascendancy *n* ascendenţă
ascertain *v* a descoperi
ascetic *adj* ascetic
ash *n* cenuşă; frasin
ashamed *adj* ruşinat
ashore *adv* pe ţărm
ashtray *n* scrumieră
aside *adv* la o parte
aside from *adv* în afară de
ask *v* a întreba; a cere
asleep *adj* adormit
asparagus *n* sparanghel
aspect *n* aspect
asphalt *n* asfalt
asphyxiate *v* a asfxia
asphyxiation *n* asfixiere
aspiration *n* aspiraţie
aspire *v* a aspira
aspirin *n* aspirină
assail *v* a ataca
assailant *n* atacator
assassin *n* asasin
assassinate *v* a asasina
assassination *n* asasinat
assault *n* asalt, atac
assault *v* a asalta
assemble *v* a asambla
assembly *n* adunare; miting
assent *v* a încuviinţa
assert *v* a afirma
assertion *n* afirmaţie
assess *v* a evalua
assessment *n* evaluare
asset *n* bun, dar
assets *n* avere, bunuri
assign *v* a repartiza
assignment *n* repartizare
assimilate *v* a asimila
assimilation *n* asimilare
assist *v* a asista
assistance *n* asistenţă
associate *v* a asocia
association *n* asociaţie
assorted *adj* asortat
assortment *n* sortiment
assume *v* a-şi asuma
assumption *n* asumare
assurance *n* asigurare
assure *v* a asigura
asterisk *n* asterisc
asteroid *n* asteroid
asthma *n* astmă
asthmatic *adj* astmatic
astonish *v* a ului

astonishing *adj* uluitor
astound *v* a ului
astounding *adj* uluitor
astray *v* a rătăci
astrologer *n* astrolog
astrology *n* astrologie
astronaut *n* astronaut
astronomer *n* astronom
astronomic *adj* astronomic
astronomy *n* astronomie
astute *adj* isteţ, deştept
asunder *adv* separat
asylum *n* azil
at *pre* la
atheism *n* ateism
atheist *n* ateu
athlete *n* atlet
athletic *adj* atletic
atmosphere *n* atmosferă
atmospheric *adj* atmosferic
atom *n* atom
atomic *adj* atomic
atone *v* a ispăşi
atonement *n* ispăşire
atrocious *adj* atroce
atrocity *n* atrocitate
atrophy *v* a atrofia
attach *v* a ataşa
attached *adj* ataşat
attachment *n* ataşament
attack *n* atac
attack *v* a ataca
attacker *n* atacator
attain *v* a atinge
attainable *adj* realizabil
attainment *n* realizare
attempt *v* a încerca
attempt *n* încercare
attend *v* a îngriji; a asista
attendance *n* îngrijire; însoţire
attendant *n* slujitor, ajutor
attention *n* atenţie
attentive *adj* atent, grijuliu
attenuate *v* a atenua
attenuating *adj* atenuant
attest *v* a dovedi
attic *n* mansardă
attitude *n* atitudine
attorney *n* avocat, procuror
attract *v* a atrage
attraction *n* atracţie
attractive *adj* atractiv
attribute *v* a atribui
auction *n* licitaţie
auction *v* a vinde la licitaţie
audacious *adj* îndrăzneţ

audacity *n* îndrăzneală
audible *adj* audibil
audience *n* audienţă
audit *v* a examina
auditorium *n* auditoriu
augment *v* a mări
August *n* august
aunt *n* matuşă
auspicious *adj* favorabil
austere *adj* auster, sever
austerity *n* stricteţe
authentic *adj* autentic
authenticate *v* a autentifica
authenticity *n* autenticitate
author *n* autor
authoritarian *adj* autoritarist
authority *n* autoritate
authorization *n* autorizaţie
authorize *v* a autoriza
auto *n* automobil
autograph *n* autograf
automatic *adj* automat
automobile *n* automobil
autonomous *adj* autonom
autonomy *n* autonomie
autopsy *n* autopsie
autumn *n* toamnă
auxiliary *adj* auxiliar
avail *v* a folosi, a ajuta
availability *n* disponibilitate
available *adj* disponibil
avalanche *n* avalanşă
avarice *n* avariţie
avaricious *adj* avar, zgârcit
avenge *v* a răzbuna
avenue *n* bulevard
average *n* medie
averse *adj* potrivnic
aversion *n* aversiune
avert *v* a abate, a evita
aviation *n* aviaţie
aviator *n* aviator
avid *adj* lacom; nerăbdător
avoid *v* a evita
avoidable *adj* evitabil
avoidance *n* evitare
avowed *adj* mărturisit
await *v* a aştepta
awake *iv* a se trezi
awake *adj* treaz
awakening *n* trezire
award *v* a acorda
award *n* premiu, distincţie
aware *adj* conştient
awareness *n* vigilenţă
away *adv* departe

awe *n* respect; teamă
awesome *adj* teribil, copleşitor
awful *adj* teribil
awkward *adj* incomod
awning *n* marchiză, cort
ax *n* topor
axiom *n* axiomă
axis *n* axă
axle *n* ax, osie

B

babble *v* a gânguri
baby *n* copilaş, prunc
babysitter *n* bonă, dădacă
bachelor *n* celibatar; licenţiat
back *n* spate
back *adv* înapoi, în spate
back *v* a sprijini
back down *v* a bate în retragere
back up *v* a susţine
backbone *n* coloană vertebrală
backdoor *n* uşa din spate
backfire *v* a da greş
background *n* fundal
backing *n* sprijin, reazem
backlash *n* reacţiune
backlog *n* listă, coadă
backpack *n* rucsac
backup *n* rezervă
backward *adj* posterior
backwards *adv* înapoi
bacon *n* slănină, costiţă
bacteria *n* bacterie
bad *adj* rău
badge *n* insignă, emblemă
badly *adv* rău; teribil
baffle *v* a zădărnici
bag *n* plasă, geantă
baggage *n* bagaj
baggy *adj* care atârnă
baguette *n* baghetă
bail *n* cauţiune
bailiff *n* uşier, aprod
bait *n* momeală
bake *v* a coace
baker *n* brutar
bakery *n* brutărie
balance *v* a balansa
balance *n* balanţă; echilibru
balcony *n* balcon
bald *adj* chel
bale *n* balot

ball *n* minge; bilă; bal
balloon *n* balon
ballot *n* buletin de vot
ballroom *n* salon de bal
balm *n* balsam
balmy *adj* balsamic
bamboo *n* bambus
ban *n* interdicţie
ban *v* a interzice
banality *n* banalitate
banana *n* banană
band *n* bandă; orchestră
bandage *n* bandaj
bandage *v* a bandaja
bandit *n* bandit
bang *v* a pocni, a lovi
banish *v* a exila, a izgoni
banishment *n* exil
bank *n* bancă
bankrupt *v* a falimenta
bankrupt *adj* falit, ruinat
bankruptcy *n* bancrută
banner *n* steag
banquet *n* banchet
baptism *n* botez
baptize *v* a boteza
bar *n* bară; bar; bufet
bar *v* a bara, a opri
barbarian *n* barbar
barbaric *adj* barbar
barbarism *n* barbarie
barbecue *n* grătar, frigare
barber *n* bărbier
bare *adj* gol, simplu
barefoot *adj* desculţ
barely *adv* abia, doar
bargain *n* tocmeală
bargain *v* a se tocmi
bargaining *n* chilipir
barge *n* şalupă, şlep
bark *v* a lătra
bark *n* lătrat; scoarţă
barley *n* orz
barmaid *n* chelneriţă
barman *n* barman
barn *n* şură, hambar
barometer *n* barometru
barracks *n* cazarmă
barrage *n* baraj, dig
barrel *n* butoi, baril
barren *adj* sterp, steril
barricade *n* baricadă
barrier *n* barieră
barring *pre* fără, în afară de
bartender *n* barman
barter *v* a face troc

base *n* bază
base *v* a baza
baseball *n* baseball
baseless *adj* neîntemeiat
basement *n* pivniţă, subsol
bashful *adj* timid, ruşinos
basic *adj* fundamental
basics *n* fundamental
basin *n* lighean, bazin
basis *n* bază
bask *v* a sta la soare
basket *n* coş, paner
basketball *n* baschet
bastard *n* bastard
bat *n* liliac; băţ; bâtă
batch *n* grup; pâlc
bath *n* baie, spălare
bathe *v* a se spăla
bathrobe *n* halat de baie
bathroom *n* baie
bathtub *n* cadă
baton *n* baston, baghetă
battalion *n* batalion
batter *v* a lovi, a izbi
battery *n* baterie
battle *n* bătălie, luptă
battle *v* a se lupta
battleship *n* vas de război
bay *n* golf
bayonet *n* baioneta
bazaar *n* bazar
be *iv* a fi; a exista
be born *v* a fi născut
beach *n* plajă
beacon *n* lumină, far
beak *n* cioc de pasăre
beam *n* grindă, prăjină
bean *n* fasole
bear *n* urs
bear *iv* a se îndrepta catre
bearable *adj* suportabil
beard *n* barbă
bearded *adj* bărbos, cu barbă
bearer *n* purtător, mesager
beast *n* bestie, fiară
beat *iv* a bate
beat *n* lovitură; cartier
beaten *adj* bătut
beating *n* bătaie, înfrângere
beautiful *adj* frumos
beautify *v* a înfrumuseţa
beauty *n* frumuseţe
beaver *n* castor
because *c* pentru că
because of *pre* din pricina
beckon *v* a chema

become *iv* a deveni
bed *n* pat; albie; strat
bedding *n* aşternut, culcuş
bedroom *n* dormitor
bedspread *n* cuvertură
bee *n* albină
beef *n* carne de vacă
beef up *v* a omorî , a întări
beehive *n* stup
beer *n* bere
beet *n* sfeclă
beetle *n* gândac
before *adv* înainte, anterior
before *pre* înaintea, în faţa
beforehand *adv* în avans
beg *v* a cerşi, a cere
beggar *n* cerşetor
begin *iv* a începe
beginner *n* începător
beginning *n* început
beguile *v* a păcăli
behalf (on) *adv* din partea
behave *v* a se purta
behavior *n* comportament
behead *v* a decapita
behind *pre* în spatele
behold *iv* a privi
being *n* fiinţă, făptură
belated *adj* întârziat
belch *v* a râgâi
belch *n* râgâială
belfry *n* clopotniţă
Belgian *adj* belgian
Belgium *n* Belgia
belief *n* credinţă
believable *adj* credibil
believe *v* a crede
believer *n* credincios
belittle *v* a diminua
bell *n* clopot
bell pepper *n* ardei gras
belligerent *adj* beligerant
belly *n* burtă, stomac
belly button *n* buric
belong *v* a aparţine
belongings *n* lucruri
beloved *adj* iubit
below *adv* mai jos, dedesubt
below *pre* sub
belt *n* curea, centură
bench *n* bancă
bend *iv* a se îndoi; a coti
bend down *v* a se apleca
beneath *pre* sub, dedesubtul
benediction *n* binecuvântare
benefactor *n* binefăcător

beneficial *adj* folositor
beneficiary *n* beneficiar
benefit *n* beneficiu
benefit *v* a profita
benevolent *adj* binevoitor
benign *adj* benign, blând
bequeath *v* a lăsa moştenire
bereaved *adj* răpit, furat
bereavement *n* nenorocire
beret *n* basc, beretă
berserk *adv* apucat de streche
berth *n* cuşetă
beseech *iv* a implora
beset *iv* a înconjura
beside *pre* alături
besides *pre* pe lângă
besiege *iv* a asedia
best *adj* cel mai bun
best man *n* cavaler de onoare
bestial *adj* bestial, animalic
bestiality *n* bestialitate
bestow *v* a acorda, a da
bet *iv* a paria, a miza
bet *n* pariu
betray *v* a trăda, a înşela
betrayal *n* trădare
better *adj* mai bun
between *pre* între
beverage *n* băutură
beware *v* a avea grijă
bewilder *v* a zăpăci
bewitch *v* a vrăji
beyond *adv* dincolo
bias *n* înclinaţie
bible *n* biblie
biblical *adj* biblic
bibliography *n* bibliografie
bicycle *n* bicicletă
bid *n* ofertă, licitare
bid *iv* a licita
big *adj* mare
bigamy *n* bigamie
bigot *adj* bigot
bigotry *n* bigotism
bike *n* bicicletă
bile *n* fiere
bilingual *adj* bilingv
bill *n* cioc; notă de plată
billiards *n* biliard
billion *n* miliard
billionaire *n* miliardar
bimonthly *adj* bilunar
bin *n* cutie, coş de gunoi
bind *iv* a lega, a lipi
binding *adj* obligator
binoculars *n* binoclu

biography *n* biografie
biological *adj* biologic
biology *n* bioligie
bird *n* pasăre
birth *n* naştere
birthday *n* zi de naştere
biscuit *n* biscuit
bishop *n* episcop
bison *n* bizon
bit *n* firimitură; sfredel
bite *iv* a muşca; a tăia
bite *n* muşcătură
bitter *adj* amar
bitterly *adv* dureros, amar
bitterness *n* amărăciune
bizarre *adj* bizar, ciudat
black *adj* negru
blackberry *n* mură
blackboard *n* tablă
blackmail *n* şantaj
blackmail *v* a şantaja
blackness *n* întuneric
blacksmith *n* fierar
bladder *n* băşică
blade *n* lamă, tăiş
blame *n* vină
blame *v* a învinovăţi
blameless *adj* nevinovat
bland *adj* amabil
blank *adj* gol, în alb
blanket *n* pătură
blaspheme *v* a blasfema
blasphemy *n* blasfemie
blast *n* răbufnire
blaze *v* a aprinde
bleach *v* a înălbi
bleach *n* înălbitor
bleak *adj* sterp, lugubru
bleed *iv* a sângera
bleeding *n* sângerare
blemish *n* pată, defect
blemish *v* a strica, a păta
blend *n* amestec
blend *v* a amesteca
blender *n* amestecător
bless *v* a binecuvânta
blessed *adj* binecuvântat
blessing *n* binecuvântare
blind *v* a orbi
blind *adj* orb
blindfold *n* legat la ochi
blindfold *v* a lega la ochi
blindly *adv* orbeşte
blindness *n* orbire
blink *v* a clipi
bliss *n* fericire

blissful *adj* fericit
blister *n* pustulă
blizzard *n* viscol
bloat *v* a umfla
bloated *adj* umflat
block *n* bloc; pietroi
block *v* a bloca
blockade *v* a bloca
blockade *n* blocadă
blockage *n* blocaj
blond *adj* blond
blood *n* sânge
bloody *adj* sângeros
bloom *v* a înflori
blossom *v* a înflori
blot *n* pată, defect
blot *v* a păta
blouse *n* bluză
blow *n* lovitură, suflu
blow *iv* a sufla; a umfla
blow out *iv* a stinge
blow up *iv* a umfla
blowout *n* izbucnire
bludgeon *v* a ciomăgi
blue *adj* albastru
blueprint *n* plan, proiect
bluff *v* a blufa
blunder *n* greşeală, gafă
blunt *adj* tocit; teşit
bluntness *n* ciuntire
blur *v* a înceţoşa
blurred *adj* înceţoşat
blush *v* a roşi
blush *n* roşeaţă
boar *n* porc mistreţ
board *n* tablă; bord
board *v* a se îmbarca
boast *v* a se lăuda cu
boat *n* vas, barcă
bodily *adj* trupesc
body *n* corp; cadavru; om
bog *n* mlaştină
bog down *v* a se împotmoli
boil *v* a fierbe
boil down to *v* a scădea la fiert
boil over *v* a da în foc
boiler *n* boiler
boisterous *adj* zgomotos, furtunos
bold *adj* curajos; îndrăzneţ
boldness *n* curaj, impertinenţă
bolster *v* a sprijini, a susţine
bolt *n* zăvor; cui
bolt *v* a zăvorî
bomb *n* bombă
bomb *v* a bombarda
bombing *n* bombardament

bombshell *n* bombă, obuz
bond *n* angajament
bondage *n* sclavie
bone *n* os
bone marrow *n* măduvă
bonfire *n* foc, rug
bonus *n* bonus, primă
book *n* carte
bookcase *n* bibliotecă
bookkeeper *n* contabil
bookkeeping *n* contabilitate
booklet *n* broşură
bookseller *n* librar
bookstore *n* librărie
boom *n* prăjină; catarg
boom *v* a bubui, a prospera
boost *v* a sălta, a mări
boost *n* sporire, mărire
boot *n* gheată, cizmă
booth *n* cabină telefonică
booty *n* captură, pradă
booze *n* băutură
border *n* frontieră; limită
border on *v* a se învecina cu
borderline *adj* linie de frontieră
bore *v* a plictisi
bored *adj* plictisit
boredom *n* plictiseală
boring *adj* plictisitor
born *adj* născut
borough *n* târg, orăşel
borrow *v* a împrumuta
bosom *n* sân, piept
boss *n* şef
boss around *v* a face pe şeful
bossy *adj* autoritar
botany *n* botanică
botch *v* a rasoli
both *adj* amândoi
bother *v* a necăji
bothersome *adj* neplăcut
bottle *n* sticlă
bottle *v* a îmbutelia
bottleneck *n* gât de sticlă
bottom *n* fund, temelie
bottomless *adj* fără fund
bough *n* ramură
boulder *n* bolovan
boulevard *n* bulevard
bounce *v* a sări, a ţopăi
bounce *n* săritură, salt
bound *adj* prins, legat
bound for *adj* cu destinaţia
boundary *n* graniţă
boundless *adj* nelimitat
bounty *n* mărinimie

bourgeois *adj* burghez
bow *n* arc; curcubeu
bow *v* a îndoi, a apleca
bow out *v* a se retrage
bowels *n* intestine, maţe
bowl *n* bol; scobitură
box *n* cutie
box office *n* casă de bilete
boxer *n* boxer
boxing *n* box
boy *n* băiat
boycott *v* a boicota
boyfriend *n* prieten
boyhood *n* adolescenţă
bra *n* sutien
brace for *v* a suporta, a prelua
bracelet *n* brăţară
bracket *n* consolă
brag *v* a face paradă de
braid *n* cosiţă, împletitură
brain *n* creier
brainwash *v* a spăla creierul
brake *n* frână
brake *v* a frâna
branch *n* ramură
branch office *n* filială, organizaţie
branch out *v* a se ramifica
brand *n* marcă
brand-new *adj* nou-nouţ
brandy *n* rachiu, coniac
brat *n* pici, puşti
brave *adj* curajos, viteaz
bravely *adv* vitejeşte
bravery *n* curaj, bravură
brawl *n* scandal, bătaie
breach *n* încălcare; abuz
bread *n* pâine
breadth *n* lăţime
break *n* ruptură; întrerupere
break *iv* a rupe, a crăpa
break away *v* a fugi
break down *v* a se strica
break free *v* a se elibera
break in *v* a intra prin efracţie
break off *v* a se întrerupe
break open *v* a se deschide
break out *v* a erupe, a izbucni
break up *v* a înceta
breakable *adj* fragil
breakdown *n* stricăciune, pană
breakfast *n* mic dejun
breakthrough *n* a pătrunde
breast *n* sân, piept
breath *n* respiraţie, suflu
breathe *v* a respira
breathing *n* respiraţie, răsuflare

breathtaking *adj* care taie respiraţia
breed *iv* a naşte; a făta
breed *n* rasă, specie
breeze *n* briză
brethren *n* frăţie de sânge
brevity *n* concizie
brew *v* a fierbe, a fermenta
brewery *n* fabrică de bere
bribe *v* a mitui
bribe *n* mită
bribery *n* corupţie
brick *n* cărămidă
bricklayer *n* zidar
bridal *adj* nupţial
bride *n* mireasă
bridegroom *n* mire
bridge *n* pod, punte
bridle *n* căpăstru, frâu
brief *adj* scurt
brief *v* a expune pe scurt
briefcase *n* servietă
briefly *adv* pe scurt
briefs *n* şort, chiloţi
brigade *n* brigadă
bright *adj* strălucitor
brighten *v* a se lumina
brightness *n* strălucire
brilliant *adj* strălucitor
brim *n* margine, bord
bring *iv* a aduce
bring back *v* a aduce înapoi
bring down *v* a dărâma
bring up *v* a creşte, a educa
brink *n* margine
brisk *adj* rapid, ager
Britain *n* Britania, Anglia
British *adj* englezesc
brittle *adj* fragil
broad *adj* larg, lat
broadcast *v* a transmite
broadcast *n* emisiune
broadcaster *n* spicher, crainic
broaden *v* a extinde, a mări
broadly *adv* în linii mari
broadminded *adj* înţelept
brochure *n* broşură
broil *v* a pârjoli, a frige
broiler *n* grătar
broke *adj* falit
broken *adj* rupt, spart
bronchitis *n* bronşită
bronze *n* bronz
broom *n* mătură
broth *n* supă, bulion
brothel *n* bordel

brother *n* frate
brotherhood *n* frăţie
brother-in-law *n* cumnat
brotherly *adj* frăţesc
brow *n* sprânceană
brown *adj* maron
browse *v* a răsfoi
browser *n* cel care răsfoieşte
bruise *n* contuzie, vânătaie
bruise *v* a învineţi
brunette *adj* brunet
brush *n* perie, pensulă
brush *v* a peria
brush aside *v* a da la o parte
brush up *v* a lustrui, a curăţa
brusque *adj* brusc, răstit
brutal *adj* brutal, violent
brutality *n* brutalitate
brutalize *v* a brutaliza
brute *adj* brut
bubble *n* bulă
buck *n* dolar
bucket *n* găleată
buckle *n* catarama
bud *n* boboc; mugur
buddy *n* amic, camarad
budge *v* a se clinti
budget *n* buget
buffalo *n* bivol
bug *n* gândac, gânganie
build *iv* a clădi
builder *n* constructor
building *n* clădire
buildup *n* acumulare
built-in *adj* încorporat
bulb *n* bulb, bec
bulge *n* umflătură
bulk *n* cantitate; volum
bulky *adj* voluminos
bull *n* taur
bull fight *n* coridă
bull fighter *n* toreador
bulldoze *v* a intimida
bullet *n* glonţ
bulletin *n* buletin
bulwark *n* bastion
bum *n* vagabond
bump *n* umflătură; cucui
bump into *v* a da peste
bumper *n* cupă plină
bumpy *adj* cu hopuri
bun *n* corn, chec
bunch *n* mănunchi
bundle *n* snop, legătură
bundle *v* a pune laolaltă
bunk bed *n* paturi suprapuse

bunker *n* buncăr, magazie
buoy *n* geamandură
burden *n* povară
burden *v* a împovăra
burdensome *adj* împovărător
bureau *n* birou, departament
bureaucracy *n* birocraţie
bureaucrat *n* birocrat
burger *n* chiftea
burglar *n* spărgător
burglarize *v* a intra prin efracţie
burglary *n* spargere, furt
burial *n* înmormântare
burly *adj* corpolent
burn *iv* a arde, a frige
burn *n* arsură
burp *v* a râgâi
burp *n* râgâială
burrow *n* vizuină
burst *iv* a izbucni
burst into *v* a năvăli în
bury *v* a îngropa
bus *n* autobuz
bush *n* tufiş
busily *adv* aferat
business *n* afacere
businessman *n* afacerist
bust *n* bust
bustling *adj* agitat
busy *adj* ocupat
but *c* dar, totuşi
butcher *n* măcelar
butchery *n* măcelărie
butler *n* majordom
butt *n* pat de puşcă; ţintă
butter *n* unt
butterfly *n* fluture
button *n* nasture, buton
buttonhole *n* butonieră
buy *iv* a cumpăra
buy off *v* a mitui, a cumpăra
buyer *n* cumpărător
buzz *n* bâzâit
buzz *v* a bâzâi
buzzard *n* pasăre de pradă
buzzer *n* sonerie
by *pre* lângă
bye *e* pa, la revedere
bypass *n* ocol
bypass *v* a ocoli
by-product *n* produs secundar
bystander *n* spectator, trecător

C

cab *n* taxi
cabbage *n* varză
cabin *n* colibă, cabină
cabinet *n* dulap; cabinet
cable *n* cablu, fir
cafeteria *n* cantină, bufet
caffeine *n* cofeină
cage *n* colivie, cuşcă
cake *n* prăjitură, tort
calamity *n* calamitate
calculate *v* a calcula
calculation *n* calcul, socoteală
calculator *n* calculator
calendar *n* calendar
calf *n* viţel
caliber *n* calibru
calibrate *v* a calibra
call *n* chemare; apel
call *v* a chema; a numi
call off *v* a anula
call on *v* a solicita
call out *v* a striga
calling *n* profesie, chemare
callous *adj* aspru, bătătorit
calm *adj* calm
calm *n* calm, linişte
calm down *v* a se linişti
calorie *n* calorie
calumny *n* calomnie
camel *n* cămilă
camera *n* aparat de fotografiat
camouflage *v* a camufla
camouflage *n* camuflaj
camp *n* tabără
camp *v* a campa
campaign *n* campanie
campfire *n* foc de tabără
can *iv* a conserva
can *v* a putea
can *n* conservă
canal *n* canal
canary *n* canar
cancel *v* a anula
cancellation *n* anulare
cancer *n* cancer
cancerous *adj* canceros
candid *adj* cinstit, sincer
candidacy *n* candidatură
candidate *n* candidat
candle *n* lumânare
candlestick *n* sfeşnic
candor *n* candoare, cinste
candy *n* dulciuri

cane *n* trestie; baston
canister *n* canistră
canned *adj* conservat
cannibal *n* canibal
cannon *n* tun
canoe *n* canoe
canonize *v* a canoniza
cantaloupe *n* pepene galben
canteen *n* bidon, cantină
canvas *n* pânză, tablou
canvas *v* a dezbate
canyon *n* canion
cap *n* şapcă; bonetă
capability *n* capacitate
capable *adj* capabil
capacity *n* capacitate
cape *n* cap; capă; etolă
capital *n* capital, capitală
capital letter *n* majusculă
capitalism *n* capitalism
capitalize *v* a capitaliza
capitulate *v* a capitula
capsize *v* a se răsturna
capsule *n* capsulă
captain *n* căpitan
captivate *v* a captiva
captive *n* prizioner, captiv
captivity *n* captivitate
capture *v* a captura
capture *n* captură
car *n* automobil
carat *n* carat
caravan *n* caravană
carburetor *n* carburator
carcass *n* carcasă
card *n* card; carte de joc
cardboard *n* carton
cardiac *adj* cardiac
cardiac arrest *n* stop cardiac
cardiology *n* cardiologie
care *n* grijă
care *v* a avea grijă
care about *v* a-i păsa de
care for *v* a se îngriji de
career *n* carieră
carefree *adj* lipsit de griji
careful *adj* grijuliu
careless *adj* neglijent
carelessness *n* neglijenţă
caress *n* mângâiere
caress *v* a mângâia
caretaker *n* îngrijitor
cargo *n* încărcătură
caricature *n* caricatură
caring *adj* grijuliu
carnage *n* carnagiu

carnal *adj* carnal
carnation *n* garoafă
carol *n* colindă
carpenter *n* tâmplar
carpentry *n* tâmplărie
carpet *n* covor
carriage *n* trăsură
carrot *n* morcov
carry *v* a căra
carry on *v* a duce
carry out *v* a îndeplini
cart *n* cărucior
cart *v* a căra
cartoon *n* desen animat
cartridge *n* cartuş
carve *v* a ciopli; a sculpta
cascade *n* cascadă
case *n* caz; situaţie
cash *n* bani gheaţă
cashier *n* casier
casino *n* cazino
casket *n* sicriu
casserole *n* caserolă
cassock *n* sutană
cast *iv* a turna; a arunca
castaway *n* naufragiat
caste *n* castă
castle *n* castel
casual *adj* degajat
casualty *n* victimă
cat *n* pisică
cataclysm *n* cataclism
catacomb *n* catacombă
catalog *n* catalog
catalog *v* a cataloga
cataract *n* cataractă
catastrophe *n* catastrofă
catch *iv* a se prinde
catch up *v* a ajunge
catching *adj* molipsitor
catchword *n* slogan, parolă
catechism *n* catehism
category *n* categorie
cater to *v* a se ocupa de
caterpillar *n* omidă
cathedral *n* catedrală
catholic *adj* catolic
Catholicism *n* catolicism
cattle *n* vite
cauliflower *n* conopidă
cause *n* cauză
cause *v* a cauza
caution *n* grijă, precauţie
cautious *adj* precaut
cavalry *n* cavalerie
cave *n* peşteră, grotă

cave in *v* a se prabuşi
cavern *n* cavernă
cavity *n* cavitate, carie
cease *v* a înceta
cease-fire *n* armistiţiu
ceaselessly *adv* neîncetat
ceiling *n* tavan
celebrate *v* a celebra
celebration *n* sărbătorire
celebrity *n* celebritate
celery *n* ţelină
celestial *adj* ceresc
celibacy *n* celibat
celibate *adj* celibatar
cellar *n* pivniţă
cellphone *n* celular
cement *n* ciment
cemetery *n* cimitir
censorship *n* cenzură
censure *v* a cenzura
census *n* recensământ
cent *n* cent
centenary *n* centenar
center *n* centru
center *v* a centra
centimeter *n* centimetru
central *adj* central
centralize *v* a centraliza
century *n* secol, veac
ceramic *n* ceramică
cereal *n* cereală
cerebral *adj* cerebral
ceremony *n* ceremonie
certain *adj* sigur, cert
certainty *n* siguranţă
certificate *n* certificat
certify *v* a certifica
chagrin *n* întristare
chain *n* lanţ
chain *v* a înlănţui
chair *n* scaun
chair *v* a prezida
chairman *n* preşedinte
chalet *n* cabană
chalice *n* potir, caliciu
chalk *n* cretă
chalkboard *n* tablă
challenge *v* a provoca
challenge *n* provocare
challenging *adj* provocator
chamber *n* cameră
champ *n* campion
champion *n* campion
champion *v* a apăra
chance *n* şansă; posibilitate
chancellor *n* cancelar

C

chandelier *n* candelabru
change *v* a schimba
change *n* schimbare
channel *n* canal
chant *n* cântec
chaos *n* haos
chaotic *adj* haotic
chapel *n* capelă
chaplain *n* capelan
chapter *n* capitol
char *v* a se carboniza
character *n* caracter, fire
characteristic *adj* caracteristic
charade *n* şaradă
charbroiled *adj* fript
charcoal *n* cărbune de lemn
charge *v* a acuza
charge *n* plată; acuzaţie
charisma *n* carismă
charismatic *adj* carismatic
charitable *adj* caritabil
charity *n* caritate
charm *v* a încânta
charm *n* şarm, farmec
charming *adj* fermecător
chart *n* hartă; grafic
charter *n* navlosire
charter *v* a navlosi
chase *n* hăituială, urmărire
chase *v* a urmări
chase away *v* a goni, a hăitui
chasm *n* spărtură
chaste *adj* cast
chastise *v* a pedepsi
chastisement *n* pedeapsă
chastity *n* castitate
chat *v* a conversa
chauffeur *n* şofer
cheap *adj* ieftin
cheat *v* a păcăli, a înşela
cheater *n* escroc, pungaş
check *n* control; cec
check *v* a controla
check in *v* a se înregistra
check up *n* verificare, control
checkbook *n* carnet de cecuri
cheek *n* obraz
cheekbone *n* os zigomatic
cheeky *adj* obraznic
cheer *v* a înveseli
cheer up *v* a se înveseli
cheerful *adj* vesel
cheers *n* noroc
cheese *n* brânză
chef *n* bucătar şef
chemical *adj* chimic

chemist *n* chimist
chemistry *n* chimie
cherish *v* a preţui
cherry *n* cireaşă
chess *n* şah
chest *n* ladă; cufăr; piept
chestnut *n* castană
chew *v* a mesteca
chicken *n* pui
chicken pox *n* vărsat de vânt
chide *v* a ocărî
chief *n* şef, conducător
chiefly *adv* mai ales
child *n* copil
childhood *n* copilărie
childish *adj* copilăros
childless *adj* fără copii
children *n* copii
chill *n* răceală; fior
chill *v* a îngheţa, a răci
chill out *v* a se calma
chilly *adj* rece, înfrigurat
chimney *n* şemineu, horn
chimpanzee *n* cimpanzeu
chin *n* bărbie
chip *n* aşchie; ciob
chisel *n* daltă
chocolate *n* ciocolată
choice *n* alegere
choir *n* cor
choke *v* a îneca
cholera *n* holeră
cholesterol *n* colesterol
choose *iv* a prefera
choosy *adj* lingav, mofturos
chop *v* a tăia, a ciopli
chop *n* bucată, cotlet
chopper *n* satâr
chore *n* treabă, muncă
chorus *n* cor, refren
christen *v* a boteza
christening *n* botez
christian *adj* creştin
Christianity *n* creştinism
Christmas *n* Crăciun
chronic *adj* cronic
chronicle *n* cronică
chronology *n* cronologie
chubby *adj* bucălat
chuckle *v* a chicoti
chunk *n* bucată
church *n* biserică
chute *n* jgheab, tobogan
cider *n* cidru
cigar *n* trabuc
cigarette *n* ţigară

C

cinder *n* cenuşă
cinema *n* cinematograf
cinnamon *n* scorţişoară
circle *n* cerc
circle *v* a încercui
circuit *n* circuit
circular *adj* circular
circulate *v* a circula
circulation *n* circulaţie
circumcise *v* a circumcide
circumcision *n* circumcizie
circumstance *n* circumstanţă
circumstancial *adj* circumstanţial
circus *n* circ
cistern *n* cisternă
citizen *n* cetăţean
citizenship *n* cetăţenie
city *n* oraş
city hall *n* primărie
civic *adj* civic
civil *adj* cetăţenesc
civilization *n* civilizaţie
civilize *v* a civiliza
claim *v* a pretinde
claim *n* pretenţie
clam *n* scoică
clamor *v* a face gălăgie
clamp *n* clemă
clan *n* clan
clandestine *adj* clandestin
clap *v* a pocni
clarification *n* clarificare
clarify *v* a clarifica
clarinet *n* clarinet
clarity *n* claritate
clash *v* a ciocni, a izbi
clash *n* ciocnire
class *n* clasă; categorie
classic *adj* clasic
classify *v* a clasifica
classmate *n* coleg de clasă
classroom *n* sală de clasă
classy *adj* elegant, la modă
clause *n* clauză
claw *n* gheară
claw *v* a zgâria
clay *n* argilă, lut
clean *adj* curat
clean *v* a curăţa
cleaner *n* curăţitor
cleanliness *n* curăţenie
cleanse *v* a face curăţenie
clear *adj* clar; curat; pur
clear *v* a curăţa; a clarifica
clearance *n* clarificare
clear-cut *adj* limpede, drept

clearly *adv* limpede, distinct
clearness *n* claritate
cleft *n* crăpătură
clemency *n* clemenţă
clench *v* a strânge
clergy *n* cler
clergyman *n* preot
clerical *adj* clerical
clerk *n* funcţionar, grefier
clever *adj* deştept
click *v* a pocni
client *n* client
clientele *n* clientelă
cliff *n* râpă
climate *n* climat, climă
climatic *adj* climateric
climax *n* punct culminant
climb *v* a se urca
climbing *n* căţărare
clinch *v* a nitui
cling *iv* a se agăţa
clinic *n* clinică
clip *v* a reteza, a prinde
clipping *n* tăietură
cloak *n* mantie
clock *n* ceas, ceasornic
clog *v* a se bloca
cloister *n* mănăstire
clone *v* a clona
cloning *n* clonare
close *v* a închide
close *adj* apropiat
close to *pre* în jur de
closed *adj* închis
closely *adv* îndeaproape
closet *n* dulap
closure *n* încheiere
clot *n* cheag
cloth *n* cârpă, pânză
clothe *v* a îmbrăca
clothes *n* haine
clothing *n* îmbrăcăminte
cloud *n* nor
cloudless *adj* senin
cloudy *adj* înnorat
clown *n* clovn
club *n* club; bâtă; crosă
club *v* a ciomăgi
clue *n* soluţie, cheie
clumsiness *n* stângăcie
clumsy *adj* stângaci
cluster *n* ciorchine
cluster *v* a se aduna
clutch *n* apucare
coach *v* a antrena
coach *n* antrenor, meditator

coaching *n* antrenare
coagulate *v* a coagula
coagulation *n* coagulare
coal *n* cărbune
coalition *n* coaliţie
coarse *adj* aspru; grosolan
coast *n* coastă, ţărm
coastal *adj* de coastă
coastline *n* linie de coastă
coat *n* haină; înveliş; strat
coax *v* a îndupleca
cob *n* lebădoi, bucată
cobblestone *n* piatră de râu
cobweb *n* pânză de păianjen
cocaine *n* cocaină
cock *n* cocoş
cockpit *n* carlingă
cocktail *n* cocteil
cocky *adj* îngâmfat
cocoa *n* cacao
coconut *n* nucă de cocos
cod *n* cod
code *n* cod; semnal
codify *v* a codifica
coefficient *n* coeficient
coerce *v* a sili
coercion *n* constrângere
coexist *v* a coexista
coffee *n* cafea
coffin *n* sicriu
cohabit *v* a coabita
coherent *adj* coerent
cohesion *n* coeziune
coin *n* monedă
coincide *v* a coincide
coincidence *n* coincidenţă
coincidental *adj* întâmplător
cold *adj* rece, calm
coldness *n* frig, răceală
colic *n* colică
collaborate *v* a colabora
collaboration *n* colaborare
collaborator *n* colaborator
collapse *v* a se prăbuşi
collapse *n* prăbuşire
collar *n* zgardă, guler
collarbone *n* claviculă
collateral *adj* colateral
colleague *n* coleg
collect *v* a colecta
collection *n* colecţie
collector *n* colector
college *n* colegiu
collide *v* a se ciocni
collision *n* ciocnire
cologne *n* apă de colonie

colon *n* intestinul gros
colonel *n* colonel
colonial *adj* colonial
colonization *n* colonizare
colonize *v* a coloniza
colony *n* colonie
color *n* culoare
color *v* a colora
colorful *adj* colorat
colossal *adj* colosal, uriaş
colt *n* mânz
column *n* coloană, rubrică
coma *n* comă
comb *n* pieptene
comb *v* a pieptăna
combat *n* luptă
combat *v* a combate
combatant *n* combatant
combination *n* combinaţie
combine *v* a combina
combustible *n* combustibil
combustion *n* combustie
come *iv* a veni
come about *v* a se întâmpla
come across *v* a întâmpina
come apart *v* a se despărţi
come back *v* a se întoarce
come down *v* a coborî, a sosi
come from *v* a născoci
come in *v* a intra
come out *v* a ieşi
come over *v* a trece pe la
come up *v* a deveni
comeback *n* revenire
comedian *n* comediant
comedy *n* comedie
comet *n* cometă
comfort *n* comfort
comfortable *adj* comfortabil
comforter *n* consolator
comical *adj* comic
coming *n* sosire, venire
coming *adj* promiţător
comma *n* virgulă
command *v* a comanda
commander *n* comandant
commandment *n* comandament
commemorate *v* a comemora
commence *v* a începe
commend *v* a lăuda, a trimite
commendation *n* laudă
comment *v* a comenta
comment *n* comentariu
commerce *n* comerţ
commercial *adj* comercial
commission *n* comision; comisie

commit *v* a comite; a angaja
commitment *n* obligaţie
committed *adj* ataşat
committee *n* comitet
common *adj* comun
commotion *n* tulburare
communicate *v* a comunica
communication *n* comunicare
communion *n* comuniune
communism *n* comunism
communist *adj* comunist
community *n* comunitate
commute *v* a comuta
compact *adj* compact
compact *v* a consolida
companion *n* companion
companionship *n* tovărăşie
company *n* companie
comparable *adj* comparabil
comparative *adj* comparativ
compare *v* a compara
comparison *n* comparaţie
compartment *n* compartiment
compass *n* busolă
compassion *n* compasiune
compassionate *adj* milos
compatibility *n* compatibilitate
compatible *adj* compatibil
compatriot *n* compatriot
compel *v* a constrânge
compelling *adj* convingător
compendium *n* compendiu
compensate *v* a compensa
compensation *n* compensaţie
compete *v* a concura
competence *n* competenţă
competent *adj* competent
competition *n* competiţie
competitive *adj* competitiv
competitor *n* competitor
compile *v* a alcătui
complain *v* a protesta
complaint *n* plângere
complement *n* complement
complete *adj* complet
complete *v* a termina
completely *adv* în întregime
completion *n* completare
complex *adj* complicat
complexion *n* ten, înfăţişare
complexity *n* complexitate
compliance *n* bunăvoinţă
compliant *adj* binevoitor
complicate *v* a complica
complication *n* complicaţie
complicity *n* complicitate

compliment *n* compliment
complimentary *adj* admirativ; gratuit
comply *v* a se supune
component *n* componentă
compose *v* a compune
composed *adj* compus; liniştit
composer *n* compozitor
composition *n* compoziţie
compost *n* bălegar
composure *n* linişte, calm
compound *n* compus
compound *v* a compune
comprehend *v* a înţelege
comprehensive *adj* cuprinzător
compress *v* a comprima
compression *n* comprimare
comprise *v* a cuprinde
compromise *n* compromis
compromise *v* a compromite
compulsion *n* constrângere
compulsive *adj* obligatoriu
compulsory *adj* obligatoriu
compute *v* a calcula
computer *n* computer
comrade *n* tovarăş
con man *n* escroc, pungaş
conceal *v* a ascunde
concede *v* a ceda, a admite
conceited *adj* încrezut
conceive *v* a concepe
concentrate *v* a concentra
concentration *n* concentrare
concentric *adj* concentric
concept *n* concept
conception *n* concepţie
concern *v* a interesa
concern *n* grijă, preocupare
concerning *pre* referitor la
concert *n* concert
concession *n* concesie, cedare
conciliate *v* a împăca
conciliatory *adj* conciliant
concise *adj* concis, succint
conclude *v* a încheia
conclusion *n* concluzie
conclusive *adj* final, convingător
concoct *v* a pregăti
concoction *n* născocire
concrete *n* beton
concrete *adj* concret
concur *v* a fi de acord
concurrent *adj* concomitent
concussion *n* lovitură, comoţie
condemn *v* a condamna
condemnation *n* condamnare

C

condensation *n* condensare
condense *v* a condensa
condescend *v* a condescinde
condiment *n* condiment
condition *n* condiţie, situaţie
conditional *adj* condiţional
condo *n* condominiu
condolences *n* condoleanţe
condone *v* a trece cu vederea
conducive *adj* duce la
conduct *n* conduită,
conduct *v* a duce; a dirija
conductor *n* dirijor
cone *n* con
confer *v* a conferi
conference *n* conferinţă
confess *v* a mărturisi
confession *n* mărturisire
confessional *n* spovedanie
confessor *n* duhovnic
confidant *n* confident
confide *v* a mărturisi
confidence *n* credinţă
confident *adj* încrezător
confidential *adj* confidenţial
confine *v* a limita; a îngrădi
confinement *n* captivitate
confirm *v* a confirma
confirmation *n* confirmare
confiscate *v* a confisca
confiscation *n* confiscare
conflict *n* conflict
conflict *v* a fi în conflict
conflicting *adj* contradictoriu
conform *v* a potrivi
conformist *adj* conformist
conformity *n* conformitate
confound *v* a confunda
confront *v* a confrunta
confrontation *n* confruntare
confuse *v* a încurca
confusing *adj* confundabil
confusion *n* confuzie
congenial *adj* plăcut
congested *adj* congestionat
congestion *n* congestie
congratulate *v* a felicita
congratulations *n* felicitări
congregate *v* a se aduna
congregation *n* congregaţie
congress *n* congres
conjecture *n* presupunere
conjugal *adj* conjugal
conjugate *v* a conjuga
conjunction *n* conjuncţie, unire
conjure up *v* a evoca

connect *v* a conecta
connection *n* conexiune
connive *v* a tăinui
connote *v* a implica
conquer *v* a cuceri
conqueror *n* cuceritor
conquest *n* cucerire
conscience *n* conştiinţă
conscious *adj* conştient
conciousness *n* conştienţă
conscript *n* recrut
consecrate *v* a consacra
consecration *n* sfinţire
consecutive *adj* consecutiv
consensus *n* consens
consent *v* a fi de acord
consent *n* acord
consequence *n* consecinţă
consequent *adj* ulterior, firesc
conservation *n* conservare
conservative *adj* conservator
conserve *v* a conserva
conserve *n* dulceaţă, gem
consider *v* a considera
considerable *adj* considerabil
considerate *adj* moderat
consideration *n* consideraţie
consignment *n* consemnare
consist *v* a consta în
consistency *n* consecvenţă
consistent *adj* solid; consistent
consolation *n* consolare
console *v* a consola
consolidate *v* a consolida
consonant *n* consoană
conspicuous *adj* evident, vizibil
conspiracy *n* conspiraţie
conspirator *n* complotist
conspire *v* a conspira
constancy *n* constanţă
constant *adj* constant
constellation *n* constelaţie
consternation *n* consternare
constipate *v* a constipa
constipated *adj* constipat
constipation *n* constipaţie
constitute *v* a constitui
constitution *n* constituţie
constrain *v* a constrânge
constraint *n* constrângere
construct *v* a construi
construction *n* construcţie
constructive *adj* constructiv
consul *n* consul
consulate *n* consulat
consult *v* a consulta

consultation *n* consultaţie
consume *v* a consuma
consumer *n* consumator
consumption *n* consumaţie
contact *v* a contacta
contact *n* contact
contagious *adj* contagios
contain *v* a conţine
container *n* conteiner
contaminate *v* a contamina
contamination *n* contaminare
contemplate *v* a contempla
contemporary *adj* contemporar
contempt *n* dispreţ, sfidare
contend *v* a susţine
contender *n* susţinător
content *adj* mulţumit
content *v* a mulţumi
contentious *adj* certăreţ
contents *n* conţinut
contest *n* concurs
contestant *n* cocurent
context *n* context
continent *n* continent
continental *adj* continental
contingency *n* eventualitate
contingent *adj* eventual
continuation *n* continuare
continue *v* a continua
continuity *n* continuitate
continuous *adj* continuu
contour *n* contur
contraband *n* contrabandă
contract *v* a contracta
contract *n* contract
contraction *n* contracţie
contradict *v* a contrazice
contradiction *n* contradicţie
contrary *adj* contrar
contrast *v* a contrasta
contrast *n* contrast
contribute *v* a contribui
contribution *n* contribuţie
contributor *n* contribuabil
contrition *n* pocăinţă
control *n* control
control *v* a controla
controversial *adj* controversat
controversy *n* controversă
convalescent *adj* convalescent
convene *v* a convoca
convenience *n* convenienţă
convenient *adj* convenabil
convent *n* mănăstire
convention *n* convenţie, acord
conventional *adj* convenţional

converge *v* a concentra
conversation *n* conversaţie
converse *v* a conversa
conversely *adv* invers
conversion *n* schimbare
convert *v* a converti
convert *n* convertit
convey *v* a transmite
convict *v* condamnat
conviction *n* convingere
convince *v* a convinge
convincing *adj* convingător
convoluted *adj* răsucit, încurcat
convoy *n* convoi, alai
convulse *v* a zgudui
convulsion *n* convulsie
cook *v* a găti
cook *n* bucătar
cookie *n* fursec
cooking *n* gătit
cool *adj* răcoros; calm
cool *v* a răci
cool down *v* a se linişti
cooling *adj* răcoritor
coolness *n* racire; calmare
cooperate *v* a coopera
cooperation *n* cooperare
cooperative *adj* cooperatist
coordinate *v* a coordona
coordination *n* coordonare
coordinator *n* coordonator
cop *n* poliţist
cope *v* a face faţă
copier *n* copist
copper *n* aramă
copy *v* a copia
copy *n* copie
copyright *n* drept de autor
cord *n* funie; coardă
cordial *adj* cordial
cordless *adj* fără fir
cordon *n* cordon
cordon off *v*
core *n* miez
cork *n* dop
corn *n* porumb
corner *n* colţ; cotlon; stoc
cornet *n* cornet, corn
corollary *n* urmare
coronary *adj* coronar
coronation *n* încoronare
corporal *adj* corporal
corporal *n* caporal
corporation *n* corporaţie
corpse *n* cadavru
corpulent *adj* gras

C

corpuscle *n* corpuscul
correct *v* a corecta
correct *adj* corect
correction *n* corecţie
correlate *v* a pune în corelaţie
correspond *v* a corespunde
corridor *n* coridor
corroborate *v* a întări
corrode *v* a roade, a rugini
corrupt *v* a corupe
corrupt *adj* corupt; stricat
corruption *n* corupţie
cosmetic *n* cosmetic
cosmic *adj* cosmic
cosmonaut *n* cosmonaut
cost *iv* a costa
cost *n* cost, preţ
costly *adj* costisitor
costume *n* costum
cottage *n* căsuţă, bordei
cotton *n* bumbac
couch *n* canapea, sofa
cough *n* tuse
cough *v* a tuşi
council *n* consiliu
counsel *v* a se sfătui
counsel *n* sfat; consilier
counselor *n* sfătuitor
count *v* a socoti
count *n* socoteală; cont
countenance *n* expresie
counter *n* tejghea
counter *v* a se opune
counteract *v* a contracara
counterfeit *v* a falsifica
counterfeit *adj* falsificat
counterpart *n* omolog
countess *n* contesă
countless *adj* nenumărat
country *n* ţară; stat
countryman *n* ţăran
countryside *n* regiune rurală
county *n* distric, judeţ
coup *n* lovitură de stat
couple *n* pereche; cuplu
coupon *n* cupon
courage *n* curaj
courageous *adj* curajos
courier *n* curier
course *n* curs; drum
court *n* curte; tribunal
court *v* a curta
courteous *adj* curtenitor
courtesy *n* curtoazie
courthouse *n* tribunal
courtship *n* curte, petiţie

courtyard *n* curtea casei
cousin *n* văr
cove *n* golf
covenant *n* acord, pact
cover *n* copertă; adăpost
cover *v* a acoperi
cover up *v* a ascunde
coverage *n* cuprindere
covert *adj* ascuns, tainic
coverup *n* acoperire
covet *v* a râvni la
cow *n* vacă
coward *n* laş
cowardice *n* laşitate
cowardly *adv* cu laşitate
cowboy *n* cowboy, văcar
cozy *adj* comfortabil
crab *n* crab
crack *n* crăpătură
crack *v* a crăpa; a plesni
cradle *n* leagăn
craft *n* viclenie; meserie
craftsman *n* meşteşugar
cram *v* a îndopa
cramp *n* crampă
cramped *adj* strâmpt
crane *n* cocor
crank *n* manivelă
cranky *adj* stricat, şubred
crap *n* rahat, prostii
crash *n* trosnet; accident
crash *v* a zdrobi; a turti
crass *adj* cras
crater *n* crater
crave *v* a tânji
craving *n* dorinţă, poftă
crawl *v* a se târî
crayon *n* pastel
craziness *n* nebunie
crazy *adj* nebun
creak *v* a scârţâi
creak *n* scârţâit
cream *n* frişcă
creamy *adj* cremos
crease *n* dungă, pliu
crease *v* a îndoi
create *v* a crea
creation *n* creaţie
creative *adj* creativ
creativity *n* creativitate
creator *n* creator
creature *n* creatură
credibility *n* credibilitate
credible *adj* credibil
credit *n* credit
creditor *n* creditor

C

creed *n* crez
creek *n* pârâu
creep *v* a-i da fiori
creepy *adj* care te înfioară
cremate *v* a incinera
crematorium *n* crematoriu
crest *n* creastă, coamă
crevice *n* crăpătură
crew *n* echipaj
crib *n* pat de copil
cricket *n* greiere
crime *n* crimă
criminal *adj* criminal
cripple *adj* invalid, infirm
cripple *v* a mutila, a ciunti
crisis *n* criză
crisp *adj* crocant
criss-cross *v* a încrucişa
crispy *adj* crocant
criterion *n* criteriu
critical *adj* critic; primejdios
criticism *n* critică
criticize *v* a critica
critique *n* critică
crockery *n* olărit, ceramică
crocodile *n* crocodil
crony *n* prieten nedespărţit
crook *n* cârje, îndoitură
crooked *adj* strâmb, încovoiat
crop *n* recoltă
cross *n* cruce, încrucişare
cross *adj* supărat, irascibil
cross *v* a traversa, a trece
cross out *v* a tăia, a şterge
crossfire *n* foc concentric
crossing *n* traversare
crossroads *n* intersecţie
crosswalk *n* trecere de pietoni
crossword *n* cuvinte încrucişate
crouch *v* a se ghemui
crow *n* cioară
crow *v* a gânguri
crowbar *n* bară de metal
crowd *n* mulţime
crowd *v* a se îngrămădi
crowded *adj* aglomerat
crown *n* coroană
crown *v* a încorona
crowning *n* încoronare
crucial *adj* crucial, decisiv
crucifix *n* crucifix
crucifixion *n* crufificare
crucify *v* a crucifica
crude *adj* crud; neterminat
cruel *adj* crud, chinuitor
cruelty *n* cruzime

crumb *n* firimitură
crumble *v* a fărâmiţa
crunchy *adj* crocant
crusade *n* cruciadă
crusader *n* cruciat
crush *v* a zdrobi
crushing *adj* zdrobit
crust *n* crustă; coajă
crusty *adj* scorţos
crutch *n* cârjă, sprijin
cry *n* plânset, strigăt
cry *v* a plânge, a striga
cry out *v* a striga, a zbiera
crying *n* plânset
crystal *n* cristal
cub *n* pui de animal
cube *n* cub
cubic *adj* cubic
cubicle *n* compartiment
cucumber *n* castravete
cuddle *v* a strânge în braţe
cuff *n* manşetă, palmă
cuisine *n* bucătărie
culminate *v* a culmina
culpability *n* vină
culprit *n* vinovat, acuzat
cult *n* cult
cultivate *v* a cultiva
cultivation *n* cultivare, cultură
cultural *adj* cultural
culture *n* cultură
cumbersome *adj* obositor, incomod
cunning *adj* viclean, abil
cup *n* ceaşcă
cupboard *n* dulap
curable *adj* vindecabil
curator *n* custode, îngrijitor
curb *v* a ţine în frâu
curb *n* frâu, bordură
curdle *v* a se închega
cure *v* a vindeca
cure *n* vindecare
curiosity *n* curiozitate
curious *adj* curios
curl *v* a suci, a răsuci
curl *n* buclă
curly *adj* ondulat
currency *n* monedă, valută
current *adj* curent
currently *adv* în mod curent
curse *v* a blestema
curtail *v* a ciunti, a reduce
curtain *n* cortină, perdea
curve *n* curbă
curve *v* a coti
cushion *n* pernă

cushion *v* a tapisa
cuss *v* a înjura
custard *n* cremă de ouă
custodian *n* custode
custody *n* pază, arest
custom *n* datină, obicei
customary *adj* obişnuit
customer *n* client
custom-made *adj* făcut la comandă
customs *n* vamă
cut *n* tăietură
cut *iv* a tăia
cut back *v* a reteza, a scurta
cut down *v* a tăia, a doborî
cut off *v* a întrerupe
cut out *v* a întrerupe
cute *adj* nostim, drăguţ
cutlery *n* tacâmuri, cuţite
cutter *n* cuter, tăietor
cyanide *n* cianat
cycle *n* ciclu
cyclist *n* ciclist
cyclone *n* ciclon
cylinder *n* cilindru
cynic *adj* cinic
cynicism *n* cinism
cypress *n* chiparos
cyst *n* chist
czar *n* ţar

D

dad *n* tati, tăticuţu
dagger *n* hanger
daily *adv* zilnic
dairy farm *n* fermă de lapte
daisy *n* margaretă
dam *n* stăvilar, baraj
damage *n* pagubă
damage *v* a strica
damaging *adj* stricător
damn *v* a blestema
damnation *n* damnaţiune
damp *adj* umed
dampen *v* a tempera
dance *n* dans
dance *v* a dansa
dancing *n* dans
dandruff *n* mătreaţă
danger *n* pericol
dangerous *adj* periculos
dangle *v* a legăna

dare *v* a îndrazni
dare *n* îndrăzneală
daring *adj* îndrăzneţ
dark *adj* întunecat
darken *v* a se întuneca
darkness *n* întuneric
darling *adj* drăguţ, scump
darn *v* a ţese ciorapi
dart *n* suliţă, săgeată
dash *v* a arunca, a ţâşni
dashing *adj* îndrăzneţ, vioi
data *n* date, fapte
database *n* bază de date
date *n* dată, întâlnire
date *v* a data, a se întâlni
daughter *n* fiică
daughter-in-law *n* noră
daunt *v* a speria
daunting *adj* înfricoşat
dawn *n* zori, răsărit
day *n* zi
daydream *v* o reverie
daze *v* a ameţi
dazed *adj* zăpăcit
dazzle *v* a străluci orbitor
dazzling *adj* orbitor
de luxe *adj* luxos
deacon *n* diacon
dead *adj* mort, stins
dead end *n* capăt, fundătură
deaden *v* a amorţi, a alina
deadline *n* limită
deadlock *adj* în impas
deadly *adj* mortal
deaf *adj* surd
deafen *v* a asurzi
deafening *adj* asurzitor
deafness *n* surzenie
deal *iv* a trata cu
deal *n* afacere, învoială
dealer *n* negustor
dealings *n* tranzacţii
dean *n* vicar, decan
dear *adj* drag, scump
dearly *adv* scump
death *n* moarte
deathbed *n* patul morţii
debase *v* a coborî
debatable *adj* discutabil
debate *v* a dezbate
debate *n* dezbatere
debit *n* debit
debrief *v* a interoga
debris *n* moloz
debt *n* datorie bănească
debtor *n* datornic

D

debunk *v* a demasca
debut *n* debut
decade *n* decadă, deceniu
decadence *n* decadenţă
decaff *adj* decofeinizat
decapitate *v* a decapita
decay *v* a decădea
decay *n* putreziciune
deceased *adj* decedat
deceit *n* înşelăciune
deceitful *adj* mincinos
deceive *v* a înşela
December *n* decembrie
decency *n* decenţă
decent *adj* decent
deception *n* decepţie
deceptive *adj* înşelător
decide *v* a decide
deciding *adj* decisiv
decimal *adj* zecimal
decimate *v* a decima
decipher *v* a descifra
decision *n* decizie
decisive *adj* decisiv
deck *n* punte
declaration *n* declaraţie
declare *v* a declara
declension *n* declinare
decline *v* a scădea
decline *n* declin, slăbire
decompose *v* a se descompune
décor *n* decor
decorate *v* a decora
decorative *adj* decorativ
decorum *n* decenţă
decrease *v* a scădea
decrease *n* descreştere
decree *n* decret
decree *v* a decreta
decrepit *adj* îmbătrânit
dedicate *v* a dedica
dedication *n* dedicaţie
deduce *v* a deduce
deduct *v* a scădea
deductible *adj* deductibil
deduction *n* deducţie
deed *n* acţiune, act
deem *v* a crede
deep *adj* adânc
deepen *v* a adânci
deer *n* cerb
deface *v* a desfigura
defame *v* a defăima
defeat *v* a învinge
defeat *n* înfrângere
defect *n* defect

defect *v* a defecta
defection *n* defecţiune
defective *adj* deficient
defend *v* a apăra
defendant *n* acuzat
defender *n* apărător
defense *n* apărare
defenseless *adj* lipsit de apărare
defer *v* a amâna
defiance *n* sfidare
defiant *adj* sfidător
deficiency *n* deficienţă
deficient *adj* deficient
deficit *n* deficit
defile *v* a spurca
define *v* a defini
definite *adj* hotărât, clar
definition *n* definiţie
definitive *adj* definitiv
deflate *v* a dezumfla
deform *v* a deforma
deformity *n* diformitate
defraud *v* a escroca
defray *v* a rambursa
defrost *v* a decongela
deft *adj* abil
defuse *v* a reduce primejdia
defy *v* a sfida, a înfrunta
degenerate *v* a degenera
degenerate *adj* degenerat
degeneration *n* degenerare
degradation *n* degradare
degrade *v* a degrada
degrading *adj* degradat
degree *n* grad, titlu
dehydrate *v* a deshidrata
deign *v* a condescinde
deity *n* zeitate
dejected *adj* trist, deprimat
delay *v* a întârzia
delay *n* întârziere
delegate *v* a delega
delegate *n* delegat
delegation *n* delegare
delete *v* a şterge
deliberate *v* a delibera
deliberate *adj* intenţionat
delicacy *n* delicateţe
delicate *adj* delicat
delicious *adj* delicios
delight *n* încântare
delight *v* a încânta
delightful *adj* încântător
delinquency *n* delicvenţă
delinquent *adj* delicvent
deliver *v* a furniza; a oferi

D

delivery *n* predare; transport
delude *v* a înşela
deluge *n* potop
delusion *n* iluzie
demand *v* a pretinde, a cere
demand *n* cerere, pretenţie
demanding *adj* pretenţios
demean *v* a condescinde
demeaning *adj* reputat
demeanor *n* comportare
demented *adj* nebun
demise *n* deces
democracy *n* democraţie
democratic *adj* democratic
demolish *v* a dărâma
demolition *n* demolare
demon *n* demon
demonstrate *v* a demonstra
demonstrative *adj* demonstrativ
demoralize *v* a demoraliza
demote *v* a retrograda
den *n* vizuină, bârlog
denial *n* negare
denigrate *v* a denigra
Denmak *n* Danemarca
denominator *n* numitor
denote *v* a indica
denounce *v* a denunţa
dense *adj* dens; gros
density *n* densitate
dent *v* a cresta
dent *n* zimţ
dental *adj* dentar
dentist *n* dentist
dentures *n* dantură
deny *v* a nega
deodorant *n* deodorant
depart *v* a pleca, a răposa
department *n* departament
departure *n* plecare
depend *v* a depinde
dependable *adj* de nădejde
dependence *n* dependenţă
dependent *adj* dependent
depict *v* a descrie
deplete *v* a goli
deplorable *adj* deplorabil
deplore *v* a deplânge
deploy *v* a desfăşura
deployment *n* desfăşurare
deport *v* a deporta
deportation *n* deportare
depose *v* a demite
deposit *n* depozit
depot *n* depozit; depou
depraved *adj* depravat

depravity *n* depravare
depreciate *v* a deprecia
depreciation *n* depreciere
depress *v* a deprima
depressing *adj* deprimant
depression *n* depresiune
deprive *v* a priva
deprived *adj* privat
deprivation *n* privare, lipsire
depth *n* adâncime
derail *v* a deraia
derailment *n* deraiare
deranged *adj* deranjat
derelict *adj* părăsit
deride *v* a ridiculiza
derivative *adj* derivat
derive *v* a proveni
derogatory *adj* peiorativ
descend *v* a coborî
descendant *n* descendent
descent *n* coborâre; origine
describe *v* a descrie
description *n* descriere
descriptive *adj* descriptiv
desert *n* pustietate, merit
desert *v* a dezerta
deserted *adj* părăsit
deserter *n* dezertor
deserve *v* a merita
deserving *adj* merituos
design *n* desen; proiect
designate *v* a desemna
desirable *adj* dezirabil
desire *n* dorinţă
desire *v* a dori
desist *v* a înceta
desk *n* pupitru; birou
desolate *adj* pustiu, părăsit
desolation *n* dezolare
despair *n* deznădejde
desperate *adj* deznădăjduit
despicable *adj* mizerabil
despise *v* a dispreţui
despite *c* dispreţ
despondent *adj* nenorocit
despot *n* tiran
despotic *adj* despotic
dessert *n* desert
destination *n* destinaţie
destiny *n* destin
destitute *adj* sărac, nevoiaş
destroy *v* a distruge
destroyer *n* distrugător
destruction *n* destrugere
destructive *adj* distructiv
detach *v* a detaşa

detachable *adj* detaşabil
detail *n* detaliu
detail *v* a detalia
detain *v* a deţine,
detect *v* a detecta
detective *n* detectiv
detector *n* detector
detention *n* reţinere, arestare
deter *v* a împiedica
detergent *n* detergent
deteriorate *v* a deteriora
deterioration *n* deteriorare
determination *n* determinare
determine *v* a determina
deterrence *n* descurajare
detest *v* a detesta
detestable *adj* detestabil
detonate *v* a detona
detonation *n* detonare
detonator *n* detonator
detour *n* ocol
detriment *n* detriment
detrimental *adj* dăunător
devaluation *n* devalorizare
devalue *v* a devaloriza
devastate *v* a devasta
devastating *adj* devastator
devastation *n* devastare
develop *v* a dezvolta
development *n* dezvoltare
deviation *n* deviere
device *n* dispozitiv
devil *n* demon, diavol
devious *adj* indirect
devise *v* a născoci
devoid *adj* lipsit de
devote *v* a dedica
devotion *n* devotament
devour *v* a devora
devout *adj* pios, serios
dew *n* rouă
diabetes *n* diabet
diabetic *adj* diabetic
diabolical *adj* diabolic
diagnose *v* a diagnostica
diagnosis *n* diagnostic
diagonal *adj* în diagonală
diagram *n* diagramă
dial *n* cadran
dial tone *n* ton la telefon
dialect *n* dialect
dialogue *n* dialog
diameter *n* diametru
diamond *n* diamant
diaper *n* scutec
diarrhea *n* diaree

diary *n* jurnal
dice *n* zaruri
dictate *v* a dicta
dictator *n* dictator
dictatorial *adj* dictatorial
dictatorship *n* dictatură
dictionary *n* dicţionar
die *v* a muri
die out *v* a se sfârşi
diet *n* dietă, regim
differ *v* a diferi
difference *n* diferenţă
different *adj* diferit
difficult *adj* dificil
difficulty *n* dificultate
diffuse *v* a difuza
dig *iv* a săpa
digest *v* a digera
digestion *n* digestie
digestive *adj* digestiv
digit *n* deget, cifră
dignify *v* a înnobila
dignitary *n* demnitar
dignity *n* demnitate
digress *v* a se abate
dilapidated *adj* dărâmat
dilemma *n* dilemă
diligence *n* silinţă
diligent *adj* silitor
dilute *v* a dilua
dim *adj* ceţos, neclar
dim *v* a se înceţoşa
dime *n* dime
dimension *n* dimensiune
diminish *v* a diminua
dine *v* a mânca
dining room *n* sufragerie
dinner *n* cină
dinosaur *n* dinozaur
diocese *n* dioceză
diphthong *n* diftong
diploma *n* diplomă
diplomacy *n* diplomaţie
diplomat *n* diplomat
diplomatic *adj* diplomatic
dire *adj* cumplit, extrem
direct *adj* direct
direct *v* a direcţiona
direction *n* direcţie
director *n* director
directory *n* ghid, îndrumar
dirt *n* ţărână, noroi
dirty *adj* murdar
disability *n* incapacitate
disabled *adj* inapt, invalid
disadvantage *n* dezavantaj

D

disagree *v* a dezaproba
disagreeable *adj* dezagreabil
disagreement *n* dezacord
disappear *v* a dispărea
disappearance *n* dispariţie
disappoint *v* a dezamăgi
disappointing *adj* dezamăgit
disapproval *n* dezaprobare
disapprove *v* a dezaproba
disarm *v* a dezarma
disarmament *n* dezarmament
disaster *n* dezastru
disastrous *adj* dezastruos
disband *v* a demobiliza
disbelief *n* neîncredere
disburse *v* a plăti
discard *v* a înlătura
discern *v* a distinge
discharge *v* a descărca
discharge *n* descărcare
disciple *n* discipol
discipline *n* disciplină
disclaim *v* a repudia
disclose *v* a dezvălui
discomfort *n* discomfort
disconnect *v* a deconecta
discontent *adj* nemulţumit
discontinue *v* a înceta
discord *n* dezacord
discordant *adj* discordant
discount *n* decont
discount *v* a deconta
discourage *v* a descuraja
discouragement *n* descurajare
discouraging *adj* descurajator
discourtesy *n* nepoliteţe
discover *v* a descoperi
discovery *n* decoperire
discredit *v* a discredita
discreet *adj* discret
discrepancy *n* discrepanţă
discretion *n* discreţie
discriminate *v* a discrimina
discrimination *n* disciminare
discuss *v* a discuta
discussion *n* discuţie
disdain *n* dispreţ
disease *n* boală
disembark *v* a debarca
disenchanted *adj* dazamăgit
disentangle *v* a descurca
disfigure *v* a desfigura
disgrace *n* dizgraţie
disgrace *v* a dezonora
disgraceful *adj* ruşinos
disgruntled *adj* nemulţumit

D

disguise *v* a deghiza
disguise *n* deghizare
disgust *n* dezgust
disgusting *adj* dezgustător
dish *n* farfurie
dishearten *v* a descuraja
dishonest *adj* necinstit
dishonesty *n* necinste
dishonor *n* dezonoare
dishonorable *adj* dezonorabil
disillusion *n* deziluzie
disinfect *v* a dezinfecta
disinfectant *n* dezinfectant
disinherit *v* a dezmoşteni
disintegrate *v* a dezintegra
disintegration *n* dezintegrare
disinterested *adj* dezinteresat
disk *n* disc
dislike *v* a antipatiza
dislike *n* antipatie
dislocate *v* a disloca
dislodge *v* a muta
disloyal *adj* necredincios
disloyalty *n* necredinţă
dismal *adj* întunecos
dismantle *v* a demonta
dismay *n* spaimă
dismay *v* a înspăimânta
dismiss *v* a concedia
dismissal *n* izgonire
dismount *v* a demonta
disobedience *n* nesupunere
disobedient *adj* nesupus
disobey *v* a nu asculta
disorder *n* dezordine
disorganized *adj* dezorganizat
disoriented *adj* dezorientat
disown *v* a renega
disparity *n* nepotrivire
dispatch *v* a expedia
dispel *v* a alunga
dispensation *n* dispensare
dispense *v* a împărţi
dispersal *n* dispersare
disperse *v* a dispersa
displace *v* a deplasa
display *n* expoziţie
display *v* a expune
displease *v* a ofensa
displeasing *adj* supărător
displeasure *n* nemulţumire
disposable *adj* disponibil
disposal *n* folosire
dispose *v* a dispune
disprove *v* a dovedi fals
dispute *n* dispută

D

dispute *v* a discuta
disqualify *v* a descalifica
disregard *v* a nesocoti
disrespect *n* nepoliteţe
disrespectful *adj* nepoliticos
disrupt *v* a fărâmiţa
disruption *n* dezbinare
dissatisfied *adj* nemulţumit
disseminate *v* a răspândi
dissent *v* a fi în dezacord
dissident *adj* disident
dissimilar *adj* diferit
dissipate *v* a risipi
dissolute *adj* destrăbălat
dissolution *n* dizolvare
dissolve *v* a dizolva
dissonant *adj* disonant
dissuade *v* a disuada
distance *n* distanţă
distant *adj* distant
distaste *n* dezgust
distasteful *adj* dezagreabil
distill *v* a distila
distinct *adj* distinct
distinction *n* distincţie
distinctive *adj* distinctiv
distinguish *v* a distinge
distort *v* a deforma
distortion *n* deformare
distract *v* a distrage
distraction *n* distragere
distraught *adj* înnebunit
distress *n* necaz
distress *v* a necăji
distressing *adj* chinuitor
distribute *v* a distribui
distribution *n* distribuţie
district *n* district, regiune
distrust *n* neîncredere
distrust *v* a suspecta
distrustful *adj* bănuitor
disturb *v* a tulbura
disturbance *n* tulburare
disturbing *adj* tulburător
disunity *n* lipsă de unitate
disuse *n* nefolosire
ditch *n* şanţ
dive *v* a plonja
diver *n* scafandru
diverse *adj* divers
diversify *v* a diversifica
diversion *n* diversiune
diversity *n* diveristate
divert *v* a distrage
divide *v* a despărţi
dividend *n* dividend

divine *adj* divin
diving *n* scufundare
divinity *n* divinitate
divisible *adj* divizibil
division *n* diviziune
divorce *n* divorţ
divorce *v* a divorţa
divorcee *n* femeie divorţată
divulge *v* a divulga
dizziness *n* ameţeală
dizzy *adj* ameţit
do *iv* a acţiona
docile *adj* docil
docility *n* docilitate
dock *n* doc
doctor *n* doctor
doctrine *n* doctrină
document *n* document
documentary *n* documentar
documentation *n* documentare
dodge *v* e evita
dog *n* câine
dogmatic *adj* dogmatic
dole out *v* a distribui
doll *n* păpuşă
dollar *n* dolar
dolphin *n* delfin
dome *n* dom
domestic *adj* domestic; intern
domesticate *v* a domestici
dominate *v* a domina
domination *n* dominare
domineering *adj* autoritar
dominion *n* dominaţie
donate *v* a dona
donation *n* donaţie
donkey *n* măgar
donor *n* donator
doom *n* soartă rea
doomed *adj* condamnat
door *n* uşă, poartă
doorbell *n* sonerie
doorstep *n* prag
doorway *n* prag, cadrul uşii
dope *n* stupefiant, dopaj
dope *v* a droga, a dopa
dormitory *n* dormitor comun
dosage *n* dozaj
dossier *n* dosar
dot *n* punct
double *adj* dublu
double *v* a dubla
double-check *v* a verifica
double-cross *v* a înşela
doubt *n* îndoială
doubtful *adl* neîncrezător

dough *n* aluat, cocă
dove *n* porumbel
down *adv* jos, la pământ
down payment *n* plată în avans
downcast *adj* deprimat
downfall *n* cădere
downhill *adv* în jos, la vale
downpour *n* ploaie torenţială
downsize *v* a micşora
downstairs *adv* jos, la parter
down-to-earth *adj* nepretenţios
downtown *n* centrul oraşului
downtrodden *adj* umilit, asuprit
downturn *n* îndoitură, îndoire
dowry *n* zestre
doze *n* aţipeală, somn
doze *v* a aţipi, a dormita
dozen *n* duzină
draft *n* plan; recrutare
draft *v* a schiţa
draftsman *n* desenator
drag *v* a trage, a târî
dragon *n* dragon, balaur
drain *v* a canaliza
drainage *n* canalizare
dramatic *adj* dramatic
dramatize *v* a dramatiza
drape *n* drapaj
drastic *adj* drastic
draw *n* tragere, atracţie
draw *iv* a trage; a atrage
drawback *n* piedică
drawer *n* sertar
drawing *n* desen, grafică
dread *v* a înspăimânta
dreaded *adj* înspăimântat
dreadful *adj* înspăimântător
dream *iv* a visa
dream *n* vis
dress *n* rochie
dress *v* a îmbrăca
dresser *n* costumier
dressing *n* îmbrăcare, sos
dried *adj* uscat
drift *v* a îndepărta, a duce
drift apart *v* a se afla în derivă
drifter *n* pierde-vară
drill *v* a sfredeli; a instrui
drill *n* sfredel; instrucţie
drink *iv* a bea
drink *n* băutură
drinkable *adj* potabil
drinker *n* băutor, beţiv
drip *v* a picura
drip *n* picătură
drive *iv* a conduce

drive away *v* a izgoni
driver *n* şofer
driveway *n* alee, străduţă
drizzle *v* a burniţa, a bura
drizzle *n* burniţă
drop *n* picătură; cădere
drop *v* a scăpa
drop off *v* a scădea
drop out *v* a se da bătut
drought *n* secetă
drown *v* a îneca
drowsy *adj* adormit
drug *n* doctorie, drog
drug *v* a droga
drugstore *n* farmacie
drum *n* tobă; rezervor
drunk *adj* beat
drunkenness *n* beţie
dry *v* a usca
dry *adj* uscat
dryclean *v* a curăţa
dryer *n* uscător
dual *adj* dual
dubious *adj* dubios
duchess *n* ducesă
duck *n* raţă
duck *v* a cufunda
duct *n* tub, canal
due *adj* datorat
duel *n* duel
dues *n* taxe, impozite
duke *n* duce
dull *adj* greoi, prost
duly *adv* la timpul potrivit
dumb *adj* mut; amuţit
dummy *n* manechin
dummy *adj* nătâng, prostuţ
dump *v* a descărca
dump *n* depozit
dung *n* bălegar
dungeon *n* temniţă, beci
dupe *v* a păcăli
duplicate *v* a reproduce
duplication *n* duplicare
durable *adj* durabil
duration *n* durată
during *pre* în timpul
dusk *n* crepuscul
dust *n* praf, pulbere
dusty *adj* prăfuit
Dutch *adj* olandez
duty *n* îndatorire
dwarf *n* pitic
dwell *iv* a locui
dwelling *n* locuinţă
dwindle *v* a se micşora

dye *v* a vopsi
dye *n* vopsea
dying *adj* muribund
dynamic *adj* dinamic
dynamite *n* dinamită
dynasty *n* dinastie

E

each *adj* fiecare
each other *adj* unul pe altul
eager *adj* doritor
eagerness *n* nerăbdare
eagle *n* vultur
ear *n* ureche; auz; spic
earache *n* durere de urechi
early *adv* devreme
earmark *v* a însemna
earn *v* a câştiga, a merita
earnestly *adv* sincer
earnings *n* salariu, câştig
earphones *n* căşti
earring *n* cercel
earth *n* pământ
earthquake *n* cutremur
earwax *n* cerumen
ease *v* a uşura, a alina
ease *n* tihnă, uşurinţă
easily *adv* uşor
east *n* est, răsărit
eastbound *adj* spre est
Easter *n* Paşte
eastern *adj* estic
easterner *n* oriental
eastward *adv* spre est
easy *adj* uşor, facil
eat *iv* a mânca
eat away *v* a înghiţi, a distruge
eavesdrop *v* a trage cu urechea
ebb *v* a decădea
eccentric *adj* excentric
echo *n* ecou
eclipse *n* eclipsă
ecology *n* ecologie
economical *adj* economic
economize *v* a economisi
economy *n* economie
ecstasy *n* extaz
ecstatic *adj* vesel
edge *n* muchie, margine
edgy *adj* ascuţit, tăios
edible *adj* comestibil
edifice *n* clădire

edit *v* a redacta, a edita
edition *n* ediţie
educate *v* a educa
educational *adj* educaţional
eerie *adj* straniu
effect *n* efect
effective *adj* efectiv
effectiveness *n* efectivitate
efficiency *n* eficienţă
efficient *adj* eficient
effigy *n* figură, efigie
effort *n* effort
effusive *adj* efuziv
egg *n* ou
egg white *n* albuş
egoism *n* egoism
egoist *n* egoist
eight *adj* opt
eighteen *adj* optsprezece
eighth *adj* al optulea
eighty *adj* optzeci
either *adj* fiecare, oricare
either *adv* de asemenea
eject *v* a scoate
elapse *v* a scurge
elastic *adj* elastic
elated *adj* entuziast
elbow *n* cot
elder *n* mai mare
elderly *adj* bătrâior
elect *v* a alege
election *n* alegere
electric *adj* electric
electrician *n* electrician
electricity *n* electricitate
electrify *v* a electriza
electrocute *v* a electrocuta
electronic *adj* electronic
elegance *n* eleganţă
elegant *adj* elegant
element *n* element
elementary *adj* elementar
elephant *n* elefant
elevate *v* a ridica
elevation *n* ridicare
elevator *n* elevator, lift
eleven *adj* unsprezece
eleventh *adj* al unsprezecelea
eligible *adj* eligibil
eliminate *v* a elimina
elm *n* ulm
eloquence *n* elocvenţă
else *adv* în plus, mai
elsewhere *adv* în altă parte
elude *v* a evita, a eluda
elusive *adj* lunecos

E

emaciated *adj* supt; înfometat
emanate *v* a emana
emancipate *v* a emancipa
embalm *v* a îmbălsăma
embark *v* a îmbarca
embarrass *v* a împiedica
embassy *n* ambasadă
embellish *v* a înfrumuseţa
embers *n* jeratic
embezzle *v* a delapida
embitter *v* a amărî
emblem *n* emblemă
embody *v* a întrupa
emboss *v* a ştanţa
embrace *v* a îmbrăţişa
embrace *n* îmbrăţişare
embroider *v* a broda
embroidery *n* broderie
embroil *v* a încâlci
embryo *n* embrion
emerald *n* smarald
emerge *v* a ieşi la iveală
emergency *n* urgenţă
emigrant *n* emigrant
emigrate *v* a emigra
emission *n* emitere
emit *v* e emite
emotion *n* emoţie
emotional *adj* emoţional
emperor *n* împărat
emphasis *n* emfază
emphasize *v* a sublinia
empire *n* imperiu
employ *v* a angaja
employee *n* salariat
employer *n* angajator
employment *n* angajare
empress *n* împărăteasă
emptiness *n* goliciune, vid
empty *adj* gol
empty *v* a goli
enable *v* a face posibil
enchant *v* a vrăji
enchanting *adj* încântător
encircle *v* a încercui
enclave *n* enclavă
enclose *v* a înconjura
enclosure *n* îngrădire
encompass *v* a cuprinde
encounter *v* a întâlni
encounter *n* întâlnire
encourage *v* a încuraja
encroach *v* a încălca
encyclopedia *n* enciclopedie
end *n* sfârşit, capăt
end *v* a sfârşi

end up *v* a sfârşi
endanger *v* a primejdui
endeavor *v* a se strădui
endeavor *n* strădanie, efort
ending *n* sfârşit
endless *adj* nesfârşit
endorse *v* a gira; a aproba
endorsement *n* gir, aprobare
endure *v* a îndura
enemy *n* inamic
energetic *adj* energic
energy *n* energie
enforce *v* a promulga
engage *v* a ocupa, a logodi
engaged *adj* logodit, ocupat
engagement *n* angajament
engine *n* motor
engineer *n* inginer
England *n* Anglia
English *adj* englezesc
engrave *v* a grava
engraving *n* gravură
engrossed *adj* absorbit
engulf *v* a înghiţi; a hăpăi
enhance *v* a spori
enjoy *v* a savura
enjoyable *adj* plăcut
enjoyment *n* plăcere
enlarge *v* a lărgi
enlargement *n* mărire
enlighten *v* a lumina
enlist *v* a înrola
enormous *adj* enorm, uriaş
enough *adv* destul
enrage *v* a supăra
enrich *v* a îmbogăţi
enroll *v* a înrola
enrollment *n* înrolare
ensure *v* a asigura
entail *v* a determina
entangle *v* a încurca
enter *v* a intra în
enterprise *n* curaj, aventură
entertain *v* a distra
entertaining *adj* distractiv
entertainment *n* distracţie
enthrall *v* a captiva
enthralling *adj* captivant
enthuse *v* a entuziasma
enthusiasm *n* entuziasm
entice *v* a momi
enticement *n* momeală
enticing *adj* ispititor
entire *adj* total, întreg
entirely *adv* complet
entrance *n* intrare

E

entreat *v* a implora
entree *n* gustare, antreu
entrenched *adj* fortificat
entrepreneur *n* antreprenor
entrust *v* a încredinţa
entry *n* intrare
enumerate *v* a enumera
envelop *v* a învălui
envelope *n* plic
envious *adj* invidios
environment *n* mediu
envisage *v* a preconiza
envoy *n* trimis, sol
envy *n* invidie
envy *v* a invidia
epidemic *n* epidemie
epilepsy *n* epilepsie
episode *n* episod
epistle *n* epistolă
epitaph *n* epitaf
epitomize *v* a rezuma
epoch *n* epocă
equal *adj* egal
equality *n* egalitate
equate *v* a egala
equation *n* ecuaţie
equator *n* ecuator
equilibrium *n* echilibru
equip *v* a echipa
equipment *n* echipament
equivalent *adj* echivalent
era *n* eră
eradicate *v* a eradica
erase *v* a şterge
eraser *n* gumă
erect *v* a ridica
erect *adj* drept, vertical
err *v* a greşi
errand *n* serviciu, comision
erroneous *adj* greşit
error *n* greşeală
erupt *v* a erupe; a izbucni
eruption *n* erupţie, izbucnire
escalate *v* a se extinde
escalator *n* scară rulantă
escapade *n* escapadă
escape *v* a evada
escort *n* escortă
esophagus *n* esofag
especially *adv* în special
espionage *n* spionaj
essay *n* eseu
essence *n* esenţă
essential *adj* esenţial
establish *v* a stabili
estate *n* moşie

esteem *v* a stima
estimate *v* a estima
estimation *n* estimare
estranged *adj* înstrăinat
estuary *n* estuar
eternity *n* eternitate
ethical *adj* moral, etic
ethics *n* morală
etiquette *n* etichetă
euphoria *n* euforie
Europe *n* Europa
European *adj* european
evacuate *v* a evacua
evade *v* a evita, a ocoli
evaluate *v* a evalua
evaporate *v* a evapora
evasion *n* sustragere
evasive *adj* evaziv
eve *n* ajun
even *adj* neted, egal
even if *c* chiar dacă
even more *c* chiar mai
evening *n* seară
event *n* eveniment
eventuality *n* eventualitate
eventually *adv* în cele din urmă
ever *adv* oricând, mereu
everlasting *adj* etern
every *adj* fiecare, toţi
everybody *pro* toată lumea
everyday *adj* zilnic
everyone *pro* toată lumea
everything *pro* tot
evict *v* a izgoni
evidence *n* dovadă, probă
evil *n* rău
evil *adj* rău, ticălos
evoke *v* a evoca, a aminti
evolution *n* evoluţie
evolve *v* a evolua
exact *adj* exact
exaggerate *v* a exagera
exalt *v* a înălţa
examination *n* examinare
examine *v* a examina
example *n* exemplu
exasperate *v* a exaspera
excavate *v* a escava
exceed *v* a depăşi
exceedingly *adv* extrem
excel *v* a excela
excellence *n* excelenţă
excellent *adj* excelent
except *pre* fără
exception *n* excepţie
exceptional *adj* excepţional

E

excerpt *n* extras
excess *n* exces
excessive *adj* excesiv
exchange *v* a schimba
excite *v* a emoţiona
excitement *n* emoţie
exciting *adj* emoţionant
exclaim *v* a exclama
exclude *v* a exclude
excruciating *adj* cumplit
excursion *n* excursie
excuse *v* a scuza
excuse *n* scuză
execute *v* a executa
executive *n* executiv
exemplary *adj* exemplar
exemplify *v* a exemplifica
exempt *adj* scutit
exemption *n* scutire
exercise *n* exerciţiu
exercise *v* a exersa
exert *v* a folosi; a exercita
exertion *n* exercitare; effort
exhaust *v* a epuiza; a evacua
exhausting *adj* epuizant
exhaustion *n* istovire
exhibit *v* a expune
exhibition *n* expoziţie
exhilarating *adj* înviorant, vesel
exhort *v* a ruga
exile *v* a exila
exile *n* exil
exist *v* a exista
existence *n* existenţă
exit *n* ieşire
exodus *n* exod
exonerate *v* a dezvinovăţi
exorbitant *adj* exorbitant
exorcist *n* exorcist
exotic *adj* exotic
expand *v* a desfăşura
expansion *n* expansiune
expect *v* a aştepta
expectancy *n* aşteptare
expectation *n* speranţă
expediency *n* convenienţă
expedient *adj* avantajos
expedition *n* expediţie
expel *v* a expulza
expenditure *n* cheltuială
expense *n* cheltuială, cost
expensive *adj* scump
experience *n* experienţă
experiment *n* experiment
expert *adj* expert
expiate *v* a ispăşi

expiation *n* ispăşire
expiration *n* expirare
expire *v* a expira
explain *v* a explica
explicit *adj* explicit
explode *v* a exploda
exploit *v* a exploata
exploit *n* ispravă
explore *v* a explora
explorer *n* explorator
explosion *n* explozie
explosive *adj* exploziv
explotation *n* exploatare
export *v* a exporta
expose *v* a demasca
exposed *adj* expus
express *adj* expres; clar
express *v* a exprima
expression *n* expresie
expressly *adv* explicit
expropriate *v* a expropria
expulsion *n* expulzare
exquisite *adj* excelent
extend *v* a extinde
extension *n* extensiune
extent *n* măsură
extenuating *adj* atenuante
exterior *adj* exterior
exterminate *v* a extermina
external *adj* extern, exterior
extinct *adj* stins, dispărut
extinguish *v* a stinge
extort *v* a stoarce
extortion *n* escrocherie
extra *adv* suplimentar
extract *v* a extrage
extradite *v* a extrăda
extradition *n* extrădare
extraneous *adj* exterior
extravagance *n* extravaganţă
extravagant *adj* extravagant
extreme *adj* extrem
extremist *adj* extremist
extremities *n* extremităţi
extricate *v* a elibera
extroverted *adj* extrovertit
exude *v* a asuda
exult *v* a exulta
eye *n* ochi, privire
eyebrow *n* sprânceană
eyeglasses *n* ochelari
eyelash *n* geană
eyelid *n* pleoapă
eyesight *n* vedere
eyewitness *n* martor ocular

F

F

fable *n* fabulă
fabric *n* ţesătură
fabricate *v* a născoci
fabulous *adj* fabulos
face *n* faţă, înfăţişare
facet *n* faţetă; aspect
facilitate *v* a uşura
facing *pre* cu faţa la
fact *n* fapt
factor *n* factor
factory *n* fabrică
factual *adj* efectiv
faculty *n* facultate
fad *n* capriciu
fade *v* a decolora
faded *adj* decolorat
fail *v* a eşua
failure *n* eşec
faint *v* a leşina
faint *n* leşin
faint *adj* slab, istovit
fair *n* târg, expoziţie
fair *adj* corect; cinstit
fairness *n* corectitudine
fairy *n* zână
faith *n* încredere; credinţă
faithful *adj* credincios
fake *v* a falsifica
fake *adj* fals
fall *n* cădere; cascadă
fall *iv* a cădea
fall back *v* a se retrage
fall behind *v* a rămâne în urmă
fall down *v* a cădea, a atârna
fall through *v* a eşua, a da greş
fallacy *n* înşelătorie
falsehood *n* minciună
falsify *v* a falsifica
falter *v* a îngăima
fame *n* faimă
familiar *adj* familiar
family *n* familie
famine *n* foamete
famous *adj* faimos
fan *n* evantai; admirator
fanatic *adj* fanatic
fancy *adj* imaginaţie
fang *n* colţ
fantastic *adj* fantastic
fantasy *n* fantezie
far *adv* departe
faraway *adj* îndepărtat
farce *n* farsă

fare *n* tarif, taxă
farewell *n* la revedere
farm *n* fermă
farmer *n* fermier
farming *n* agricultură
farmyard *n* fermă
farther *adv* mai departe
fascinate *v* a fascina
fashion *n* modă
fashionable *adj* la modă
fast *adj* strâns, rapid
fasten *v* a fixa
fat *n* grăsime
fat *adj* gras
fatal *adj* fatal
fate *n* soartă
fateful *adj* fatal, vital
father *n* tată, părinte
fatherhood *n* paternitate
father-in-law *n* socru
fatherly *adj* patern
fathom out *v* a înţelege
fatigue *n* oboseală
fatten *v* a se îngrăşa
fatty *adj* gras
faucet *n* robinet
fault *n* vină, vinovăţie
faulty *adj* deficient
favor *n* favoare
favorable *adj* favorabil
favorite *adj* favorit
fear *n* frică, teamă
fearful *adj* înspăimântător
feasible *adj* realizabil
feast *n* ospăţ
feat *n* faptă
feather *n* pană
feature *n* trăsătură
February *n* februarie
fed up *adj* sătul
federal *adj* federal
fee *n* taxă
feeble *adj* plăpând
feed *iv* a mânca
feedback *n* reacţie inversă
feel *iv* a se simţi
feeling *n* sentiment
feelings *n* sentimente
feet *n* labele picioarelor
feign *v* a simula
fellow *n* individ
fellowship *n* tovărăşie
felon *n* criminal
felony *n* crimă
female *n* femelă
feminine *adj* feminin

fence *n* gard
fencing *n* scrimă
fend *v* a feri
fender *n* apărătoare
ferment *v* a fermenta
ferment *n* ferment
ferocious *adj* feroce
ferocity *n* ferocitate
ferry *n* bac
fertile *adj* fertil
fertility *n* fertilitate
fertilize *v* a fertiliza
fervent *adj* fierbinte
festive *adj* festiv
festivity *n* festivitate
fetid *adj* rău mirositor
fetus *n* făt
feud *n* vrajbă
fever *n* febră
feverish *adj* febril
few *adj* puţini
fewer *adj* mai puţin
fiancé *n* logodnic
fiber *n* fibră
fickle *adj* schimbător
fiction *n* ficţiune
fictitious *adj* fictiv
fiddle *n* scripcă
fidelity *n* fidelitate
field *n* câmp
fierce *adj* violent, rău
fiery *adj* arzător
fifteen *adj* cincisprezece
fifth *adj* al cincelea
fifty *adj* cincizeci
fifty-fifty *adv* pe din două
fig *n* smochin
fight *iv* a se lupta
fight *n* luptă, bătaie
fighter *n* luptător
figure *n* cifră, siluetă
figure out *v* a descifra
file *v* a înregistra
file *n* dosar; arhivă
fill *v* a umple
filling *n* umplere
film *n* film
filter *n* filtru
filter *v* a filtra
filth *n* murdărie
filthy *adj* murdar
fin *n* aripioară
final *adj* final
finalize *v* a finaliza
finance *v* a finanţa
financial *adj* financiar

find *iv* a găsi
find out *v* a afla
fine *n* amendă
fine *v* a amenda
fine *adv* fin, precis
fine *adj* frumos, bun
finger *n* deget de la mână
fingernail *n* unghie
fingerprint *n* amprentă
fingertip *n* buricul degetului
finish *v* a încheia
Finland *n* Finlanda
Finnish *adj* finlandez
fire *v* a incendia
fire *n* foc, incendiu
firearm *n* armă de foc
firecracker *n* pocnitoare
fireman *n* pompier
fireplace *n* şemineu
firewood *n* lemne de foc
fireworks *n* focuri de artificii
firm *adj* ferm
firm *n* firmă
firmness *n* fermitate
first *adj* prim, întâi
fish *n* peşte
fisherman *n* pescar
fishy *adj* suspect
fist *n* pumn
fit *n* potrivire
fit *v* a potrivi, a proba
fitting *adj* potrivit, nimerit
five *adj* cinci
fix *v* a fixa
fjord *n* fiord
flag *n* steag
flagpole *n* catarg de steag
flamboyant *adj* ţipător
flame *n* flacără
flammable *adj* inflamabil
flank *n* flanc
flare *n* pâlpâit, flacără
flare-up *v* a se aprinde
flash *n* fulgerare
flashlight *n* fulger
flashy *adj* ţipător
flat *n* apartament
flat *adj* plat, turtit
flatten *v* a turti
flatter *v* a flata, a măguli
flattery *n* flatare
flaunt *v* a etala
flavor *n* savoare, aromă
flaw *n* lipsă, deficienţă
flawless *adj* impecabil
flea *n* purice

flee *iv* a fugi de
fleece *n* caier, nor
fleet *n* flotă
fleeting *adj* efemer
flesh *n* carne, trup
flex *v* a curba
flexible *adj* flexibil
flicker *v* licărire
flier *n* zburător; flaier
flight *n* zbor; stol; fugă
flimsy *adj* subţire
flip *v* a pocni
flirt *v* a flirta
float *v* a lansa pe apă
flock *n* turmă
flog *v* a biciui
flood *v* a inunda
floodgate *n* ecluză
flooding *n* inundare
floodlight *n* reflector
floor *n* podea, etaj
flop *n* cădere, eşec
floss *n* puf, aţă de dinţi
flour *n* făină
flourish *v* a înflori
flow *v* a curge
flow *n* curent, vărsare
flower *n* floare
flowerpot *n* ghiveci
flu *n* gripă
fluctuate *v* a fluctua
fluently *adv* fluent
fluid *n* fluid
flunk *v* a trânti
flush *v* torent, îmbujorare
flute *n* flaut
flutter *v* a flutura
fly *iv* a zbura
fly *n* muscă, zbor
foam *n* spumă
focus *n* focar, centru
focus on *v* a se concentra
foe *n* duşman
fog *n* ceaţă, pâclă
foggy *adj* ceţos
foil *v* a depăşi
fold *v* a îndoi
folder *n* pliant
folks *n* oameni
folksy *adj* popular
follow *v* a urma
follower *n* însoţitor
folly *n* prostie
fond *adj* tandru; preferat
fondle *v* a mângâia
fondness *n* tandreţe

food *n* mâncare
foodstuff *n* alimente
fool *v* a păcăli
fool *adj* prost
foolproof *adj* inofensiv
foot *n* laba piciorului
football *n* fotbal
footnote *n* notă de subsol
footprint *n* urmă de picior
footstep *n* pas
footwear *n* încălţăminte
for *pre* pentru
forbid *iv* a interzice
force *n* forţă, putere
force *v* a forţa
forceful *adj* puternic
forcibly *adv* prin forţă
forecast *iv* a prognoza
forefront *n* partea din faţă
foreground *n* prim plan
forehead *n* frunte
foreign *adj* străin; extern
foreigner *n* străin
foreman *n* maistru
foremost *adj* principal
foresee *iv* a prevedea
foreshadow *v* a prevesti
foresight *n* previziune
forest *n* pădure
foretaste *n* degustare
foretell *v* a prezice
forever *adv* pururi, mereu
forewarn *v* a avertiza
foreword *n* prefaţă
forfeit *v* a pierde
forge *v* a forja
forgery *n* falsificare
forget *v* a uita
forgive *v* a ierta
forgiveness *n* iertare
fork *n* furculiţă
form *n* formă
formal *adj* formal
formality *n* formalitate
formalize *v* a da o formă
formally *adv* în mod formal
format *n* format
formation *n* formare, formaţie
former *adj* fost, anterior
formerly *adv* pe vremuri
formidable *adj* formidabil
formula *n* formulă
forsake *iv* a părăsi
fort *n* fort
forthcoming *adj*
forthright *adj* deschis, sincer

F

fortify *v* a fortifica
fortitude *n* vitejie, bravură
fortress *n* fortăreaţă
fortunate *adj* norocos
fortune *n* noroc
forty *adj* patruzeci
forward *adv* înainte
fossil *n* fosilă
foster *v* a creşte; a hrăni
foul *adj* urât, murdar
foundation *n* fundaţie
founder *n* întemeietor
foundry *n* topitorie
fountain *n* fântână
four *adj* patru
fourteen *adj* paisprezece
fourth *adj* al patrulea
fox *n* vulpe
foxy *adj* şiret
fraction *n* fracţie
fracture *n* fractură
fragile *adj* fragil
fragment *n* fragment
fragrance *n* aromă, parfum
fragrant *adj* parfumat
frail *adj* firav, plăpând
frailty *n* slăbiciune
frame *n* cadru; construcţie
frame *v* a încadra
framework *n* cadru; context
France *n* Franţa
franchise *n* franciză
frank *adj* sincer
frankly *adv* deschis
frankness *n* francheţe
frantic *adj* nebunesc
fraternal *adj* frăţesc
fraternity *n* fraternitate
fraud *n* fraudă
fraudulent *adj* necinstit
freckle *n* pistrui
freckled *adj* pistruiat
free *v* a elibera
free *adj* liber; gratuit
freedom *n* libertate
freeway *n* autostradă
freeze *iv* a îngheţa
freezer *n* frigider
freezing *adj* glacial
freight *n* marfă, transport
French *adj* franţuzesc
frenetic *adj* frenetic
frenzied *adj* frenetic
frenzy *n* frenezie
frequency *n* frecvenţă
frequent *adj* frecvent

frequent *v* a frecventa
fresh *adj* proaspăt
freshen *v* a împrospăta
freshness *n* prospeţime
friar *n* călugăr
friction *n* frecare; fricţiune
Friday *n* vineri
fried *adj* beat, prăjit
friend *n* prieten, amic
friendship *n* prietenie
fries *n* cartofi prăjiţi
frigate *n* fregată
fright *n* spaimă
frighten *v* a speria
frightening *adj* înspăimântător
frigid *adj* frigid, rece
fringe *n* franjuri; breton
frivolous *adj* frivol
frog *n* broască
from *pre* de la, din
front *n* faţă; front; faţadă
front *adj* frontal
frontage *n* faţadă
frontier *n* frontieră
frost *n* ger, frig
frostbite *n* degerătură
frostbitten *adj* degerat
frosty *adj* geros
frown *v* a se încrunta
frozen *adj* îngheţat
frugal *adj* frugal
frugality *n* frugalitate
fruit *n* fruct
fruitful *adj* rodnic
frustrate *v* a împiedica
frustration *n* frustrare
fry *v* a prăji
frying pan *n* tigaie
fuel *n* combustibil
fuel *v* a alimenta
fugitive *n* fugitiv, fugar
fulfill *v* a împlini
fulfillment *n* împlinire
full *adj* plin, complet
fully *adv* cu desăvârşire
fumes *n* abur
fumigate *v* a afuma
fun *n* distracţie, veselie
function *n* funcţie, funcţiune
fund *n* fond
fund *v* a furniza
fundamental *adj* fundamental
funds *n* resurse
funeral *n* înmormântare
fungus *n* ciupercă
funny *adj* nostim, amuzant

fur *n* blană
furious *adj* furios
furiously *adv* furios, cu furie
furnace *n* furnal, coş
furnish *v* a mobila
furnishings *n* mobilier, furnituri
furniture *n* mobilă
furor *n* furie
furrow *n* brazdă
furry *adj* îmblănit
further *adv* mai departe
furthermore *adv* pe deasupra
fury *n* furie
fuse *n* fitil
fusion *n* fuziune
fuss *n* agitaţie, zarvă
fussy *adj* agitat
futile *adj* inutil, de prisos
futility *n* zădărnicie
future *n* viitor
fuzzy *adj* estompat, vag

G

gadget *n* dispozitiv
gag *n* căluş, truc
gag *v* a face să tacă
gage *v* a pune în joc
gain *v* a câştiga
gain *n* câştig
gal *n* fată, femeie
galaxy *n* galaxie
gale *n* vânt puternic
gall bladder *n* vezica biliară
gallant *adj* elegant, galant
gallery *n* galerie
gallon *n* galon
gallop *v* a galopa
gallows *n* spânzutătoare
galvanize *v* a galvaniza
game *n* joc, partidă
gang *n* grup, bandă
gangrene *n* cangrenă
gangster *n* gangster
gap *n* gol; lipsă
garage *n* garaj
garbage *n* gunoi
garden *n* grădină
gardener *n* grădinar

gargle *v* a gargarisi
garland *n* ghirlandă
garlic *n* usturoi
garment *n* confecţii
garnish *v* a garnisi
garnish *n* garnitură
garrison *n* garnizoană
garrulous *adj* flecar, guraliv
garter *n* jartieră
gas *n* gaz
gash *n* tăietură, rană
gasoline *n* gazolină
gasp *v* a gâfâi
gastric *adj* gastric
gate *n* poartă
gather *v* a aduna
gathering *n* adunare
gauge *v* a măsura
gauze *n* tifon, voal
gaze *v* a se uita insistent
gear *n* angrenaj, viteză
geese *n* gâşte
gem *n* nestemată
gender *n* gen
gene *n* genă
general *n* general
generalize *v* a generaliza
generate *v* a genera
generation *n* generaţie
generator *n* generator
generic *adj* generic
generosity *n* generozitate
genetic *adj* genetic
genial *adj* genial
genius *n* geniu
genocide *n* genocid
genteel *adj* rafinat
gentle *adj* gentil
gentleman *n* gentleman
gentleness *n* tandreţe
genuflect *v* a îngenunchia
genuine *adj* veritabil, sincer
geography *n* geografie
geology *n* geologie
geometry *n* geometrie
germ *n* germen, microb
German *adj* german
Germany *n* Germania
germinate *v* a încolţi
gerund *n* gerunziu
gestation *n* gestaţie
gesticulate *v* a gesticula
gesture *n* gest
get *iv* a ajunge
get along *v* a se împăca
get away *v* a scăpa

get back *v* a reveni
get by *v* a reuşi să treacă
get down *v* a coborî
get down to *v* a ajunge la
get in *v* a pătrunde
get off *v* a scăpa de
get out *v* a ieşi
get over *v* a trece dincolo
get together *v* a aduna
get up *v* a ridica
geyser *n* gheizer
ghastly *adj* groaznic
ghost *n* fantomă
giant *n* uriaş
gift *n* dar, cadou
gifted *adj* înzestrat
gigantic *adj* gigantic
giggle *v* a chicoti
gimmick *n* păcăleală
ginger *n* ghimbir
gingerly *adv* blând
giraffe *n* girafă
girl *n* fată
girlfriend *n* prietenă
give *iv* a da
give back *v* a înapoia
give in *v* a ceda
give out *v* a se epuiza
give up *v* a renunţa
glacier *n* gheţar
glad *adj* bucuros
gladiator *n* gladiator
glamorous *adj* fermecător
glance *v* a privi
glance *n* privire
gland *n* glandă
glare *n* strălucire
glass *n* sticlă, pahar
glasses *n* ochelari
glassware *n* sticlărie
gleam *n* licărire
gleam *v* a licări
glide *v* a aluneca
glimmer *n* licărire
glimpse *n* privire
glimpse *v* a privire
glitter *v* a străluci
globe *n* glob
globule *n* globulă
gloom *n* întuneric
gloomy *adj* întunecos
glorify *v* a glorifica
glorious *adj* glorios
glory *n* glorie
gloss *n* luciu
glossary *n* glosar

glossy *adj* lucios
glove *n* mănuşă
glow *v* a străluci
glucose *n* glucoză
glue *n* lipici, clei
glue *v* a lipi
glut *n* ghiftuire
glutton *n* lacom
gnaw *v* a roade
go *iv* a merge
go ahead *v* a merge înainte
go away *v* a pleca
go back *v* a se întoarce
go down *v* a coborî
go in *v* a intra
go on *v* a continua
go out *v* a ieşi
go through *v* a trece prin
go under *v* a se scufunda
go up *v* a merge în sus
goad *v* a îndemna
goal *n* ţintă; gol
goalkeeper *n* portar
goat *n* capră
gobble *v* a înfuleca
God *n* Dumnezeu
goddess *n* zeiţă
godless *adj* ateu
gold *n* aur
golden *adj* auriu
good *adj* bun
good-looking *adj* chipeş
goodness *n* bunătate
goods *n* bunuri
goodwill *n* bunăvoinţă
goof *v* a se prosti
goof *n* bufon, fraier
goose *n* gâscă
gorge *n* strâmtoare
gorgeous *adj* minunat
gorilla *n* gorilă
gory *adj* însângerat
gospel *n* evanghelie
gossip *v* a bârfi
gossip *n* bârfă
gout *n* gută
govern *v* a guverna
government *n* guvern
governor *n* guvernator
gown *n* halat, rochie
grab *v* a apuca
grace *n* graţie
graceful *adj* graţios
gracious *adj* graţios
grade *n* rang, grad
gradual *adj* gradual

graduate *v* a absolvi
graduation *n* absolvire
graft *v* a altoi, a mitui
graft *n* altoi, mită
grain *n* bob, grână
gram *n* gram
grammar *n* gramatică
grand *adj* măreţ
grandchild *n* nepot de bunic
granddad *n* bunic
grandfather *n* bunic
grandmother *n* bunică
grandparents *n* bunici
grandson *n* nepot de bunic
grandstand *n* tribună oficială
granite *n* granit
granny *n* bunicuţă
grant *v* a acorda
grant *n* alocaţie, dar
grape *n* strugure
grapefruit *n* grepfrut
grapevine *n* viţă de vie
graphic *adj* grafic
grasp *n* strânsoare, apucare
grasp *v* a apuca; a strânge
grass *n* iarbă
grassroots *adj* de bază
grateful *adj* recunoscător
gratify *v* a gratifica
gratifying *adj* încântător
gratitude *n* recunoştinţă
gratuity *n* gratuitate
grave *adj* grav
grave *n* mormânt
gravel *n* pietriş
gravely *adv* grav, solemn
gravestone *n* piatră de mormânt
graveyard *n* cimitir
gravitate *v* a gravita
gravity *n* gravitate
gravy *n* sos
gray *adj* cenuşiu
grayish *adj* gri, cenuşiu
graze *v* a roade, a paşte
graze *n* rosătură; julitură
grease *v* a unge
grease *n* untură; grăsime
greasy *adj* unsuros
great *adj* mare, măreţ
greatness *n* măreţie
Greece *n* Grecia
greed *n* lăcomie
greedy *adj* lacom
Greek *adj* grecesc
green *adj* verde
green bean *n* mazăre

greenhouse *n* seră
Greenland *n* Groenlanda
greet *v* a întâmpina
greetings *n* salutări
gregarious *adj* gregar
grenade *n* grenadă
greyhound *n* ogar
grief *n* necaz, supărare
grievance *n* necaz, plângere
grieve *v* a se necăji
grill *v* a frige la grătar
grill *n* grătar
grim *adj* aspru, sever
grimace *n* grimasă
grime *n* murdărie
grind *iv* a trudi
grip *v* a apuca
grip *n* apucare
gripe *n* înşfăcare
grisly *adj* oribil, sinistru
groan *v* a geme
groan *n* geamăt
groceries *n* articole de băcănie
groin *n* arcadă, stinghie
groom *n* mire, servitor
groove *n* scobitură, şanţ
gross *adj* grosolan; greoi
grossly *adv* grosolan, scabros
grotesque *adj* grotesc
grotto *n* grotă
grouch *v* a fi bosumflat
grouchy *adj* bosumflat
ground *n* teren, pământ
ground floor *n* parter
groundless *adj* neîntemeiat
groundwork *n* fundaţie, temelie
group *n* grup
grow *iv* a creşte
grow up *v* a creşte
growl *v* a mârâi
grown-up *n* adult
growth *n* creştere
grudge *n* ciudă, ranchiună
grudgingly *adv* cu zgârcenie
gruelling *adj* groaznic
gruesome *adj* înspăimântător
grumble *v* a mormăi
grumpy *adj* ţâfnos
guarantee *v* a garanta
guarantee *n* garanţie
guarantor *n* girant
guard *n* pază, gardă
guardian *n* gardian
guerrilla *n* gherilă
guess *v* a ghici
guess *n* ghiceală

guest *n* oaspete
guidance *n* călăuzire
guide *v* a călăuzi
guide *n* călăuză, ghid
guidebook *n* ghid
guidelines *n* linie de ghidare
guild *n* organizaţie
guile *n* viclenie
guillotine *n* ghilotină
guilt *n* vină
guilty *adj* vinovat
guise *n* veşmânt
guitar *n* chitară
gulf *n* golf
gull *n* pescăruş, fraier
gullible *adj* naiv, credul
gulp *v* a înghiţi
gulp *n* înghiţitură
gum *n* gingie; gumă
gun *n* pistol
gun down *v* a împuşca
gunfire *n* împuşcătură
gunman *n* puşcaş
gunpowder *n* praf de puşcă
gunshot *n* împuşcătură
gust *n* rafală, torent
gusto *n* savoare
gusty *adj* impetuos
gut *n* maţ
guts *n* curaj
gutter *n* jgheab; rigolă
guy *n* tip, individ
guzzle *v* a sorbi
gymnasium *n* gimnaziu
gynecology *n* ginecologie
gypsy *n* ţigan

H

habit *n* obicei
habitable *adj* locuibil
habitual *adj* obişnuit
hack *v* a ciopârţi, a tăia
haggle *v* a se tocmi
hail *n* grindină
hail *v* a turna
hair *n* păr
hairbrush *n* perie de cap
haircut *n* tunsoare
hairdo *n* coafură, coafat
hairdresser *n* coafor, frizer
hairpiece *n* meşă
hairy *adj* păros

half *n* jumătate
half *adj* pe jumătate
hall *n* sală, hol
hallucinate *v* a halucina
hallway *n* culoar, hol
halt *v* a opri
halve *v* a înjumătăţi
ham *n* şuncă
hamburger *n* hamburger
hamlet *n* cătun
hammer *n* ciocan
hammock *n* hamac
hand *n* mână
hand in *v* a înmâna
hand out *v* a elibera
hand over *v* a preda
handbag *n* poşetă
handbook *n* manual
handcuff *v* a încătuşa
handcuffs *n* cătuşe
handful *n* un pumn
handicap *n* handicap
handkerchief *n* batistă
handle *v* a mânui
handle *n* manivelă
handmade *adj* lucrat manual
handout *n* dar, pomană
handrail *n* balustradă
handshake *n* strângere de mână
handsome *adj* frumos
handwritting *n* scris
handy *adj* îndemânatic
hang *iv* a atârna
hang around *v* a vagabonda
hang on *v* a se ţine de
hang up *v* a închide telefonul
hanger *n* umeraş
hangup *n* încurcătură
happen *v* a se întâmpla
happening *n* întâmplare
happiness *n* fericire
happy *adj* fericit
harass *v* a hărţui
harassment *n* hărţuire
harbor *n* port
hard *adj* greu, tare
harden *v* a întări
hardly *adv* abia, cu greu
hardness *n* duritate
hardship *n* dificultate
hardy *adj* tare, rezistent
hare *n* iepure de câmp
harm *v* a avaria, a răni
harm *n* rău, stricăciune
harmful *adj* dăunător
harmless *adj* inofensiv

harmonize *v* a se armoniza
harmony *n* armonie
harp *n* harpă
harpoon *n* harpon
harrowing *adj* grăpat
harsh *adj* aspru
harshly *adv* aspru, riguros
harshness *n* asprime
harvest *n* recoltă
harvest *v* a recolta
hashish *n* haşiş
hassle *v* a hărţui, a se certa
hassle *n* ceartă, dezacord
haste *n* grabă
hasten *v* a se grăbi
hastily *adv* în grabă
hasty *adj* grăbit, grabnic
hat *n* pălărie
hatchet *n* baltag, toporişcă
hate *v* a urî
hateful *adj* urâcios
hatred *n* ură
haughty *adj* semeţ, arogant
haul *v* a trage
haunt *v* a bântui
have *iv* a avea, a poseda
have to *v* a trebui să
haven *n* port
havoc *n* dezastru
hawk *n* şoim
hay *n* fân
haystack *n* şura de fân
hazard *n* şansă, hazard
hazardous *adj* hazardat
haze *n* ceaţă uşoară
hazelnut *n* alună
hazy *adj* ceţos, neclar
he *pro* el
head *n* cap
head for *v* a se îndrepta către
headache *n* durere de cap
heading *n* titlu
head-on *adv* frontal
headphones *n* căşti
headquarters *n* cartier general
headway *n* progres
heal *v* a vindeca
healer *n* vindecător
health *n* sănătate
healthy *adj* sănătos
heap *n* morman
heap *v* a îngrămădi
hear *iv* a auzi
hearing *n* auz, ascultare
hearsay *n* vorbe, zvon
hearse *n* dric

heart *n* inimă
heartbeat *n* bătaia inimii
heartburn *n* arsură la stomac
hearten *v* a încuraja
heartfelt *adj* sincer, profund
hearth *n* vatră, cămin
heartless *adj* neîndurător
hearty *adj* sincer, profund
heat *v* a încălzi
heat *n* căldură
heater *n* sobă, radiator
heathen *n* păgân
heating *n* încălzire
heatstroke *n* insolaţie
heatwave *n* val de căldură
heaven *n* rai, paradis
heavenly *adj* divin
heaviness *n* povară, apăsare
heavy *adj* greu
heckle *v* a hărţui cu întrebări
hectic *adj* aprins
heed *v* a băga de seamă
heel *n* călcâi
height *n* înălţime
heighten *v* a înălţa
heinous *adj* criminal, ticălos
heir *n* moştenitor
heiress *n* moştenitoare
heist *n* jaf
helicopter *n* elicopter
hell *n* iad
hello *e* alo, bună
helm *n* cârmă
helmet *n* cască
help *v* a ajuta
help *n* ajutor
helper *n* ajutor
helpful *adj* util, de ajutor
helpless *adj* neputincios
hem *n* tiv, poale
hemisphere *n* emisferă
hemorrhage *n* hemoragie
hen *n* găină
hence *adv* de aici înainte
henchman *n* agent, acolit
her *adj* ei, său, sa, săi
herald *v* a vesti
herald *n* vestitor
herb *n* iarbă
here *adv* aici
hereafter *adv* în viitor
hereby *adv* astfel
hereditary *adj* ereditar
heresy *n* erezie
heretic *adj* eretic
heritage *n* moştenire

hermetic *adj* ermetic
hermit *n* pustnic
hernia *n* hernie
hero *n* erou
heroic *adj* eroic
heroin *n* eroină
heroism *n* eroism
hers *pro* al ei, a ei, ai ei
herself *pro* însăşi
hesitant *adj* ezitant
hesitate *v* a ezita, a şovăi
hesitation *n* ezitare
heyday *n* înflorire
hiccup *n* sughiţ
hidden *adj* ascuns
hide *iv* a ascunde
hideaway *n* ascunzătoare
hideous *adj* hidos
hierarchy *n* ierarhie
high *adj* înalt, acut
highlight *n* lumină puternică
highly *adv* extrem de, foarte
Highness *n* Alteţa
highway *n* autostradă
hijack *v* a deturna
hijack *n* deturnare
hijacker *n* jefuitor
hike *v* a se plimba
hike *n* plimbare
hilarious *adj* hilar, vesel
hill *n* deal
hillside *n* coastă de deal
hilltop *n* vârf de deal
hilly *adj* deluros
hinder *v* a împiedica
hindrance *n* obstacol
hinge *n* balama
hint *n* sugestie
hint *v* a sugera
hip *n* şold
hire *v* a închiria
his *adj* lui, său, sa
his *pro* al lui, a lui
Hispanic *adj* spaniol
hiss *v* a fluiera
historian *n* istoric
history *n* istorie
hit *n* atac; succes
hit *iv* a lovi
hit back *v* a se apăra
hitch *n* hop, salt
hitchhike *n* autostop
hitherto *adv* până acum
hive *n* stup
hoard *v* a aduna
hoarse *adj* răguşit

hoax *n* păcăleală
hobby *n* pasiune
hog *n* porc îngrăşat
hoist *v* a ridica
hoist *n* ridicare
hold *iv* a se ţine
hold back *v* a reţine
hold on to *v* a o ţine tot aşa
hold out *v* a ţine, a dăinui
hold up *v* a arăta, a întârzia
holdup *n* jaf, atac
hole *n* gaură
holiday *n* sărbătoare
holiness *n* sfinţenie
Holland *n* Olanda
hollow *adj* scobit
holocaust *n* holocaust
holy *adj* sfânt
homage *n* omagiu
home *n* casă, domiciliu
homeland *n* ţară, patrie
homeless *adj* fără adăpost
homely *adj* obişnuit
homemade *adj* făcut în casă
homesick *adj* nostalgic
homework *n* temă
homicide *n* omucidere
homily *n* predică
honest *adj* cinstit
honesty *n* cinste
honey *n* miere, iubit
honeymoon *n* lună de miere
honk *v* a claxona
honor *n* onoare
hood *n* glugă
hoodlum *n* cuţitar, bătăuş
hoof *n* copită
hook *n* cârlig; croşetă
hooligan *n* huligan
hop *v* a sări, a omite
hope *n* speranţă
hopeful *adj* încrezător
hopeless *adj* disperat
horizon *n* orizont
horizontal *adj* orizontal
hormone *n* hormon
horn *n* corn
horrendous *adj* îngrozitor
horrible *adj* oribil
horrify *v* a îngrozi
horror *n* oroare
horse *n* cal
hose *n* furtun
hospital *n* spital
hospitality *n* ospitalitate
hospitalize *v* a spitaliza

host *n* gazdă
hostage *n* ostatec
hostess *n* gazdă
hostile *adj* ostil
hostility *n* ostilitate
hot *adj* fierbinte
hotel *n* hotel
hour *n* oră
hourly *adv* din oră în oră
house *n* casă, locuinţă
household *n* gospodărie
housekeeper *n* gospodină
housewife *n* stăpâna casei
housework *n* treburile casnice
how *adv* cum
however *c* totuşi
howl *v* a urla
howl *n* urlet
hub *n* centru
huddle *v* a învălmăşi
hug *v* a îmbrăţişa
hug *n* îmbrăţişare
huge *adj* uriaş
hull *n* coajă, păstaie
hum *v* a zumzăi
human *adj* uman
human being *n* fiinţă umană
humanities *n* umanistică
humankind *n* omenire
humble *adj* umil
humbly *adv* umil
humid *adj* umed
humidity *n* umiditate
humiliate *v* a umili
humility *n* modestie
humor *n* umor
humorous *adj* comic
hump *n* umflătură
hunch *n* cocoaşă, bucată
hunchback *n* cocoşat
hunched *adj* cocoşat
hundred *adj* sută
hundredth *adj* al o sutălea
hunger *n* foame
hungry *adj* flămând
hunt *v* a vâna
hunter *n* vânător
hunting *n* vânătoare
hurdle *n* obstacol
hurl *v* a arunca
hurricane *n* uragan
hurriedly *adv* în grabă
hurry *v* a grăbi
hurry up *v* a se grăbi
hurt *iv* a durea, a suferi
hurt *adj* rană, durere

hurtful *adj* dureros
husband *n* soţ
hush *n* tăcere
hush up *v* a tăinui
husky *adj* voinic
hustle *n* învălmăşeală
hut *n* colibă, baracă
hydraulic *adj* hidraulic
hydrogen *n* hidrogen
hyena *n* hienă
hygiene *n* igienă
hymn *n* imn religios
hyphen *n* liniuţă, cratimă
hypnosis *n* hipnoză
hypnotize *v* a hipnotiza
hypocrisy *n* ipocrizie
hypocrite *adj* ipocrit
hypothesis *n* ipoteză
hysteria *n* isterie
hysterical *adj* isteric

I

I *pro* eu
ice *n* gheaţă
ice cream *n* îngheţată
ice cube *n* cub de gheaţă
ice skate *v* patină
iceberg *n* aisberg
icebox *n* răcitor
ice-cold *adj* rece ca gheaţa
icon *n* icoană, imagine
icy *adj* glacial, îngheţat
idea *n* idee
ideal *adj* ideal
identical *adj* identic
identify *v* a identifica
identity *n* identitate
ideology *n* ideologie
idiom *n* limbă, dialect
idiot *n* idiot
idiotic *adj* idiot, prostesc
idle *adj* trândav, leneş
idol *n* idol
idolatry *n* idolatrie
if *c* dacă
ignite *v* a aprinde
ignorance *n* ignoranţă

ignorant *adj* ignorant
ignore *v* a ignora
ill *adj* rău, bolnav
illegal *adj* ilegal
illegible *adj* necitet̜
illegitimate *adj* nelegitim
illicit *adj* ilicit
illiterate *adj* incult
illness *n* boală
illogical *adj* ilogic
illuminate *v* a ilumina
illusion *n* iluzie
illustrate *v* a ilustra
illustration *n* ilustraţie
illustrious *adj* ilustru
image *n* imagine
imagination *n* imaginaţie
imagine *v* a imagina
imbalance *n* dezechilibru
imitate *v* a imita
imitation *n* imitaţie
immaculate *adj* imaculat
immature *adj* imatur
immaturity *n* imaturitate
immediately *adv* imediat
immense *adj* imens
immensity *n* imensitate
immerse *v* a înmuia
immersion *n* imersiune
immigrant *n* imigrant
immigrate *v* a imigra
immigration *n* imigraţie
imminent *adj* iminent
immobile *adj* imobil
immobilize *v* a imobiliza
immoral *adj* imoral
immorality *n* imoralitate
immortal *adj* imortal
immortality *n* imortalitate
immune *adj* imun
immunity *n* imunitate
immunize *v* a imuniza
immutable *adj* imuabil
impact *n* impact
impact *v* a ciocni, a lovi
impair *v* a slăbi, a afecta
impartial *adj* imparţial
impatience *n* nerăbdare
impatient *adj* nerăbdător
impeccable *adj* impecabil
impediment *n* împiedicare
impending *adj* care împiedică
imperfection *n* imperfecţiune
imperial *adj* imperial
imperialism *n* imperialism
impersonal *adj* impersonal

impertinence *n* impertinenţă
impertinent *adj* impertinent
impetuous *adj* impetuos
implacable *adj* implacabil
implant *v* a implanta
implement *v* a aplica
implicate *v* a implica
implication *n* implicaţie
implicit *adj* implicit
implore *v* a implora
imply *v* a implica
impolite *adj* nepoliticos
import *v* a importa
importance *n* importanţă
importation *n* import
impose *v* a impune
imposing *adj* impunător
imposition *n* impunere
impossibility *n* imposibilitate
impossible *adj* imposibil
impotent *adj* impotent
impound *v* a confisca
impoverished *adj* sărăcit
impractical *adj* impracticabil
imprecise *adj* imprecis
impress *v* a imprima
impressive *adj* impresionant
imprison *v* a întemniţa
improbable *adj* improbabil
improper *adj* nepotrivit
improve *v* a îmbunătăţi
improvement *n* îmbunătăţire
improvise *v* a improviza
impulse *n* impuls
impulsive *adj* impulsiv
impunity *n* impunitate
impure *adj* impur
in *pre* în, la
in depth *adv* îndatorat
inability *n* incapacitate
inaccessible *adj* inaccesibil
inaccurate *adj* inexact
inadmissible *adj* inadmisibil
inappropriate *adj* nepotrivit
inasmuch as *c* întrucât
inaugurate *v* a inaugura
inauguration *n* inaugurare
incalculable *adj* nemăsurat
incapable *adj* incapabil
incarcerate *v* a încarcera
incense *n* tămâie
incentive *n* stimulent
inception *n* început
incessant *adj* neîncetat
inch *n* inch, ţol
incident *n* incident

incidentally *adv* întâmplător
incision *n* incizie
incite *v* a stârni
incitement *n* incitare
inclination *n* înclinaţie
incline *v* a înclina
include *v* a include
inclusive *adv* cuprinzător
incoherent *adj* incoerent
income *n* venit
incoming *adj* care intră
incompatible *adj* incompatibil
incompetence *n* incompetenţă
incompetent *adj* incompetent
incomplete *adj* incomplet
inconsistent *adj* inconsistent
incontinence *n* incontinenţă
inconvenient *adj* supărător
incorporate *v* a integra
incorrect *adj* incorect
incorrigible *adj* incorigibil
increase *v* a creşte, a spori
increase *n* creştere, spor
increasing *adj* care creşte
incredible *adj* incredibil
increment *n* sporire
incriminate *v* a acuza
incurable *adj* incurabil
indecency *n* indecenţă
indecision *n* nehotărâre
indecisive *adj* nehotărât
indeed *adv* într-adevăr
indefinite *adj* indefinit
indemnify *v* a compensa
indemnity *n* garanţie
independence *n* independenţă
independent *adj* independent
index *n* indice
indicate *v* a indica
indication *n* indicaţie
indifference *n* indiferenţă
indifferent *adj* indiferent
indigent *adj* sărac
indigestion *n* indigestie
indirect *adj* indirect
indiscreet *adj* indiscret
indiscretion *n* indiscreţie
indispensable *adj* indispensabil
indisposed *adj* indispus
indisputable *adj* indisputabil
indivisible *adj* indivizibil
indoctrinate *v* a îndoctrina
indoor *adv* înăuntru
induce *v* a determina
indulge *v* a răsfăţa
indulgent *adj* indulgent

industrious *adj* muncitor
industry *n* industrie
ineffective *adj* ineficace
inefficient *adj* ineficient
inept *adj* stupid
inequality *n* inegalitate
inevitable *adj* inevitabil
inexcusable *adj* de neiertat
inexpensive *adj* ieftin
inexperienced *adj* nepriceput
inexplicable *adj* inexplicabil
infallible *adj* infailibil
infamous *adj* infam
infancy *n* copilărie
infant *n* copil mic
infantry *n* infanterie
infect *v* a infecta
infection *n* infecţie
infectious *adj* molipsitor
infer *v* a deduce
inferior *adj* inferior
infertile *adj* nefertil
infested *adj* infestat
infidelity *n* infideliatate
infiltrate *v* a infiltra
infiltration *n* infiltrare
infinite *adj* infinit
infirmary *n* infirmerie
inflammation *n* inflamare
inflate *v* a umfla
inflation *n* inflaţie
inflexible *adj* neclintit
inflict *v* a impune
influence *n* influenţă
influential *adj* important
influenza *n* gripă
influx *n* aflux
inform *v* a informa
informal *adj* neoficial
informant *n* informator
information *n* informaţie
informer *n* informator
infraction *n* infracţiune
infrequent *adj* rar
infuriate *v* a înfuria
infusion *n* infuzie
ingenuity *n* ingeniozitate
ingest *v* a ingera
ingot *n* lingou
ingrained *adj* imprimat
ingratitude *n* nerecunoştinţă
ingredient *n* ingredient
inhabit *v* a ocupa
inhabitable *adj* locuibil
inhabitant *n* locuitor
inhale *v* a inhala

inherit *v* a moşteni
inheritance *n* moştenire
inhibit *v* a inhiba
inhuman *adj* inuman
initial *adj* iniţial
initially *adv* la început
initials *n* iniţiale
initiate *v* a iniţia
initiative *n* iniţiativă
inject *v* a injecta
injection *n* injecţie
injure *v* a jigni
injurious *adj* dăunător
injury *n* rană
injustice *n* nedreptate
ink *n* cerneală
inkling *n* bănuială
inlaid *adj* încrustat
inland *adj* intern
in-laws *n* rude prin alianţă
inmate *n* locatar
inn *n* han
innate *adj* înnăscut
inner *adj* interior
innocence *n* inoceţă
innocent *adj* inocent
innovation *n* inovaţie
innuendo *n* aluzie
innumerable *adj* nenumărat
input *n* alimentare
inquest *n* anchetă
inquire *v* a chestiona
inquiry *n* cercetare
inquisition *n* inchiziţie
insane *adj* nebun
insanity *n* nebunie
insatiable *adj* nesăţios
inscription *n* inscripţie
insect *n* insectă
insecurity *n* nesiguranţă
insensitive *adj* insensibil
inseparable *adj* inseparabil
insert *v* a insera
insertion *n* inserare
inside *adj* interior
inside *pre* în, înăuntrul
inside out *adv* întors pe dos
insignificant *adj* neimportant
insincere *adj* nesincer
insincerity *n* nesinceritate
insinuate *v* a insinua
insinuation *n* insinuare
insipid *adj* insipid
insist *v* a insista
insistence *n* insistenţă
insolent *adj* obraznic

insoluble *adj* insolubil
insomnia *n* insomnie
inspect *v* a inspecta
inspection *n* inspecţie
inspector *n* inspector
inspiration *n* inspiraţie
inspire *v* a inspira
instability *n* instabilitate
install *v* a instala
installation *n* instalare
installment *n* rată, acont
instance *n* exemplu
instant *n* clipă, moment
instantly *adv* imediat
instead *adv* în schimb
instigate *v* a instiga
instil *v* a introduce
instinct *n* instinct
institute *v* a institui
institution *n* instituţie
instruct *v* a instrui
instructor *n* instructor
insufficient *adj* insuficient
insulate *v* a izola
insulation *n* izolare
insult *v* a insulta
insult *n* insultă
insurance *n* asigurare
insure *v* a asigura
insurgency *n* insurgenţă
insurrection *n* insurecţie
intact *adj* neatins, intact
intake *n* înghiţire
integrate *v* a integra
integration *n* integrare
integrity *n* integritate
intelligent *adj* inteligent
intend *v* a intenţiona
intense *adj* intens
intensify *v* a intensifica
intensity *n* intensitate
intensive *adj* intens
intention *n* intenţie
intercede *v* a interveni
intercept *v* a intercepta
intercession *n* intervenţie
interchange *n* schimb reciproc
interest *n* interes
interested *adj* interesat, atent
interesting *adj* interesant
interfere *v* a interveni
interference *n* amestec
interior *adj* interior, intern
interlude *n* interludiu
intermediary *n* intermediar
intern *v* a interna

I

interpret *v* a interpreta
interpretation *n* interpretare
interpreter *n* interpret
interrogate *v* a întreba
interrupt *v* a întrerupe
interruption *n* întrerupere
intersect *v* a intersecta
intertwine *v* a se răsuci
interval *n* interval
intervene *v* a interveni
intervention *n* intervenţie
interview *n* interviu
intestine *n* intestin
intimacy *n* intimitate
intimate *adj* intim
intimidate *v* a intimida
intolerable *adj* insuportabil
intolerance *n* intoleranţă
intoxicated *adj* îmbătat
intravenous *adj* intravenos
intrepid *adj* îndrăzneţ
intricate *adj* complicat
intrigue *n* intrigă
intriguing *adj* intrigant
intrinsic *adj* intrinsec
introduce *v* a introduce
introduction *n* introducere
introvert *adj* introvertit
intrude *v* a deranja
intruder *n* intrus
intrusion *n* deranj
intuition *n* intuiţie
inundate *v* a inunda
invade *v* a invada
invader *n* invadator
invalid *n* invalid
invalidate *v* a anula
invaluable *adj* nepreţuit
invasion *n* invazie
invent *v* a inventa
invention *n* invenţie
inventory *n* inventar
invest *v* a investi
investigate *v* a investiga
investigation *n* investigaţie
investment *n* investiţie
investor *n* investitor
invincible *adj* invincibil
invisible *adj* invizibil
invitation *n* invitaţie
invite *v* a invita
invoice *n* factură
invoke *v* a invoca
involve *v* a implica
involved *v* implicat
involvement *n* implicare

inward *adj* interior, intern
inwards *adv* spre interior
iodine *n* iod
irate *adj* furios
Ireland *n* Irlanda
Irish *adj* irlandez
iron *n* fier
iron *v* a călca rufe
ironic *adj* ironic
irony *n* ironie
irrational *adj* iraţional
irrefutable *adj* irefutabil
irregular *adj* neregular
irrelevant *adj* nerelevant
irreparable *adj* ireparabil
irresistible *adj* irezistibil
irrespective *adj* indiferent
irreversible *adj* ireversibil
irrevocable *adj* irevocabil
irrigate *v* a iriga
irrigation *n* irigaţie
irritate *v* a irita
irritating *adj* iritant
Islamic *adj* islamic
island *n* insulă
isle *n* insulă
isolate *v* a izola
isolation *n* izolare
issue *n* problemă
Italian *adj* italian
italics *adj* caractere cursive
Italy *n* Italia
itch *v* a mânca
itchiness *n* mâncărime
item *n* articol
itemize *v* a detalia
itinerary *n* itinerar
ivory *n* fildeş

J

jackal *n* şacal
jacket *n* jachetă
jackpot *n* lozul cel mare
jaguar *n* jaguar
jail *n* temniţă, închisoare
jail *v* a închide
jailer *n* temnicer
jam *n* gem; aglomeraţie
janitor *n* îngrijitor
January *n* ianuarie
Japan *n* Japonia
Japanese *adj* japonez

jar *n* borcan
jasmine *n* iasomie
jaw *n* falcă
jealous *adj* gelos
jealousy *n* gelozie
jeans *n* blugi, ginşi
jeopardize *v* a primejdui
jerk *v* a zdruncina
jerk *n* smucitură
jersey *n* jerseu
Jew *n* evreu
jewel *n* bijuterie
jeweler *n* bijutier
jewelry store *n* magazin de bijuterii
Jewish *adj* evreiesc
jigsaw *n* ferăstrău mecanic
job *n* treabă, slujbă
jobless *adj* fără serviciu
join *v* a îmbina, a uni
joint *n* articulaţie; îmbinare
jointly *adv* în comun
joke *n* glumă
joke *v* a glumi
jokingly *adv* în glumă
jolly *adj* vesel, plăcut
jolt *v* a zdruncina
jolt *n* zdruncinătură
journal *n* ziar; revistă; jurnal
journalist *n* jurnalist, ziarist
journey *n* călătorie
jovial *adj* jovial
joy *n* bucurie, veselie
joyful *adj* vesel, voios
joyfully *adv* vesel, cu voioşie
jubilant *adj* triumfător
Judaism *n* iudaism
judge *n* judecător
judgment *n* jedecată
judicious *adj* înţelept
jug *n* ulcior, închisoare
juggler *n* jongler
juice *n* suc
juicy *adj* zemos, suculent
July *n* iulie
jump *v* a sări
jump *n* săritură, salt
jumpy *adj* nerăbdător
junction *n* conjunctură, joncţiune
June *n* iunie
jungle *n* junglă; tufăriş; desiş
junior *adj* junior, tânăr
junk *n* gunoi, resturi
jury *n* juraţi, juriu
just *adj* just, drept
justice *n* justiţie, judecată
justify *v* a îndreptăţi, a justifica

justly *adv* corect, pe merit
juvenile *n* tânăr, adolescent
juvenile *adj* juvenil, de tineret

K

kangaroo *n* cangur
karate *n* karate
keep *iv* a rămâne, a continua
keep on *v* a continua
keep up *v* a menţine
keg *n* butoiaş
kennel *n* cuşcă de câine
kettle *n* ceainic, ibric
key *n* cheie; cifru;
key ring *n* portchei
keyboard *n* claviatură
kick *v* a lovi cu piciorul
kickback *n* mită
kid *n* ied; piele fină
kidnap *v* a răpi
kidnapper *n* răpitor de oameni
kidnapping *n* răpire de oameni
kidney *n* rinichi
kidney bean *n* fasole mare
kill *v* a omorî, a ucide
killer *n* asasin, ucigaş
killing *n* ucidere
kilogram *n* kilogram
kilometer *n* kilometru
kilowatt *n* kilowatt
kind *adj* blând, prietenos
kindle *v* a se aprinde
kindly *adv* prietenos, bun
kindness *n* amabilitate
king *n* rege
kingdom *n* regat
kinship *n* înrudire, asemănare
kiosk *n* chioşc
kiss *v* a săruta
kiss *n* sărut
kitchen *n* bucătărie
kite *n* zmeu
kitten *n* pisicuţă
knee *n* genunchi
kneecap *n* rotulă
kneel *iv* a îngenunchea
knife *n* cuţit
knight *n* cavaler
knit *v* a împleti, a tricota
knob *n* mâner rotund
knock *n* lovitură
knock *v* a ciocăni

knot *n* nod, nucleu
know *iv* a fi informat
know-how *n* îndemânare
knowingly *adv* cu bună ştiinţă
knowledge *n* cunoaştere

L

lab *n* laborator
label *n* etichetă
labor *n* muncă, sarcină
laborer *n* muncitor
labyrinth *n* labirint
lace *n* dantelă, ornament
lack *v* a fi lipsit de
lack *n* lipsă
lad *n* flăcău, tânăr
ladder *n* scară, trepte
laden *adj* încărcat
lady *n* doamnă
ladylike *adj* elegant, nobil
lagoon *n* lagună
lake *n* lac
lamb *n* miel
lame *adj* şchiop
lament *v* a plânge
lament *n* lamentare, bocet
lamp *n* lampă
lamppost *n* felinar
lampshade *n* abajur
land *n* pământ, teritoriu
land *v* a debarca, a ateriza
landfill *n* groapă de gunoi
landing *n* debarcare, aterizare
landlady *n* proprietăreasă
landlord *n* moşier, proprietar
landscape *n* peisaj
lane *n* uliţă, culoar
language *n* limbă, limbaj
languish *v* a lâncezi
lantern *n* felinar
lap *n* poală; genunchi
lapse *n* greşeală; scăpare
lapse *v* a cădea, a aluneca
larceny *n* furt, furtişag
lard *n* untură
large *adj* mare, larg
larynx *n* laringe
laser *n* laser
lash *n* geană; biciuire
lash *v* a bate, a stârni
lash out *v* a vorbi urât
last *v* a dura, a ţine

last *adj* ultim
last name *n* nume de familie
last night *adv* aseară
lasting *adj* permanent, trainic
lastly *adv* în sfârşit
latch *n* zăvor, iale
late *adv* târziu
lately *adv* în ultima vreme
later *adv* mai târziu
later *adj* mai târziu, ulterior
lateral *adj* lateral
latest *adj* cel mai recent
lather *n* spumă de săpun
latitude *n* latitudine
latter *adj* ultimul din doi
laugh *v* a râde
laugh *n* râs
laughable *adj* amuzant
laughing stock *n* cal de bătaie
laughter *n* râs
launch *n* lansare
launch *v* a lansa, a iniţia
laundry *n* spălătorie
lavatory *n* toaletă
lavish *adj* generos, darnic
lavish *v* a irosi
law *n* lege
law-abiding *adj* paşnic, legal
lawful *adj* legal; legitim
lawmaker *n* legislator
lawn *n* peluză, pajişte
lawsuit *n* proces
lawyer *n* jurist, avocat
lax *adj* neglijent, lejer
laxative *adj* laxativ
lay *n* aşezare, poziţie
lay *iv* a oua; a paria
lay off *v* a înceta să
layer *n* strat, parior
layman *n* mirean, profan
lay-out *n* aşezare, plan
laziness *n* lene
lazy *adj* leneş
lead *iv* a duce, a conduce
lead *n* plumb; conducere
leaded *adj* plumbuit
leader *n* conducător
leadership *n* conducere
leading *adj* conducător
leaf *n* frunză, foaie
leaflet *n* manifest
league *n* leghe, ligă
leak *v* a se scurge
leak *n* spărtură, scurgere
leakage *n* scurgere
lean *adj* slab; carne macră

lean *iv* a apleca, a înclina
lean back *v* a se lăsa pe spate
lean on *v* a se biziu pe
leaning *n* înclinaţie
leap *iv* a sări
leap *n* salt
leap year *n* an bisect
learn *iv* a învăţa, a studia
learned *adj* învăţat
learner *n* începător
learning *n* învăţătură
lease *v* a închiria
lease *n* închiriere
leash *n* lesă
least *adj* cel mai puţin
leather *n* piele
leave *iv* a pleca, a porni
leave out *v* a omite
lectern *n* strană, pupitru
lecture *n* prelegere
ledger *n* registru
leech *n* lipitoare
leftovers *n* resturi
leg *n* picior
legacy *n* moştenire
legal *adj* legal, juridic
legality *n* legalitate
legalize *v* a legaliza
legend *n* legendă
legible *adj* lizibil, clar
legion *n* legiune
legislate *v* a legifera
legislation *n* legislaţie
legislature *n* legislatură
legitimate *adj* legitim
leisure *n* răgaz, timp liber
lemon *n* lămâie
lemonade *n* limonadă
lend *iv* a da, a împrumuta
length *n* lungime
lengthen *v* a lungi
lengthy *adj* prea lung
leniency *n* îngăduinţă
lenient *adj* îngăduitor
lens *n* lentilă
Lent *n* postul Paştelui
lentil *n* linte
leopard *n* leopard
leper *n* lepros
leprosy *n* lepră
less *adj* mai puţin, mai mic
lessee *n* arendaş, chiriaş
lessen *v* a micşora
lesser *adj* mai puţin important
lesson *n* lecţie
let *iv* a închiria

let down *v* a dezamăgi
let go *v* a lăsa să plece
let in *v* a primi
let out *v* a lăsa să iasă
lethal *adj* letal, mortal
letter *n* literă; scrisoare
lettuce *n* salată verde
leukemia *n* leucemie
level *v* a nivela, a egaliza
level *n* nivel; suprafaţă
lever *n* pârghie
leverage *n* mecanism cu pârghii
levy *v* a ridica, a percepe
lewd *adj* obscen, lasciv
liability *n* obligaţie
liable *adj* supus, susceptibil
liaison *n* legătură
liar *adj* mincinos
libel *n* calomnie
liberate *v* a elibera
liberation *n* eliberare
liberty *n* libertate
librarian *n* bibliotecar
library *n* bibliotecă
lice *n* păduchi
licence *n* permisiune
license *v* a autoriza
lick *v* a linge
lid *n* capac, pleoapă
lie *iv* a minţi
lie *v* a sta culcat
lie *n* minciună
lieu *n* loc
lieutenant *n* locotenent
life *n* viaţă, existenţă
lifeguard *n* salvamar
lifeless *adj* mort, neînsufleţit
lifestyle *n* stil de viaţă
lifetime *adj* toată viaţa
lift *v* a ridica, a înălţa
lift off *v* a decola
lift-off *n* decolare
ligament *n* ligament
light *iv* a lumina
light *adj* uşor, luminos
light *n* lumină
lighter *n* brichetă
lighthouse *n* far
lighting *n* aprindere
lightly *adv* fără efort, uşor
lightning *n* fulger
lightweight *n* categorie uşoară
likable *adj* plăcut
like *pre* ca
like *v* a plăcea
likelihood *n* probabilitate

likely *adv* probabil
likeness *n* asemănare
likewise *adv* asemenea
liking *n* simpatie
limb *n* membru, creangă
lime *n* tei, lămâie
limestone *n* calcar
limit *n* limită; graniţă
limit *v* a limita, a îngrădi
limitation *n* limită, limitare
limp *v* a şchiopăta
limp *n* şchipătat
linchpin *n* cui de osie, splint
line *n* linie, dungă
line up *v* a se alinia
linen *n* pânză de in, rufărie
linger *v* a persista, a zăbovi
lingerie *n* lenjerie, pânzeturi
lingering *adj* încetinitor
lining *n* căptuşeală
link *v* a uni, a lega
link *n* verigă, legătură
lion *n* leu
lioness *n* leoaică
lip *n* buză, margine
liqueur *n* lichior
liquid *n* lichid
liquidate *v* a lichida
liquidation *n* lichidare
liquor *n* alcoolică
list *v* a lista, a înşira
list *n* listă
listen *v* a asculta
listener *n* ascultător
litany *n* litanie
liter *n* litru
literal *adj* literal, exact
literally *adv* exact
literate *adj* literat
literature *n* literatură
litigate *v* a fi în litigiu
litigation *n* litigiu
litre *n* litru
litter *n* litieră, resturi
little *adj* puţin
little bit *n* puţin
little by little *adv* treptat
liturgy *n* liturghie
live *adj* viu; activ; în direct
live *v* a trăi, a locui
live up *v* a fi la înălţime
livelihood *n* trai, existenţă
lively *adj* vioi, viu
liver *n* ficat
livestock *n* şeptel
livid *adj* livid

living room *n* sufragerie
lizard *n* şopârlă
load *v* a încărca
load *n* încărcătură
loaded *adj* încărcat; ameţit
loaf *n* pâine, franzelă
loan *v* a da cu împrumut
loan *n* împrumut
loathe *v* a detesta
loathing *n* silă, scârbă
lobby *n* hol; foaier
lobster *n* homar
local *adj* local
localize *v* a localiza
locate *v* a localiza, a găsi
located *adj* localizat
location *n* locaţie, aşezare
lock *v* a închide, a încuia
lock *n* lacăt, încuietoare
locker room *n* vestiar
locksmith *n* lăcătuş
locust *n* lăcustă
lodge *v* a găzdui, a băga
lodging *n* găzduire
lofty *adj* înalt, distins
log *n* butuc; jurnal de bord
log *v* a tăia copaci
logic *n* logică
logical *adj* logic
loin *n* muşchi, file
loiter *v* a zăbovi, a întârzia
loneliness *n* singurătate
lonely *adv* singuratic
loner *n* solitar, singuratic
lonesome *adj* tânjitor
long *adj* lung
long for *v* a năzui la
longing *n* dor
longitude *n* longitudine
long-standing *adj* de lungă durată
long-term *adj* pe termen lung
look *n* privire; înfăţişare
look *v* a privi; a arăta
look after *v* a îngriji
look at *v* a urmări, a se uita la
look down *v* a privi în pământ
look for *v* a căuta
look into *v* a cerceta
look out *v* a băga de seamă
look over *v* a cerceta, a examina
look through *v* a se uita prin
looking glass *n* oglindă
looks *n* aspect
loom *n* război de ţesut
loom *v* a se ivi; a apărea
loophole *n* deschizătură

loose *v* a dezlega, a slăbi
loose *adj* liber, slobod
loosen *v* a slăbi
loot *v* a prăda
loot *n* pradă
lord *n* lord
lordship *n* stăpânire, autoritate
lose *iv* a pierde, a scăpa
loser *n* învins, cel care pierde
loss *n* pierdere, înfrângere
lot *adv* foarte mult
lotion *n* loţiune
lots *adj* o mulţime de
lottery *n* loterie
loud *adj* tare, răsunător
loudly *adv* zgomotos
loudspeaker *n* megafon, difuzor
lounge *n* trândăveală
louse *n* păduche
lousy *adj* păduchios
lovable *adj* atrăgător, simpatic
love *v* a iubi
love *n* dragoste, amor
lovely *adj* atrăgător
lover *n* iubit, amant
loving *adj* iubitor
low *adj* jos, scund
lower *adj* inferior, de jos
lowkey *adj* sobru
lowly *adj* modest, umil
loyal *adj* loial, credincios
loyalty *n* credinţă, lealitate
lubricate *v* a unge
lubrication *n* lubrifiere
lucid *adj* clar, lucid
luck *n* noroc, şansă
lucky *adj* norocos
lucrative *adj* rentabil
ludicrous *adj* ridicol, absurd
luggage *n* bagaj
lukewarm *adj* călduţ
lull *n* linişte, răgaz
lumber *n* lemne, cherestea
luminous *adj* luminos
lump *n* bucată; bulgăr
lump sum *n* plată completă
lump together *v* a socoti împreună
lunacy *n* nebunie
lunatic *adj* nebun
lunch *n* prânz
lung *n* plămân
lure *v* a momi, a ademeni
lurid *adj* strălucitor
lurk *v* a sta ascuns
lush *adj* luxuriant
lust *v* a pofti

L

lust *n* poftă, voluptate
lustful *adj* pofticios, voluptuos
luxurious *adj* luxos
luxury *n* lux
lynch *v* a linşa
lynx *n* linx
lyrics *n* text de cântec

M

machine *n* maşină, aparat
machine gun *n* mitralieră
mad *adj* nebun, turbat
madam *n* doamnă
madden *v* a scoate din minţi
madly *adv* nebuneşte
madman *n* nebun, dement
madness *n* nebunie
magazine *n* revistă ilustrată
magic *n* magie
magical *adj* magic
magician *n* magician
magistrate *n* magistrat
magnet *n* magnet
magnetic *adj* magnetic
magnetism *n* magnetism
magnificent *adj* măreţ
magnify *v* a mări
magnitude *n* magnitudine
maid *n* fată în casă
maiden *n* fecioară
mail *v* corespondenţă
mail *n* a expedia prin poştă
mailbox *n* cutie poştală
mailman *n* poştaş
maim *v* a mutila
main *adj* principal
mainland *n* continent, uscat
mainly *adv* în special
maintain *v* a menţine
maintenance *n* întreţinere
majestic *adj* maiestuos
majesty *n* maiestate
major *n* major, maior
major *adj* major, principal
major in *v* a se specializa în
majority *n* majoritate
make *n* fabricaţie, alcătuire
make *iv* a face, a crea
make up *v* a elabora, a machia
make up for *v* a compensa
maker *n* creator, fabricant
makeup *n* machiaj, fard

malaria *n* malarie
male *n* mascul
malevolent *adj* răuvoitor
malfunction *v* a defecta
malfunction *n* defect
malice *n* răutate, duşmănie
malign *v* a bârfi
malignancy *n* răutate
malignant *adj* rău, malign
mall *n* mall
malnutrition *n* malnutriţie
malpractice *v* tratament greşit
mammal *n* mamifer
mammoth *n* mamut
man *n* om, bărbat
manage *v* a conduce
manageable *adj* realizabil
management *n* conducere
manager *n* manager
mandate *n* mandat
mandatory *adj* poruncitor
maneuver *n* manevră
manger *n* iesle
mangle *v* a stoarce, a ciopârţi
manhunt *n* razie
maniac *adj* maniac
manifest *v* a manifesta
manipulate *v* a manipula
mankind *n* omenire
manliness *n* bărbăţie, virilitate
manly *adj* bărbătesc
manner *n* mod, manieră
mannerism *n* manierism
manners *n* maniere
manpower *n* mână de lucru
mansion *n* conac, casă mare
manslaughter *n* omucidere
manual *n* manual
manual *adj* manual
manufacture *v* a fabrica
manure *n* bălegar
manuscript *n* manuscris
many *adj* mulţi
map *n* hartă
marble *n* marmură
march *v* a mărşălui
march *n* marş, mărşăluire
March *n* martie
mare *n* iapă
margin *n* margine
marginal *adj* marginal
marinate *v* a marina
marine *adj* marin, maritim
marital *adj* conjugal
mark *n* semn, particularitate
mark *v* a marca, a însemna

mark down *v* a nota, a însemna
marker *n* indicator, marcator
market *n* piaţă, târg
marksman *n* ţintaş
marmalade *n* dulceaţă de citrice
marriage *n* căsătorie
married *adj* căsătorit
marrow *n* măduvă
marry *v* a se căsători
Mars *n* Marte
marshal *n* mareşal; şerif
martyr *n* martir
martyrdom *n* calvar
marvel *n* minune
marvelous *adj* minunat
marxist *adj* marxist
masculine *adj* masculin
mash *v* a terciui
mask *n* mască
masochism *n* masochism
mason *n* zidar, francmason
masquerade *v* mascaradă
mass *n* mulţime; amestec
massacre *n* masacru
massage *n* masaj
massage *v* a masa
masseur *n* masor
masseuse *n* maseza
massive *adj* masiv
mast *n* catarg, stâlp
master *n* stăpân, domn
master *v* a stăpâni
mastermind *n* intelect superior
mastermind *v* a pune la cale
masterpiece *n* capodoperă
mastery *n* stăpânire, pricepere
mat *n* rogojină, preş
match *n* chibrit; meci
mate *n* tovarăş, partener
material *n* material; subiect
materialism *n* materialism
maternal *adj* matern
maternity *n* maternitate
math *n* matematică
matriculate *v* a primi la facultate
matrimony *n* căsătorie
matter *n* materie; subiect
mattress *n* somieră, saltea
mature *adj* matur
maturity *n* maturitate
maul *v* a maltrata
maxim *n* maximă
maximum *adj* maxim
May *n* mai
may *iv* a avea voie
may-be *adv* poate

mayhem *n* schilodire, mutilare
mayor *n* primar
maze *n* labirint, încurcătură
meadow *n* pajişte, luncă
meager *adj* slab, anemic
meal *n* masă, mâncare
mean *iv* a însemna
mean *adj* mediocru, meschin
meaning *n* înţeles
meaningful *adj* plin de înţeles
meaningless *adj* fără sens
meanness *n* sărăcie
means *n* metodă
meantime *adv* între timp
meanwhile *adv* între timp
measles *n* pojar
measure *v* măsură, cantitate
measurement *n* măsură
meat *n* carne
meatball *n* chiftea
mechanic *n* mecanic
mechanism *n* mecanism
mechanize *v* a mecaniza
medal *n* medalie
medallion *n* medalion
meddle *v* a interveni
mediate *v* a media
mediator *n* mediator
medication *n* medicaţie
medicinal *adj* medicinal
medicine *n* medicină
medieval *adj* medieval
mediocre *adj* mediocru
mediocrity *n* mediocritate
meditate *v* a medita, a chibzui
meditation *n* meditaţie
medium *adj* mediu
meek *adj* supus, cuminte
meekness *n* supunere, umilinţă
meet *iv* a se întâlni
meeting *n* întâlnire
melancholy *n* melancolie
mellow *adj* copt, matur
mellow *v* a se coace
melodic *adj* melodic
melody *n* melodie
melon *n* pepene galben
melt *v* a topi
member *n* membru
membership *n* calitate de membru
membrane *n* membrană
memento *n* avertisment
memo *n* memorandum
memoirs *n* memorii
memorable *adj* memorabil
memorize *v* a memora

memory *n* memorie
men *n* bărbaţi
menace *n* ameninţare
mend *v* a repara
meningitis *n* meningită
menopause *n* menopauză
menstruation *n* menstruaţie
mental *adj* mental
mentality *n* mentalitate
mentally *adv* mintal
mention *v* a menţiona
mention *n* menţiune, referire
menu *n* meniu
merchandise *n* marfă
merchant *n* negustor
merciful *adj* îndurător
merciless *adj* neîndurător
mercury *n* mercur
mercy *n* îndurare, milă
merely *adv* numai, doar
merge *v* a fuziona, a uni
merger *n* fuziune; contopire
merit *n* merit, valoare
merit *v* a merita
mermaid *n* sirenă
merry *adj* vesel, fericit
mesh *n* plasă, fire
mesmerize *v* a fascina
mess *n* încurcătură
mess around *v* a pierde vremea
mess up *v* a da de necaz
message *n* mesaj
messenger *n* mesager, curier
Messiah *n* Mesia
messy *adj* murdar
metal *n* metal
metallic *adj* metalic
metaphor *n* metaforă
meteor *n* meteor
meter *n* metru
method *n* metodă
methodical *adj* metodic
meticulous *adj* meticulos
metric *adj* metric
metropolis *n* metropolă
Mexican *adj* mexican
mice *n* şoareci
microbe *n* microb
microphone *n* microfon
microscope *n* microscop
microwave *n* microundă
midair *n* punct înalt în spaţiu
midday *n* amiază
middle *n* mijloc, centru
middleman *n* intermediar
midget *n* pitic

midnight *n* miezul nopţii
midsummer *n* miezul verii
midwife *n* moaşă
mighty *adj* puternic, mare
migraine *n* migrenă
migrant *n* nomad, migrator
migrate *v* a migra
mild *adj* blând, slab
mildew *n* mucegai
mile *n* milă
mileage *n* distanţa în mile
milestone *n* borna kilometrică
militant *adj* activist, militant
milk *n* lapte
milky *adj* lăptos
mill *n* moară, râşniţă
millennium *n* mileniu
milligram *n* miligram
millimeter *n* milimetru
million *n* milion
millionaire *n* milionar
mime *v* a mima
mince *v* a toca
mincemeat *n* tocătură
mind *v* a observa
mind *n* minte, hotărâre
mind-boggling *adj* uluitor
mindful *adj* atent
mindless *adj* stupid
mine *n* mină
mine *v* a săpa, a scobi
mine *pro* al meu
minefield *n* câmp de mine
miner *n* miner
mineral *n* mineral
mingle *v* a se amesteca
miniature *n* miniatură
minimize *v* a minimaliza
minimum *n* minim
miniskirt *n* fustă mini
minister *n* ministru
minister *v* a servi, a fi preot
ministry *n* minister; preoţie
minor *adj* minor
minority *n* minoritate
mint *n* mentă
mint *v* a fabrica monede
minus *adj* minus, negativ
minute *n* minut
miracle *n* miracol
miraculous *adj* miraculos
mirage *n* miraj
mirror *n* oglindă
misbehave *v* a se purta rău
miscalculate *v* a calcula greşit
miscarriage *n* pierdere

M

miscarry *v* a pierde, a avorta
mischief *n* ticăloşie, năzbâtie
mischievous *adj* ticălos
misconduct *n* purtare rea
misconstrue *v* a interpreta greşit
misdemeanor *n* nelegiuire
miser *n* zgârcit
miserable *adj* nenorocit, sărac
misery *n* mizerie, sărăcie
misfit *adj* inadaptabil
misfortune *n* nenorocire
misgiving *n* prevestire
misguided *adj* prost îndrumat
misinterpret *v* a interpreta greşit
misjudge *v* a judeca greşit
mislead *v* a înşela
misleading *adj* greşit
mismanage *v* a administra prost
misprint *n* greşeală de tipar
miss *v* a scăpa
miss *n* scăpare
missile *n* proiectil
missing *adj* dispărut
mission *n* misiune
missionary *n* misionar
mist *n* ceaţă
mistake *iv* a greşi, a confunda
mistake *n* greşeală, confuzie
mistaken *adj* greşit
mister *n* domnul
mistreat *v* a se purta urât
mistreatment *n* maltratare
mistress *n* stăpână, amantă
mistrust *n* neîncredere
mistrust *v* a suspecta, a bănui
misty *adj* ceţos
misunderstand *v* a înţelege greşit
misuse *n* folosire greşită
mitigate *v* a îmblânzi, a înmuia
mix *v* a amesteca
mixed-up *adj* amestecat, implicat
mixer *n* mixer, malaxor
mixture *n* amestec
mix-up *n* a încurca, a încâlci
moan *v* a geme
moan *n* geamăt
mob *v* a se îngrămădi
mob *n* gloată, mulţime
mobile *adj* mobil
mobilize *v* a mobiliza
mobster *n* gangster
mock *v* a batjocori
mockery *n* batjocură
mode *n* mod
model *n* model
moderate *adj* moderat

moderation *n* moderaţie
modern *adj* modern
modernize *v* a moderniza
modest *adj* modest
modesty *n* modestie
modify *v* a modifica
module *n* modul
moisten *v* a umezi
moisture *n* umezeală
molar *n* măsea
mold *v* a mucegăi
mold *n* mucegai
moldy *adj* acoperit de mucegai
mole *n* aluniţă, cârtiţă
molecule *n* moleculă
molest *v* a necăji
mom *n* mamă
moment *n* moment
momentarily *adv* pentru o clipă
momentous *adj* foarte important
monarch *n* monarh
monarchy *n* monarhie
monastery *n* mănăstire
monastic *adj* mănăstiresc, ascetic
Monday *n* luni
money *n* bani
money order *n* mandat poştal
monitor *v* a urmări, a verifica
monk *n* călugăr
monkey *n* maimuţă
monogamy *n* monogamie
monologue *n* monolog
monopolize *v* a monopoliza
monopoly *n* monopol
monotonous *adj* monoton
monotony *n* monotonie
monster *n* monstru
monstrous *adj* monstruos
month *n* lună
monthly *adv* lunar
monument *n* monument
monumental *adj* monumental
mood *n* dispoziţie, toană
moody *adj* capricios
moon *n* lună
moor *v* a priponi
mop *v* a şterge
moral *adj* moral, etic
moral *n* morală, etică
morality *n* morală, moralitate
more *adj* mai mult, în plus
moreover *adv* pe deasupra
morning *n* dimineaţă
moron *adj* cretin, înapoiat
morphine *n* morfină
morsel *n* bucăţică, fărâmă

mortal *adj* mortal, muritor
mortality *n* mortalitate
mortar *n* tencuială
mortgage *n* ipotecă
mortification *n* ruşine, umilinţă
mortify *v* a umili
mortuary *n* capelă funerară
mosaic *n* mozaic
mosque *n* moschee
mosquito *n* ţânţar
moss *n* muşchi
most *adj* cel mai mult
mostly *adv* mai ales, în special
motel *n* motel
moth *n* molie
mother *n* mamă
motherhood *n* maternitate
mother-in-law *n* soacră
motion *n* mişcare, moţiune
motionless *adj* nemişcat
motivate *v* a motiva
motive *n* motiv
motor *n* motor
motorcycle *n* motocicletă
motto *n* moto, deviză
mouldy *adj* mucegăit, vechi
mount *n* cal înşeuat, căţărare
mount *v* a se căţăra,
mountain *n* munte
mountainous *adj* muntos
mourn *v* a boci, a jeli
mourning *n* doliu, supărare
mouse *n* şoarece
mouth *n* gură
move *n* mişcare, mutare
move *v* a mişca, a muta
move back *v* a se retrage
move forward *v* a înainta
move out *v* a se muta
move up *v* a promova
movement *n* mişcare, mutare
movie *n* film
mow *v* a cosi
much *adv* mult, în mare măsură
mucus *n* mucozitate
mud *n* noroi
muddle *n* încurcătură
muddy *adj* noroios
muffle *v* a înfofoli, a înfăşura
muffler *n* fular, înveliş
mug *n* cană, halbă
mug *v* a jefui, a ataca
mugging *n* jaf, asalt
mule *n* catâr
multiple *adj* multiplu
multiplication *n* multiplicare

multiply *v* a înmulţi
multitude *n* mulţime
mumble *v* a mormăi
mummy *n* mămică, mumie
mumps *n* oreion
munch *v* a molfăi
munitions *n* muniţii
murder *n* crimă, omor
murderer *n* criminal, ucigaş
murky *adj* întunecos
murmur *v* a şopti, a murmura
murmur *n* murmur
muscle *n* muşchi
museum *n* muzeu
mushroom *n* ciupercă
music *n* muzică
musician *n* muzician
Muslim *adj* musulman
must *iv* a trebui
mustache *n* mustaţă
mustard *n* muştar
muster *v* a aduna, a mobiliza
mutate *v* a alterna, a schimba
mute *adj* mut
mutilate *v* a mutila
mutiny *n* rebeliune
mutually *adv* în mod reciproc
muzzle *v* a pune botniţă
muzzle *n* botniţă
my *adj* meu
myopic *adj* miop
myself *pro* pe mine, mă
mysterious *adj* misterios
mystery *n* mister
mystic *adj* mistic
mystify *v* a mistifica
myth *n* mit, legendă

N

nag *v* a necăji, a cicăli
nagging *adj* cicălitor
nail *n* unghie, cui
naive *adj* naiv
naked *adj* gol, dezbrăcat
name *n* nume
namely *adv* adică, şi anume
nanny *n* guvernantă
nap *n* pui de somn
napkin *n* şerveţel
narcotic *n* narcotic
narrate *v* a povesti
narrow *adj* îngust, limitat

narrowly *adv* abia, de abia
nasty *adj* neplăcut, murdar
nation *n* naţiune
national *adj* naţional
nationality *n* naţionaliate
nationalize *v* a naţionaliza
native *adj* nativ
natural *adj* natural
naturally *adv* în mod firesc
nature *n* natură, fire
naughty *adj* obraznic, afurisit
nausea *n* greaţă
nave *n* naos
navel *n* buric, miez
navigate *v* a naviga
navigation *n* navigaţie
navy *n* marină
navy blue *adj* bleumarin
near *pre* aproape de
nearby *adj* în apropiere
nearly *adv* aproape
nearsighted *adj* miop
neat *adj* curat, net
neatly *adv* cu acurateţe
necessary *adj* necesar
necessitate *v* a necesita
necessity *n* necesitate
neck *n* gât, guler
necklace *n* colier
necktie *n* cravată
need *v* a trebui
need *n* nevoie, necesitate
needle *n* ac
needless *adj* inutil
needy *adj* nevoiaş
negative *adj* negativ
neglect *v* a neglija
neglect *n* neglijare
negligence *n* neglijenţă
negligent *adj* neglijent
negotiate *v* a negocia
negotiation *n* negociere
neighbor *n* vecin
neighborhood *n* vecinătate
neither *adj* nici unul
neither *adv* nici
nephew *n* nepot de unchi
nerve *n* nerv, îndrăzneală
nervous *adj* nervos, agitat
nest *n* cuib
net *n* plasă, capcană
Netherlands *n* Olanda
network *n* reţea
neurotic *adj* nevrotic
neutral *adj* neutru
neutralize *v* a neutraliza

never *adv* niciodată
nevertheless *adv* totuşi
new *adj* nou
newborn *n* nou-născut
newcomer *n* nou-venit
newly *adv* de curând
newlywed *adj* proaspăt căsătorit
news *n* ştiri, informaţii
newscast *n* buletin de ştiri
newspaper *n* ziar
newsstand *n* chioşc de ziare
next *adj* următorul
next door *adj* alături
nibble *v* a ciuguli, a ronţăi
nice *adj* drăguţ
nicely *adv* cum se cuvine
nickel *n* nichel
nickname *n* poreclă
nicotine *n* nicotină
niece *n* nepoată de unchi
night *n* noapte
nightfall *n* căderea nopţii
nightingale *n* privighetoare
nightmare *n* coşmar
nine *adj* nouă
nineteen *adj* nouăsprezece
ninety *adj* nouăzeci
ninth *adj* al nouălea
nip *n* muşcătură
nip *v* a ciupi, a muşca
nipple *n* sfârcul sânului
nitpicking *adj* de chiţibuşar
nitrogen *n* azot
nobility *n* nobleţe, nobilime
noble *adj* nobil
nobleman *n* nobil
nobody *pro* nimeni
nocturnal *adj* nocturn
nod *v* a încuviinţa
noise *n* zgomot
noisily *adv* zgomotos
noisy *adj* zgomotos
nominate *v* a numi, a propune
none *pro* nici unul
nonetheless *c* cu toate acestea
nonsense *n* nonsens, fleacuri
nonsmoker *n* nefumător
nonstop *adv* fără oprire
noon *n* amiază
noose *n* laţ, ştreang
no one *pro* nimeni
nor *c* nici
norm *n* normă
normal *adj* normal
normalize *v* a normaliza
normally *adv* normal

north *n* nord
northeast *n* nord-est
northern *adj* nordic
northerner *adj* nordic
Norway *n* Norvegia
Norwegian *adj* norvegian
nose *n* nas
nosedive *v* a descinde în picaj
nostalgia *n* nostalgie
nostril *n* nară
nosy *adj* băgăcios
not *adv* nu
notable *adj* remarcabil
notably *adv* considerabil
notary *n* notar
notation *n* notaţie, notare
note *v* a nota, a însemna
notebook *n* caiet, carnet
noteworthy *adj* remarcabil
nothing *n* nimic
notice *v* a observa
notice *n* anunţ; observaţie
noticeable *adj* remarcabil
notification *n* notificare
notify *v* a anunţa
notion *n* noţiune
notorious *adj* notoriu
noun *n* substantiv
nourish *v* a hrăni, a nutri
nourishment *n* alimentare
novel *n* roman
novelist *n* romanicier
novelty *n* noutate
November *n* noiembrie
novice *n* novice
now *adv* acum, imediat
nowadays *adv* în zilele noastre
nowhere *adv* nicăieri
noxious *adj* dăunător
nozzle *n* gură de furtun
nuance *n* nuanţă
nuclear *adj* nuclear
nude *adj* nud
nudism *n* nudism
nudist *n* nudist
nudity *n* nuditate
nuisance *n* supărare
null *adj* nul
nullify *v* a anula
numb *adj* amorţit
number *n* număr
numbness *n* amorţeală
numerous *adj* numeros
nun *n* călugăriţă
nurse *n* infirmieră
nurse *v* a alăpta, a îngriji

nursery *n* camera copiilor
nurture *v* a hrăni, a îngriji
nut *n* nucă; alună
nutrition *n* hrană, nutriţie
nutritious *adj* hrănitor
nut-shell *n* coajă de nucă
nutty *adj* cu gust de nucă

O

oak *n* stejar
oar *n* vâslă, vâslaş
oasis *n* oază
oath *n* jurământ
oatmeal *n* fulgi de ovăz
obedience *n* supunere
obedient *adj* supus, ascultător
obese *adj* obez
obey *v* a se supune
object *v* a obiecta
object *n* obiect
objection *n* obiecţie
objective *n* obiectiv
obligate *v* a obliga
obligation *n* obligaţie
obligatory *adj* obligatoriu
oblige *v* a obliga
obliged *adj* îndatorat
oblique *adj* oblic
obliterate *v* a distruge
oblivion *n* uitare
oblivious *adj* neatent, uituc
oblong *adj* alungit
obnoxious *adj* nesuferit
obscene *adj* obscen
obscenity *n* obscenitate
obscure *adj* obscur
obscurity *n* obscuritate
observation *n* observaţie
observatory *n* observator
observe *v* a observa
obsess *v* a obseda
obsession *n* obsesie
obsolete *adj* demodat
obstacle *n* obstacol
obstinacy *n* încăpăţânare
obstinate *adj* încăpăţânat
obstruct *v* a împiedica
obstruction *n* obstrucţie
obtain *v* a obţine
obvious *adj* evident
obviously *adv* în mod evident
occasion *n* ocazie, prilej

occasionally *adv* ocazional
occult *adj* ocult, magic
occupant *n* ocupant
occupation *n* ocupaţie
occupy *v* a ocupa
occur *v* a se întâmpla
ocean *n* ocean
October *n* octombrie
octopus *n* caracatiţă
ocurrence *n* întâmplare
odd *adj* ciudat
oddity *n* ciudăţenie
odds *n* şanse
odious *adj* odios, oribil
odometer *n* contor de parcurs
odor *n* miros
odyssey *n* odisee
of *pre* al, a, ai, ale
off *adv* deoparte
offend *v* a ofensa, a jigni
offense *n* ofensă, jignire
offensive *adj* ofensiv
offer *v* a oferi
offer *n* ofertă
offering *n* ofertă
office *n* birou
officer *n* ofiţer
official *adj* oficial
officiate *v* a oficia
offset *v* a compensa
offspring *n* odraslă
off-the-record *adj* neoficial
often *adv* adesea
oil *n* ulei, petrol
ointment *n* alifie
okay *adv* în regulă
old *adj* vechi, bătrân
old age *n* bătrâneţe
old-fashioned *adj* de modă veche
olive *n* măslină
olympics *n* olimpiadă
omelette *n* omletă
omen *n* semn, prevestire
ominous *adj* prevestitor de rău
omission *n* omisiune
omit *v* a omite
on *pre* pe
once *adv* cândva
once *c* îndată ce
one *adj* unul
oneself *pre* se, însuşi
ongoing *adj* neîntrerupt
onion *n* ceapă
onlooker *n* privitor, spectator
only *adv* numai
onset *n* invazie

onslaught *n* atac
onwards *adv* înainte
opaque *adj* opac
open *v* a deschide
open *adj* deschis, sincer
open up *v* a deschide larg
opening *n* deschidere
open-minded *adj* receptiv
openness *n* sinceritate
opera *n* operă
operate *v* a mânui; a conduce
operation *n* operaţie
opinion *n* opinie, părere
opinionated *adj* încăpăţânat
opium *n* opiu
opponent *n* adversar
opportune *adj* oportun
opportunity *n* oportunitate
oppose *v* a se împotrivi
opposite *adj* opus
opposite *adv* opus
opposite *n* contrariul
opposition *n* opoziţie
oppress *v* a asupri
oppression *n* asuprire
opt for *v* a opta pentru
optical *adj* optic
optician *n* optician
optimism *n* optimism
optimistic *adj* optimist
option *n* opţiune
optional *adj* opţional
opulence *n* opulenţă
or *c* sau
oracle *n* oracol
orally *adv* verbal, oral
orange *n* portocală, oranj
orangutan *n* urangutan
orbit *n* orbită
orchard *n* livadă
orchestra *n* orchestră
ordain *v* a hirotonisi
ordeal *n* tortură, calvar
order *n* ordin, aranjament
ordinarily *adv* în mod obişnuit
ordinary *adj* obişnuit, normal
ordination *n* hirotonisire
ore *n* minereu
organ *n* organ, orgă
organism *n* organism
organist *n* organist
organization *n* organizaţie
organize *v* a organiza
orient *n* orient
oriental *adj* oriental
orientation *n* orientare

oriented *adj* orientat
origin *n* origine
original *adj* original, originar
originally *adv* iniţial
originate *v* a iniţia, a inventa
ornament *n* ornament
ornamental *adj* ornamental
orphan *n* orfan
orphanage *n* orfelinat
orthodox *adj* ortodox
ostentatious *adj* ostentativ
ostrich *n* struţ
other *adj* alt
otherwise *adv* în caz contrar
otter *n* vidră
ought to *iv* a fi dator să
ounce *n* uncie
our *adj* nostru
ours *pro* al nostru
ourselves *pro* ne, înşine, noi
oust *v* a izgoni
out *adv* afară
outbreak *n* izbucnire, erupţie
outburst *n* izbucnire, acces
outcast *adj* surghiunit
outcome *n* rezultat
outcry *n* ţipăt, exclamaţie
outdated *adj* depăşit
outdo *v* a întrece
outdoor *adv* în aer liber
outdoors *adv* în aer liber, afară
outer *adj* exterior
outfit *n* echipament
outgoing *adj* fost, care pleacă
outgrow *v* a depăşi
outing *n* plimbare
outlet *n* debit; livrare
outline *n* contur; schiţă
outline *v* a schiţa, a contura
outlive *v* a supravieţui
outlook *n* concepţie
outmoded *adj* demodat
outnumber *v* a întrece numeric
outpouring *n* scurgere, debit
output *n* producţie
outrage *n* insultă, ultraj
outrageous *adj* scandalos
outright *adj* total, categoric
outrun *v* a întrece
outset *n* început
outshine *v* a întrece
outside *adv* afară
outsider *n* intrus
outskirts *n* suburbii
outspoken *adj* deschis, sincer
outstanding *adj* remarcabil

outstretched *adj* întins
outward *adj* exterior
oval *adj* oval
ovary *n* ovar
ovation *n* ovaţie
oven *n* cuptor
over *pre* peste, deasupra
overall *adv* general, total
overbearing *adj* arogant
overboard *adv* peste bord
overcast *adj* întunecat, noros
overcharge *v* a supraîncărca
overcoat *n* pardesiu, palton
overcome *v* a învinge
overcrowded *adj* supraaglomerat
overdo *v* a exagera
overdone *adj* exagerat
overdose *n* supradoză
overdue *adj* întârziat
overestimate *v* a supraaprecia
overflow *v* a inunda
overhaul *v* a revizui
overlap *v* a se suprapune
overnight *adv* peste noapte
overpower *v* a depăşi
overrate *v* a supraestima
override *v* a istovi
overrule *v* a anula
overrun *v* a invada
overseas *adv* în străinătate
oversee *v* a supraveghea
overshadow *v* a eclipsa
oversight *n* neglijenţă
overstate *v* a exagera
overstep *v* a depăşi
overtake *v* a ajunge din urmă
overthrow *v* a răsturna
overthrow *n* răsturnare
overtime *adv* suplimentar
overturn *v* a răsturna
overweight *adj* în surplus
overwhelm *v* a copleşi
owe *v* a datora
owing to *adv* din pricina
owl *n* bufniţă
own *v* a recunoşte
own *adj* propriu, personal
owner *n* proprietar
ownership *n* proprietate
ox *n* bou, bovină
oxen *n* bovine
oxygen *n* oxigen
oyster *n* stridie

P

pace *v* a măsura, a regla
pace *n* pas, ritm
pacify *v* a pacifica
pack *v* a împacheta
package *n* pachet
pact *n* pact
pad *v* a căptuşi, a matlasa
padding *n* căptuşeală groasă
paddle *v* a vâsli
padlock *n* lacăt
pagan *adj* păgân
page *n* pagină; paj; uşier
pail *n* găleată
pain *n* durere
painful *adj* dureros
painless *adj* nedureros
paint *v* a vopsi, a picta
paint *n* vopsea, culoare
paintbrush *n* pensulă
painter *n* pictor, zugrav
painting *n* pictură; tablou
pair *n* pereche
pajamas *n* pijama
pal *n* tovarăş, prieten
palace *n* palat
palate *n* cerul gurii, gust
pale *adj* palid
paleness *n* gălbeneală
palm *n* palmă
palpable *adj* palpabil
paltry *adj* mic, prăpădit
pamper *v* a răsfăţa
pamphlet *n* pamflet, broşură
pan *n* tigaie
pancreas *n* pancreas
pander *v* a fi codoş
pang *n* junghi
panic *n* panică
panorama *n* panoramă
panther *n* panteră
pantry *n* cămară
pants *n* pantaloni
pantyhose *n* ciorap-pantalon
papacy *n* papalitate
paper *n* hârtie, document
paperclip *n* agrafă de papetărie
parable *n* parabolă
parachute *n* paraşută
parade *n* paradă
paradise *n* paradis
paradox *n* paradox
paragraph *n* paragraf
parakeet *n* specii de papagal

parallel *n* paralelă
paralysis *n* paralizie
paralyze *v* a paraliza
parameters *n* parametri, indici
paramount *adj* suprem
paranoid *adj* paranoid
parasite *n* parazit
paratrooper *n* soldat paraşurist
parcel *n* parcelă
parcel post *n* colete
parch *v* a se coace
parchment *n* pergament
pardon *v* a ierta
pardon *n* iertare
parenthesis *n* paranteză
parents *n* părinţi
parish *n* parohie
parishioner *n* enoriaş
parity *n* paritate
park *v* a parca
park *n* parc
parking *n* parcare
parliament *n* parlament
parochial *adj* parohial
parrot *n* papagal
parsley *n* pătrunjel
parsnip *n* păstârnac
part *v* a separa
part *n* parte, fragment
partial *adj* parţial
partially *adv* parţial
participate *v* a participa
participation *n* participare
participle *n* participiu
particle *n* particulă
particular *adj* specific, distinct
particularly *adv* în special
parting *n* despărţire
partisan *n* partizan
partition *n* despărţitură
partly *adv* parţial
partner *n* partener
partnership *n* parteneriat
partridge *n* potârniche
party *n* petrecere; partid
pass *n* trecere
pass *v* a trece
pass around *v* a circula
pass away *v* a dispărea, a muri
pass out *v* a leşina
passage *n* pasaj, trecere
passenger *n* pasager
passer-by *n* trecător
passion *n* pasiune, patimă
passionate *adj* pasionat, pătimaş
passive *adj* pasiv

passport *n* paşaport
password *n* parolă
past *adj* trecut
paste *v* a lipi
paste *n* pastă, lipici
pasteurize *v* a pasteuriza
pastime *n* distracţie, joc
pastor *n* pastor
pastoral *adj* pastoral
pastry *n* patiserie
pasture *n* păşune, imaş
pat *n* mângâiere
patch *v* a cârpi, a repara
patch *n* petic, cârpeală
patent *n* patent, licenţă
patent *adj* evident, patentat
paternity *n* paternitate
path *n* cale, potecă
pathetic *adj* patetic
patience *n* răbdare
patient *adj* răbdător
patio *n* curte interioară
patriarch *n* patriarh
patrimony *n* patrimoniu
patriot *n* patriot
patriotic *adj* patriotic
patrol *n* patrulă
patron *n* patron; susţinător
patronage *n* patronaj
patronize *v* a patrona
pattern *n* model, tipar
pavement *n* trotuar
pavilion *n* pavilion
paw *n* labă
pawn *v* a amaneta, a risca
pawnbroker *n* cămătar
pay *n* plată, salariu
pay *iv* a plăti
pay back *v* a restitui bani
pay off *v* a achita
payable *adj* plătibil
paycheck *n* cec de plată
payment *n* plată
payroll *n* fond salarial
payslip *n* stat de plată
pea *n* mazăre
peace *n* pace
peaceful *adj* paşnic
peach *n* piersică
peacock *n* păun
peak *n* vârf, culme
peanut *n* alună arahidă
pear *n* pară
pearl *n* perlă
peasant *n* ţăran
pebble *n* pietricică

peck *v* a lovi cu ciocul
peck *n* baniţă, ciocănit
peculiar *adj* particular, special
pedagogy *n* pedagogie
pedal *n* pedală
pedantic *adj* pedant
pedestrian *n* pieton
peel *v* a coji
peel *n* coajă
peep *v* a iscodi
peer *n* egal, pereche
pelican *n* pelican
pellet *n* ghemotoc de hârtie
pen *n* stilou, condei
penalize *v* a pedepsi
penalty *n* pedeapsă; penalti
penance *n* penitenţă
penchant *n* predilecţie
pencil *n* creion
pendant *n* pandantiv
pending *adj* nehotărât
pendulum *n* pendulă
penetrate *v* a penetra
penguin *n* pinguin
penicillin *n* penicilină
peninsula *n* peninsulă
penitent *n* pocăit
penniless *adj* lefter
penny *n* peni
pension *n* pensie
pentagon *n* pentagon
pent-up *adj* stăpânit, înăbuşit
people *n* lume, oameni
pepper *n* piper, ardei
per *pre* pe
perceive *v* a observa
percent *adv* la sută
percentage *n* procentaj
perception *n* percepţie
perennial *adj* peren, etern
perfect *adj* perfect
perfection *n* perfecţiune
perforate *v* a perfora
perforation *n* perforare
perform *v* a îndeplini
performance *n* îndeplinire
perfume *n* parfum
perhaps *adv* poate
peril *n* primejdie
perilous *adj* periculos
perimeter *n* perimetru
period *n* perioadă
perish *v* a pieri
perishable *adj* perisabil
perjury *n* sperjur
permanent *adj* permanent

permeate *v* a pătrunde
permission *n* permisiune
permit *v* a permite
pernicious *adj* periculos
perpetrate *v* a comite
persecute *v* a persecuta
persevere *v* a persevera
persist *v* a persista
persistence *n* persistenţă
persistent *adj* persistent
person *n* persoană
personal *adj* personal
personality *n* personalitate
personify *v* a personifica
personnel *n* personal
perspective *n* perspectivă
perspiration *n* transpiraţie
perspire *v* a transpira
persuade *v* a convinge
persuasion *n* convingere
persuasive *adj* convingător
pertain *v* a aparţine,
pertinent *adj* potrivit, util
perturb *v* a tulbura
perverse *adj* pervers
pervert *v* a perverti
pervert *adj* pervers
pessimism *n* pesimism
pessimistic *adj* pesimist
pest *n* ciumă, pestă
pester *v* a necăji
pesticide *n* pesticid
pet *n* animal de casă
petal *n* petală
petite *adj* minion
petition *n* petiţie, cerere
petrified *adj* pietrificat
petroleum *n* ţiţei
pettiness *n* micime
petty *adj* mic; meschin
pew *n* strană, jilţ
phantom *n* fantomă
pharmacist *n* farmacist
pharmacy *n* farmacie
phase *n* fază
pheasant *n* fazan
phenomenon *n* fenomen
philosopher *n* filozof
philosophy *n* filozofie
phobia *n* fobie
phone *n* telefon
phone *v* a telefona
phoney *adj* fals, prefăcut
phosphorus *n* fosfor
photo *n* fotografie
photocopy *n* fotocopie

photograph *v* a fotografia
photographer *n* fotograf
photography *n* fotografie
phrase *n* expresie
physician *n* doctor, medic
physics *n* fizică
pianist *n* pianist
piano *n* pian
pick *v* a culege; a alege
pick up *v* a ridica de jos
pickup *n* ridicare
picture *n* tablou, poză
picture *v* a imagina
picturesque *adj* pitoresc
pie *n* plăcintă
piece *n* bucată
piecemeal *adv* treptat
pier *n* dig, picior de pod
pierce *v* a străpunge
piety *n* pietate, smerenie
pig *n* porc, mitocan
pigeon *n* porumbel
pile *v* a bate în ţăruşi
pile *n* stâlp, pilon
pile up *v* a distruge
pilfer *v* a şterpeli
pilgrim *n* pelerin, călător
pilgrimage *n* pelerinaj
pill *n* pilulă, pastilă
pillage *v* a prăda
pillar *n* stâlp, pilon
pillow *n* pernă
pillowcase *n* faţă de pernă
pilot *n* pilot
pimple *n* coş
pin *n* broşă
pincers *n* cleşte
pinch *v* a ciupi
pinch *n* ciupit; o mână de
pine *n* pin
pineapple *n* ananas
pink *adj* roz
pint *n* halbă
pioneer *n* pionier
pious *adj* pios
pipe *n* ţeavă, conductă
pipeline *n* sistem de ţevi
piracy *n* piraterie, plagiat
pirate *n* pirat
pistol *n* pistol
pit *n* groapă, gaură
pitchfork *n* furcă
pitfall *n* capcană; primejdie
pitiful *adj* milos, jalnic
pity *n* milă, păcat
placard *n* afiş, placardă

placate *v* a pacifica, a împăca
place *n* loc, poziţie
placid *adj* placid, calm
plague *n* ciumă, năpastă
plain *n* câmpie
plain *adj* limpede; simplu
plainly *adv* în mod clar, desluşit
plaintiff *n* reclamant
plan *v* a plănui, a planifica
plan *n* plan
plane *n* avion
planet *n* planetă
plant *v* a planta
plant *n* plantă
plaster *n* plasture, ghips
plaster *v* a tencui
plastic *n* plastic
plate *n* farfurie
plateau *n* platou
platform *n* platformă
platinum *n* platină
platoon *n* pluton
plausible *adj* plauzibil
play *v* a juca
play *n* joc; joacă
player *n* jucător
playful *adj* jucăuş
playground *n* teren de joacă
plea *n* pledoarie
plead *v* a susţine
pleasant *adj* plăcut
please *v* a încânta
pleasing *adj* încântător
pleasure *n* plăcere
pleat *n* cută, pliseu
pleated *adj* pliat, cutat
pledge *v* a amaneta
pledge *n* gaj, garanţie
plentiful *adj* abundent
plenty *n* mulţime, abundenţă
pliable *adj* pliant, flexibil
pliers *n* cleşte, pensă
plot *v* a plănui, a complota
plot *n* parcelă, subiect
plow *v* a ara
ploy *n* truc, tactică
pluck *v* a smulge, a trage
plug *v* a astupa
plug *n* dop; priză
plum *n* prună
plumber *n* instalator
plumbing *n* instalaţii sanitare
plump *adj* rotund, dolofan
plunder *v* a prăda, a jefui
plunge *v* a plonja
plunge *n* plonjon, încercare

plural *n* plural
plus *adj* în plus, suplimentar
plush *adj* luxos, somptuos
plutonium *n* plutoniu
pneumonia *n* pneumonie
pocket *n* buzunar
poem *n* poem, poezie
poet *n* poet
poetry *n* lirică, versuri
poignant *adj* ascuţit, muşcător
point *n* vârf; ascuţiş
point *v* a indica, a sublinia
pointed *adj* direct, ascuţit
pointless *adj* tocit, fără sens
poise *n* ţinută, echilibru
poison *v* a otrăvi
poison *n* otravă
poisoning *n* otrăvire
poisonous *adj* otrăvitor
Poland *n* Polonia
polar *adj* polar
pole *n* pol, opus
police *n* poliţie
policeman *n* poliţist
policy *n* politică,
Polish *adj* polonez
polish *n* lustru, luciu
polish *v* a lustrui
polite *adj* politicos
politeness *n* politeţe
politician *n* politician
politics *n* politică
poll *n* voturi
pollen *n* polen
pollute *v* a murdări
pollution *n* poluare
polygamist *adj* poligam
polygamy *n* poligamie
pomegranate *n* rodie
pomposity *n* pompozitate
pond *n* eleşteu
ponder *v* a chibzui
pontiff *n* pontif, episcop
pool *n* piscină; biliard
pool *v* a pune de acord
poor *n* sărăcime
poorly *adv* sărăcăcios
popcorn *n* floricele
Pope *n* Papa
poppy *n* mac
popular *adj* popular
popularize *v* a populariza
populate *v* a popula
population *n* populaţie
porcelain *n* porţelan
porch *n* verandă

porcupine *n* porc spinos
pore *n* por
pork *n* carne de porc
porous *adj* poros
port *n* port
portable *adj* portabil
portent *n* semn rău
porter *n* hamal, portar
portion *n* porţiune, porţie
portrait *n* portret
portray *v* a portretiza
Portugal *n* Portugalia
Portuguese *adj* portughez
pose *v* a pune de acord
pose *n* poză, atitudine
posh *adj* elegant, şic
position *n* poziţie, rang
positive *adj* pozitiv, precis
possess *v* a poseda
possession *n* posesie
possibility *n* posibilitate
possible *adj* posibil
post *n* post; stâlp; poziţie
post office *n* oficiu poştal, poştă
postage *n* tarif poştal, timbre
postcard *n* carte poştală
poster *n* afiş
posterity *n* posteritate
postman *n* poştaş
postmark *n* ştampila poştală
postpone *v* a amâna
postponement *n* amânare
pot *n* oală; ceainic
potato *n* cartof
potent *adj* puternic
potential *adj* potenţial
pothole *n* gaură, groapă
poultry *n* carne de pasăre
pound *v* a zdrobi, a pisa
pound *n* livră, liră
pour *v* a turna, a vărsa
poverty *n* sărăcie
powder *n* pudră
power *n* putere
powerful *adj* puternic
powerless *adj* neputincios
practical *adj* practic
practice *n* practică
practise *v* a practica
practising *adj* exersare
pragmatist *adj* pragmatic
prairie *n* stepă, prerie
praise *v* a lăuda, a adora
praise *n* laudă, cult
praiseworthy *adj* merituos
prank *n* zbenguială, joc

prawn *n* specie de crevetă
pray *v* a se ruga
prayer *n* rugăciune
preach *v* a predica
preacher *n* predicator
preaching *n* predicare
preamble *n* preambul
precarious *adj* nesigur, riscant
precaution *n* precauţie
precede *v* a preceda
precedent *n* precedent
preceding *adj* precedent
precept *n* precept, ordin
precious *adj* preţios
precipice *n* prăpastie
precipitate *v* a precipita
precise *adj* precis
precision *n* precizie
precocious *adj* precoce
precursor *n* înaintaş
predecessor *n* predecesor
predicament *n* situaţie grea
predict *v* a prezice
prediction *n* prezicere
predilection *n* predilecţie
predisposed *adj* predispus
predominate *v* a predomina
preempt *v* a avea prioritate
prefabricate *v* a prefabrica
preface *n* prefaţă
prefer *v* a prefera
preference *n* preferinţă
prefix *n* prefix
pregnancy *n* graviditate
pregnant *adj* gravidă
prehistoric *adj* preistoric
prejudice *n* prejudecată
preliminary *adj* preliminar
prelude *n* preludiu
premature *adj* prematur
premeditate *v* a premedita
premeditation *n* premeditare
premier *adj* premier
premise *n* premisă
premises *n* incintă, sediu
premonition *n* premoniţie
preoccupation *n* preocupare
preoccupy *v* a preocupa
preparation *n* preparare
prepare *v* a prepara
preposition *n* prepoziţie
prerequisite *n* condiţie
prerogative *n* privilegiu
prescribe *v* a prescrie
prescription *n* prescriere
presence *n* prezenţă

present *adj* prezent
present *v* a prezenta
presentation *n* prezentare
preserve *v* a păstra
preside *v* a acţiona, a oficia
presidency *n* preşedinţie
president *n* preşedinte
press *n* presă; tipografie
press *v* a presa; a strânge
pressing *adj* urgent, presant
pressure *n* presiune
prestige *n* prestigiu
presume *v* a presupune
presumption *n* presupunere
presuppose *v* a presupune
presupposition *n* presupoziţie
pretend *v* a pretinde
pretense *n* pretenţie
pretension *n* pretenţie
pretty *adj* drăguţ
prevail *v* a triumfa
prevalent *adj* predominant
prevent *v* a împiedica
prevention *n* prevenire
preventive *adj* preventiv
preview *n* avanpremieră
previous *adj* precedent
previously *adv* în prealabil
prey *n* pradă, victimă
price *n* preţ, valoare
pricey *adj* scump, costisitor
prick *v* a înţepa, a găuri
pride *n* mândrie
priest *n* preot
priestess *n* preoteasă
priesthood *n* preoţie, cler
primacy *n* primat, întâietate
primarily *adv* în primul rând
prime *adj* număr prim
primitive *adj* primitiv
prince *n* prinţ
princess *n* prinţesă
principal *adj* principal
principle *n* principiu
print *v* a tipări, a imprima
print *n* tipăritură
printer *n* imprimantă
printing *n* imprimerie
prior *adj* anterior
priority *n* prioritate
prism *n* prismă
prison *n* închisoare
prisoner *n* prizonier
privacy *n* intimitate
private *adj* personal, intim
privilege *n* privilegiu

prize *n* premiu
probability *n* probabilitate
probable *adj* probabil
probe *v* a sonda, a cerceta
probing *n* cercetare
problem *n* problemă
problematic *adj* problematic
procedure *n* procedură
proceed *v* a înainta, a continua
proceedings *n* dezbateri
proceeds *n* profit
process *v* a prelucra
process *n* proces, procedeu
procession *n* procesiune
proclaim *v* a proclama
proclamation *n* proclamare
procrastinate *v* a amâna
procreate *v* a procrea
procure *v* a procura
prod *v* a înghionti
prodigious *adj* uriaş, uluitor
prodigy *n* minune, raritate
produce *v* a produce
produce *n* produs
product *n* produs
production *n* producţie
productive *adj* productiv
profane *adj* profan
profess *v* a declara
profession *n* profesie
professional *adj* profesional
professor *n* profesor
proficiency *n* îndemânare
proficient *adj* expert, priceput
profile *n* profil
profit *v* a profita, a câştiga
profit *n* profit
profitable *adj* profitabil
profound *adj* profund
program *n* program
programmer *n* programator
progress *v* a progresa
progress *n* progres
progressive *adj* progresiv
prohibit *v* a interzice
prohibition *n* interzicere
project *v* a proiecta
project *n* proiect
projectile *n* proiectil
prologue *n* prolog
prolong *v* a prelungi
promenade *n* promenadă
prominent *adj* proeminent
promiscuous *adj* promiscuu
promise *n* promisiune
promote *v* a promova

promotion *n* promovare
prompt *adj* prompt
prone *adj* înclinat
pronoun *n* pronume
pronounce *v* a pronunţa
proof *n* dovadă, probă
propaganda *n* propagandă
propagate *v* a propaga
propel *v* a împinge
propensity *n* înclinaţie
proper *adj* corespunzător
properly *adv* cum se cuvine
property *n* proprietate
prophecy *n* profeţie
prophet *n* profet
proportion *n* proporţie
proposal *n* propunere
propose *v* a propune
proposition *n* afirmaţie
prose *n* proză
prosecute *v* a urmări în justiţie
prosecutor *n* procuror
prospect *n* perspectivă
prosper *v* a prospera
prosperity *n* prosperitate
prosperous *adj* prosper
prostate *n* prostată
prostrate *adj* învins, istovit
protect *v* a proteja
protection *n* protecţie
protein *n* proteină
protest *v* a protesta
protest *n* protest
protocol *n* protocol
prototype *n* prototip
protract *v* a prelungi
protracted *adj* prelungit
protrude *v* a ieşi în afară
proud *adj* mândru, orgolios
proudly *adv* cu mândrie
prove *v* a dovedi
proven *adj* dovedit
proverb *n* proverb
provide *v* a furniza
providence *n* providenţă
providing that *c* cu condiţia
province *n* provincie
provision *n* grijă, pregătire
provisional *adj* provizoriu
provocation *n* provocare
provoke *v* a provoca
prow *n* proră
prowl *v* a sta la pândă
prowler *n* prădător, jefuitor
proximity *n* apropiere
proxy *n* delegat, procură

prudence *n* prudenţă
prudent *adj* prudent
prune *n* prună uscată
prurient *adj* obscen, lasciv
pseudonym *n* pseudonim
psychiatrist *n* psihiatru
psychiatry *n* psihiatrie
psychic *adj* mediu, psihic
psychology *n* psihologie
psychopath *n* psihopat
puberty *n* pubertate
public *adj* public
publication *n* publicaţie
publicity *n* publicitate
publicly *adv* în mod public
publish *v* a publica
publisher *n* editor
pudding *n* budincă
puerile *adj* puril, naiv
puff *n* pufăit, puf
puffy *adj* pufăitor, gâfâitor
pull *v* a trage
pull ahead *v* a obţine avantaj
pull down *v* a demola
pull out *v* a se îndepărta
pulley *n* scripete
pulp *n* pulpă
pulpit *n* amvon
pulsate *v* a pulsa, a vibra
pulse *n* puls
pulverize *v* a se pulveriza
pump *v* a pompa
pump *n* pompă
pumpkin *n* dovleac
punch *v* a perfora
punch *n* punci
punctual *adj* punctual
puncture *n* înţepătură
punish *v* a pedepsi
punishment *n* pedeapsă
pupil *n* elev, pupilă
puppet *n* marionetă
puppy *n* căţeluş
purchase *v* a cumpăra
purchase *n* cumpărare
pure *adj* pur
puree *n* piure
purgatory *n* purgatoriu
purge *n* purgativ, epurare
purge *v* a curăţi, a epura
purification *n* purificare
purify *v* a purifica
purity *n* puritate
purple *adj* purpuriu, vineţiu
purpose *n* scop
purposely *adv* intenţionat

purse *n* poşetă
pursue *v* a urma; a urmări
pursuit *n* urmărire; căutare
pus *n* puroi
push *v* a împinge
pushy *adj* insistent, stăruitor
put *iv* a pune, a aşeza
put aside *v* a pune la o parte
put away *v* a lăsa deoparte
put off *v* a amâna
put out *v* a stinge, a scoate
put up *v* a înălţa, a clădi
put up with *v* a tolera
putrid *adj* descompus
puzzle *n* enigmă
puzzling *adj* încurcat, enigmatic
pyramid *n* piramidă
python *n* piton

Q

quagmire *n* mlaştină
quail *n* prepeliţă
quake *v* cutremur, fior
qualify *v* a califica
quality *n* calitate
qualm *n* remuşcare
quandary *n* îndoială, dilemă
quantity *n* cantitate
quarrel *v* a se certa
quarrel *n* ceartă
quarrelsome *adj* certăreţ
quarry *n* carieră de piatră
quarter *n* sfert, pătrime
quarterly *adj* trimestrial
quarters *n* cantonament
quash *v* a anula; a nimici
queen *n* regină
queer *adj* straniu, dubios
quell *v* a înăbuşi
quench *v* a stinge, a răci
quest *n* căutare, anchetă
question *v* a întreba
question *n* întrebare
questionable *adj* îndoielnic
questionnaire *n* chestionar

queue *n* coadă
quick *adj* rapid, iute
quicken *v* a se grăbi
quickly *adv* repede
quicksand *n* nisip mişcător
quiet *adj* calm, tăcut
quietness *n* linişte, tăcere
quilt *n* plapumă
quit *iv* a matlasa
quite *adv* foarte, destul de
quiver *v* a tremura
quiz *v* a interoga, a tachina
quotation *n* citat, cotă
quote *v* a cita, a menţiona
quotient *n* cât

R

rabbi *n* rabin
rabbit *n* iepure
rabies *n* turbare, rabie
raccoon *n* raton
race *v* a participa la curse
race *n* cursă; rasă
racism *n* rasism
racist *adj* rasist
racket *n* rachetă; zarvă
racketeering *n* escrocherie
radar *n* radar
radiation *n* radiaţie
radiator *n* radiator
radical *adj* radical
radio *n* radio
radish *n* ridiche
radius *n* rază
raffle *n* tombolă
raft *n* plută
rag *n* cârpă, zdreanţă
rage *n* furie
ragged *adj* aspru, colţuros
raid *n* incursiune
raid *v* a invada
rail *n* balustradă
railroad *n* cale ferată
rain *n* ploaie
rain *v* a ploua
rainbow *n* curcubeu
raincoat *n* pardesiu de ploaie
rainfall *n* ploaie torenţială
rainy *adj* ploios
raise *n* spor de salariu
raise *v* a ridica; a spori
raisin *n* stafidă

rake *n* greblă
rally *n* strângere, adunare
ram *n* berbec
ram *v* a zdrobi, a izbi
ramification *n* ramificaţie
ramp *n* rampă
rampage *v* a fi furios
rampant *adj* furios
ramson *n* usturoi sălbatic
ranch *n* fermă de animale
rancor *n* ranchiună, pică
randomly *adv* la întâmplare
range *n* rând, distanţă
rank *n* rând; rang
rank *v* a rândui
ransack *v* a scotoci
rape *v* a viola
rape *n* viol
rapid *adj* rapid
rapist *n* violator
rapport *n* raport, relaţie
rare *adj* rar
rarely *adv* rar, rareori
rascal *n* ticălos
rash *v* a rupe în două
rash *n* erupţie, urticarie
raspberry *n* zmeură
rat *n* şobolan
rate *n* ritm; viteză; raport
rather *adv* mai degrabă
ratification *n* ratificare
ratify *v* a ratifica
ratio *n* raport, proporţie
ration *v* a raţionaliza
ration *n* raţie
rational *adj* raţional
rationalize *v* a judeca raţional
rattle *v* a zornăi
ravage *v* a distruge
ravage *n* distrugere
raven *n* corb
ravine *n* râpă
raw *adj* crud, necopt
ray *n* rază
raze *v* a nărui, a rade
razor *n* brici
reach *v* a atinge
reach *n* atingere
react *v* a reacţiona
reaction *n* reacţie
read *iv* a citi
reader *n* cititor
readiness *n* pregătire
reading *n* lectură, citire
ready *adj* pregătit, gata
real *adj* real

realism *n* realism
reality *n* realitate
realize *v* a realiza
really *adv* într-adevăr
realm *n* regat, tărâm
realty *n* realitate, credinţă
reap *v* a secera
reappear *v* a reapărea
rear *v* a îngriji, a ridica
rear *n* spate, urmă
rear *adj* dinapoi, din spate
reason *v* a raţiona, a gândi
reason *n* raţiune, cauză
reasonable *adj* rezonabil
reasoning *n* raţionament
reassure *v* a linişti
rebate *n* rabat, reducere
rebel *v* a răzvrăti
rebel *n* rebel
rebellion *n* rebeliune
rebirth *n* renaştere
rebound *v* a ricoşa, a da înapoi
rebuff *v* a respinge
rebuff *n* ripostă, refuz
rebuild *v* a reclădi, a reface
rebuke *v* a admonesta
rebuke *n* ocară, reproş
rebut *v* a respinge
recall *v* a rechema
recant *v* a retracta
recap *v* a revedea
recapture *v* a recăpăta
recede *v* a se retrage
receipt *n* chitanţă
receive *v* a primi
recent *adj* recent
reception *n* primire, recepţie
receptionist *n* recepţioner
receptive *adj* receptiv
recess *n* pauză, răgaz
recession *n* retragere
recharge *v* a reîncărca
recipe *n* reţetă
reciprocal *adj* reciproc
recital *n* recital
recite *v* a recita
reckless *adj* nepăsător
reckon *v* a socoti, a calcula
reckon on *v* a se baza pe
reclaim *v* a recupera
recline *v* a se bizui pe
recluse *n* pustnic
recognition *n* recunoaştere
recognize *v* a recunoaşte
recollect *v* a-şi aminti
recollection *n* amintire

R

recommend *v* a recomanda
recompense *v* a recompensa
recompense *n* recompensă
reconcile *v* a împăca
reconsider *v* a reconsidera
reconstruct *v* a reconstrui
record *v* a înregistra
record *n* document; urmă
recorder *n* grefier
recording *n* înregistrare
recount *n* relatare
recoup *v* a compensa
recourse *v* a face recurs
recourse *n* recurgere
recover *v* a recăpăta
recovery *n* recuperare
recreate *v* a destinde
recreation *n* distracţie
recruit *v* a recruta
recruit *n* recrut
recruitment *n* recrutare
rectangle *n* dreptunghi
rectangular *adj* dreptunghiular
rectify *v* a rectifica
rector *n* preot, rector
rectum *n* rect
recuperate *v* a recupera
recur *v* a reveni
recurrence *n* revenire
recycle *v* a recicla
red *adj* roşu
red tape *n* formalism
redden *v* a se înroşi
redeem *v* a răscumpăra
redemption *n* îndeplinire
red-hot *adj* încins
redo *v* a reface
redouble *v* a îndoi
redress *v* a îndrepta, a redresa
reduce *v* a reduce
redundant *adj* redundant
reed *n* stuf, trestie
reef *n* recif, stâncă
reel *n* mosor; rolă
reelect *v* a realege
reenactment *n* readoptare
reentry *n* reintrare
refer to *v* a se referi la
referee *n* arbitru
reference *n* referinţă, referire
referendum *n* referendum
refill *v* a reumple
refinance *v* a refinanţa
refine *v* a rafina
refinery *n* rafinărie
reflect *v* a oglindi, a reflecta

reflection *n* reflecţie
reflexive *adj* reflexiv
reform *v* a reforma
reform *n* reformă
refrain *v* a înfrâna
refresh *v* a reîmprospăta
refreshing *adj* răcoritor
refreshment *n* întremare
refrigerate *v* a răci, a îngheţa
refuel *v* a face plinul
refuge *n* refugiu
refugee *n* refugiat
refund *v* a rambursa
refund *n* rambursare, plată
refurbish *v* a renova
refusal *n* refuz, respingere
refuse *v* a refuza
refuse *n* refuz
refute *v* a respinge
regain *v* a recâştiga
regal *adj* regal
regard *v* a privi, a considera
regarding *pre* cu privire la
regardless *adv* indiferent de
regards *n* complimente
regeneration *n* regenerare
regent *n* regent
regime *n* regim
regiment *n* regiment
region *n* regiune
regional *adj* regional
register *v* a înregistra
registration *n* înregistrare
regret *v* a regreta
regret *n* regret
regrettable *adj* regretabil
regularity *n* regularitate
regularly *adv* regulat, mereu
regulate *v* a regla, a regula
regulation *n* reglare
rehabilitate *v* a restabili
rehearsal *n* repetiţie
rehearse *v* a repeta,
reign *v* a domni, a stăpâni
reign *n* domnie, stăpânire
reimburse *v* a rambursa
reimbursement *n* rambursare
rein *v* a înfrâna,
rein *n* frâu
reindeer *n* ren
reinforce *v* a întări
reinforcements *n* întăriri
reiterate *v* a repeta
reject *v* a respinge
rejection *n* respingere
rejoice *v* a se bucura

rejoin *v* a reveni, a reintra în
rejuvenate *v* a întineri
relapse *n* recidivă
related *adj* raportat la, legat de
relationship *n* relaţie
relative *adj* relativ
relative *n* rudă
relax *v* a relaxa
relaxation *n* relaxare
relaxing *adj* odihnitor, relaxant
relay *v* a retransmite
release *v* a elibera
relegate *v* a arunca, a trimite
relent *v* a se îmblânzi
relentless *adj* necruţător
relevant *adj* relevant, important
reliable *adj* demn de încredere
reliance *n* sprijin, suport
relic *n* relicvă
relief *n* uşurare, alinare
relieve *v* a uşura; a alina
religion *n* religie
religious *adj* religios
relinquish *v* a renunţa la
relish *v* a savura
relive *v* a potoli
relocate *v* a se muta
relocation *n* mutare
reluctant *adj* şovăitor
reluctantly *adv* în silă
rely on *v* a se bizui pe
remain *v* a rămâne
remainder *n* rest, rămăşiţă
remaining *adj* care rămâne
remains *n* rămăşiţe
remake *v* a reface
remark *v* a remarca
remark *n* remarcă
remarkable *adj* remarcabil
remarry *v* a se recăsători
remedy *v* a remedia
remedy *n* remediu
remember *v* a ţine minte
remembrance *n* amintire
remind *v* a aminti
reminder *n* memento
remission *n* retragere, iertare
remit *v* a remite
remittance *n* plată, stipendiu
remnant *n* rămăşiţă, rest
remodel *v* a remodela
remorse *n* remuşcare
remorseful *adj* pocăit
remote *adj* îndepărtat
removal *n* îndepărtare
remove *v* a îndepărta

remunerate *v* a remunera
renew *v* a reînnoi
renewal *n* reînnoire
renounce *v* a renunţa la
renovate *v* a renova
renovation *n* renovare
renowned *adj* renumit
rent *v* a închiria
rent *n* chirie
reorganize *v* a reorganiza
repair *v* a repara
reparation *n* reparaţie
repatriate *v* a repatria
repay *v* a răsplăti, a restitui
repayment *n* achitare
repeal *v* a abroga, a anula
repeal *n* anulare
repeat *v* a repeta
repel *v* a respinge
repent *v* a regreta
repentance *n* regret
repetition *n* repetiţie
replace *v* a înlocui
replacement *n* înlocuire
replay *n* reluare, rejucare
replenish *v* a umple
replete *adj* plin
replica *n* reproducere, copie
replicate *v* a reproduce
reply *v* a răspunde
reply *n* răspuns, replică
report *v* a relata, a raporta
report *n* relatare, raport
reportedly *adv* chipurile, pare-se
reporter *n* reporter
repose *v* a odihni
repose *n* odihnă, repaus
represent *v* a reprezenta
repress *v* a reprima
repression *n* reprimare
reprieve *n* amânare
reprint *v* a republica
reprint *n* republicare
reprisal *n* represalie
reproach *v* a reproşa
reproach *n* reproş
reproduce *v* a reproduce
reproduction *n* reproducere
reptile *n* reptilă
republic *n* republică
repudiate *v* a respinge
repugnant *adj* respingător
repulse *v* a respinge
repulse *n* respingere, ripostă
repulsive *adj* respingător
reputation *n* reputaţie

request *v* a cere, a solicita
request *n* cerere, rugăminte
require *v* a cere, a solicita
requirement *n* cerinţă
rescue *v* a salva
rescue *n* salvare
research *v* a cerceta
research *n* cercetare
resemblance *n* asemănare
resemble *v* a semăna cu
resent *v* a detesta
resentment *n* resentiment
reservation *n* rezervare
reserve *v* a rezerva
reservoir *n* rezervor
reside *v* a locui, a se afla
residence *n* rezidenţă, locuinţă
residue *n* reziduu
resign *v* a părăsi
resignation *n* demisie
resilient *adj* elastic, ager
resist *v* a rezista
resistance *n* rezistenţă
resolute *adj* hotărât, decis
resolution *n* hotărâre
resolve *v* a rezolva
resort *v* a recurge
resounding *adj* reprodus
resource *n* resursă
respect *v* a respecta
respect *n* respect
respectful *adj* respectuos
respective *adj* respectiv
respiration *n* respiraţie
respite *n* răgaz
respond *v* a răspunde
response *n* răspuns
responsibility *n* responsabilitate
responsible *adj* responsabil
responsive *adj* corespunzător
rest *v* a odihni
rest *n* odihnă, tihnă
rest room *n* toaletă
restaurant *n* restaurant
restful *adj* odihnitor, liniştitor
restitution *n* restituire
restless *adj* nestatornic
restoration *n* restaurare
restore *v* a reda, a restaura
restrain *v* a restrânge
restraint *n* restricţie
restrict *v* a restrânge
result *n* rezultat
resume *v* a rezuma
resumption *n* reluare
resurrection *n* înviere

resuscitate *v* a resuscita
retain *v* a reţine
retaliate *v* a se răzbuna
retaliation *n* revanşă
retarded *adj* întârziat
retention *n* reţinere
retire *v* a se retrage
retirement *n* retragere
retract *v* a retracta
retreat *v* a se retrage
retreat *n* retragere
retrieval *n* recuperare
retrieve *v* a recupera
retroactive *adj* retroactiv
return *v* a întoarce
return *n* întoarcere
reunion *n* reuniune
reveal *v* a dezvălui
revealing *adj* revelator
revel *v* a petrece, a chefui
revelation *n* revelaţie
revenge *v* a răzbuna
revenge *n* răzbunare
revenue *n* venit, percepţie
reverence *n* reverenţă
reversal *n* răsturnare
reverse *n* revers
reversible *adj* reversibil
revert *v* a reveni
review *v* a revedea
review *n* revedere
revise *v* a revizui
revision *n* revizie
revive *v* a învia
revoke *v* a revoca
revolt *v* a revolta
revolt *n* revoltă
revolting *adj* revoltător
revolve *v* a învârti, a chibzui
revolver *v* revolver
revulsion *n* schimbare totală
reward *v* a răsplăti, a premia
reward *n* răsplată, premiu
rewarding *adj* profitabil
rheumatism *n* reumatism
rhinoceros *n* rinocer
rhyme *n* rimă
rhythm *n* ritm
rib *n* coastă, creastă
ribbon *n* panglică
rice *n* orez
rich *adj* bogat
rid of *iv* a îndepărta
riddle *n* ghicitoare, enigmă
ride *iv* a călări; a mâna
ridge *n* creastă

R

ridicule *v* a ridiculiza
ridicule *n* ridicol, batjocură
ridiculous *adj* ridicol, absurd
rifle *n* carabină, puşcă
rift *n* spărtură
right *adv* drept
right *adj* drept; just; corect
right *n* dreapta, dreptate
rigid *adj* rigid
rigor *n* rigoare
rim *n* jantă; ramă
ring *iv* a suna
ring *n* inel; cerc; ring
ringleader *n* căpetenie
rinse *v* a clăti
riot *v* a-şi face de cap
riot *n* dezordine, tulburare
rip *v* a spinteca, a despica
rip apart *v* a rupe în bucăţi
rip off *v* a smulge
ripe *adj* copt, matur
ripen *v* a coace, a maturiza
ripple *n* val mic
rise *iv* a se ridica, a se trezi
risk *v* a risca
risk *n* risc
risky *adj* riscant
rite *n* rit, ritual
rival *n* rival
rivalry *n* rivalitate
river *n* râu, fluviu
rivet *v* a nitui
riveting *adj* nituit
road *n* drum, cale
roam *v* a străbate
roar *v* a urla, a rage
roar *n* urlet, răget
roast *v* a frige, a prăji
roast *n* friptură
rob *v* a jefui
robber *n* bandit, tâlhar
robbery *n* jaf, tâlhărie
robe *n* robă
robust *adj* robust
rock *n* rocă, piatră
rocket *n* rachetă
rocky *adj* tare, stâncos
rod *n* vergea, nuia
rodent *n* rozător
roll *v* a rula, a suci
romance *n* romantism
roof *n* acoperiş
room *n* cameră; spaţiu
roomy *adj* spaţios
rooster *n* cocoş
root *n* rădăcină

rope *n* funie, frânghie
rosary *n* mătănii
rose *n* trandafir
rosy *adj* trandafiriu
rot *v* a putrezi
rot *n* putregai
rotate *v* a rota
rotation *n* rotaţie
rotten *adj* putred, stricat
rough *adj* aspru
round *adj* rotund
roundup *n* adunare
rouse *v* a stârni
rousing *adj* aţâţător
route *n* rută
routine *n* rutină
row *v* a vâsli
row *n* şir, vâslit
rowdy *adj* scandalagiu
royal *adj* regal, regesc
royalty *n* regalitate
rub *v* a freca
rubber *n* cauciuc, gumă
rubbish *n* gunoi, prostii
rubble *n* dărâmături, moloz
ruby *n* rubin
rudder *n* cârmă
rude *adj* nepoliticos
rudeness *n* insolenţă
rudimentary *adj* rudimentar
rug *n* carpetă, covor
ruin *v* a ruina
ruin *n* ruină
rule *v* a stăpâni, a guverna
rule *n* regulă
ruler *n* conducător
rum *n* rom
rumble *v* a dudui, a bubui
rumble *n* duduit, bubuit
rumor *n* zvon
run *iv* a alerga, a fugi
run away *v* a fugi
run into *v* a se ciocni de
run out *v* a nu ajunge
run over *v* a da pe dinafară
run up *v* a se urca
runner *n* alergător, fugar
runway *n* pistă de alergare
rupture *n* ruptură
rupture *v* a rupe
rural *adj* rural
ruse *n* truc, şiretlic
rush *v* a se grăbi
Russia *n* Rusia
Russian *adj* rusesc
rust *v* a rugini

rust *n* rugină
rustic *adj* rustic
rust-proof *adj* rezistent la rugină
rusty *adj* ruginit, ruginiu
ruthless *adj* inoxidabil
rye *n* secară

S

sabotage *v* a sabota
sabotage *n* sabotaj
sack *n* sac; concediere
sacrament *n* sacrament
sacred *adj* sacru
sacrifice *n* sacrificiu
sacrilege *n* sacrilegiu
sad *adj* trist
sadden *v* a întrista
saddle *n* şa, spinare
sadist *n* sadic
sadness *n* tristeţe
safe *adj* sigur, precaut
safeguard *n* garanţie, ocrotire
safety *n* siguranţă
sail *v* a naviga
sail *n* corabie
sailboat *n* vas cu pânze
sailor *n* marinar
saint *n* sfânt
salad *n* salată
salary *n* salariu
sale *n* vânzare
salesman *n* vânzător
saliva *n* salivă
salmon *n* somon
saloon *n* cârciumă, prăvălie
salt *n* sare
salty *adj* sărat
salvage *v* a salva
salvation *n* salvare
same *adj* acelaşi, identic
sample *n* mostră
sanctify *v* a sfinţi
sanction *v* a aproba
sanction *n* sancţiune
sanctity *n* sfinţenie
sanctuary *n* sanctuar
sand *n* nisip
sandal *n* sanda
sandpaper *n* glaspapir
sandwich *n* sandviş
sane *adj* sănătos la minte
sanity *n* minte sănătoasă

sap *n* sevă, vigoare
sap *v* a săpa
saphire *n* safir
sarcasm *n* sarcasm
sarcastic *adj* sarcastic
sardine *n* sardină, sardea
satanic *adj* satanic, drăcesc
satellite *n* satelit
satire *n* satiră
satisfaction *n* satisfacţie
satisfactory *adj* satisfăcător
satisfy *v* a satisface
saturate *v* a satura
Saturday *n* sâmbătă
sauce *n* sos
saucepan *n* sosieră
saucer *n* farfurioară
sausage *n* cârnat
savage *adj* sălbatic
savagery *n* sălbăticie
save *v* a salva; a economisi
savings *n* economii
savior *n* salvator, mântuitor
savor *v* a gusta, a savura
saw *iv* a tăia cu ferăstrăul
saw *n* ferăstrău
say *iv* a spune, a zice
saying *n* zicală
scaffolding *n* schelărie
scald *v* a opări
scale *v* a cântări
scale *n* cântar; solz; crustă
scalp *n* scalp
scam *n* escrocherie
scan *v* a cerceta; a scruta
scandal *n* scandal
scandalize *v* a scandaliza
scapegoat *n* ţap ispăşitor
scar *n* cicatrice
scarce *adj* insuficient
scarcely *adv* abia
scarcity *n* lipsă, insuficienţă
scare *v* a speria
scare *n* panica, alarmă
scare away *v* a speria, a alunga
scarf *n* eşarfă
scary *adj* înspăimântător
scatter *v* a împrăştia
scenario *n* scenariu
scene *n* scenă; episod
scenery *n* decor, peisaj
scenic *adj* pitoresc; teatral
scent *n* parfum, miros
sceptic *adj* sceptic
schedule *v* a programa
schedule *n* orar; program

scheme *n* plan; schemă
schism *n* dezbinare
scholar *n* învăţat, şcolar
scholarship *n* bursă
school *n* şcoală
science *n* ştiinţă
scientific *adj* ştiinţific
scientist *n* savant
scissors *n* foarfecă
scoff *v* a-şi bate joc
scold *v* a ocărî
scolding *n* ocară
scooter *n* scuter
scope *n* înţelegere
scorch *v* a arde, a jigni
score *n* scor
score *v* a marca, a înregistra
scorn *v* a dispreţui
scornful *adj* dispreţuitor
scorpion *n* scorpion
scoundrel *n* ticălos
scour *v* a cutreiera, a curăţa
scourge *n* bici
scout *n* cercetaş
scramble *v* a se târî
scrambled *adj* omletă
scrap *n* bucăţică
scrap *v* a face bucăţele
scrape *v* a freca, a zgâria
scratch *v* a zgâria, a scărpina
scratch *n* zgârietură
scream *v* a ţipa, a striga
scream *n* ţipăt, strigăt
screech *v* a ţipa sinistru
screen *n* ecran; paravan
screen *v* a ecraniza
screw *v* a înşuruba
screw *n* şurub
screwdriver *n* şurubelniţă
scribble *v* a mâzgăli
script *n* scenariu
scroll *n* sul de hârtie
scrub *v* a freca cu peria
scruples *n* scrupul
scrupulous *adj* scrupulos
scrutiny *n* scrutare
scuffle *n* încăierare
sculptor *n* sculptor
sculpture *n* sculptură
sea *n* mare
seafood *n* fructe de mare
seagull *n* pescăruş
seal *v* a sigila, a pecetlui
seal *n* focă; sigiliu; pecete
seal off *v* a izola, a etanşa
seam *n* cusătură, îmbinare

seamless *adj* fără cusătură
seamstress *n* cusătoreasă
search *v* a cerceta
search *n* cercetare, căutare
seashore *n* ţărmul mării
seasick *adj* rău de mare
seaside *adj* litoral
season *n* anotimp, sezon
seasonal *adj* sezonier
seasoning *n* condiment
seat *n* loc
seated *adj* aşezat
secede *v* a ieşi, a se retrage
secluded *adj* singuratic
seclusion *n* izolare
second *n* secundă, secund
secondary *adj* secundar
secrecy *n* taină, discreţie
secret *n* secret
secretary *n* secretar
secretly *adv* în secret
sect *n* sectă
section *n* secţiune
sector *n* sector
secure *v* a asigura
secure *adj* sigur, în siguranţă
security *n* securitate
sedate *v* a seda
sedation *n* liniştire, calmare
seduce *v* a seduce
seduction *n* seducţie
see *iv* a vedea
seed *n* sămânţă
seedless *adj* fără sămânţă
seedy *adj* plin de seminţe
seek *iv* a căuta
seem *v* a părea
segment *n* segment
segregate *v* a separa, a izola
segregation *n* segregaţie
seize *v* a profita; a prinde
seizure *n* confiscare, apucare
seldom *adv* rareori
select *v* a selecta, a alege
selection *n* selecţie
self-concious *adj* timid, complexat
self-evident *adj* de la sine înţeles
self-interest *n* egoism
selfish *adj* egoist
selfishness *n* egoism
self-respect *n* demnitate
sell *iv* a vinde
seller *n* vânzător
sellout *n* vânzare
semblance *n* asemănare
semester *n* semestru

seminary *n* seminar
senate *n* senat
senator *n* senator
send *iv* a trimite
sender *n* expeditor
senile *adj* senil
senior *adj* senior, mai mare
seniority *n* bătrâneţe
sensation *n* senzaţie
sense *v* a simţi
sense *n* simţ; sentiment
senseless *adj* inconştient
sensible *adj* sensibil, rezonabil
sensitive *adj* sensibil
sensual *adj* senzual
sentence *v* a condamna
sentence *n* sentinţă; propoziţie
sentiment *n* sentiment
sentimental *adj* sentimental
sentry *n* sentinelă
separate *v* a separa
separate *adj* separat
separation *n* separare
September *n* septembrie
sequel *n* urmare, continuare
sequence *n* succesiune
serenade *n* serenadă
serene *adj* calm, senin
serenity *n* seninătate
sergeant *n* sergent
series *n* serie
serious *adj* serios; grav
seriousness *n* seriozitate
sermon *n* predică
serpent *n* şarpe
serum *n* ser
servant *n* servitor
serve *v* a servi; a sluji
service *n* serviciu, folos
service *v* a servi
session *n* sesiune
set *n* serviciu, set
set *iv* a apune, a porni
set about *v* a răspândi, a lansa
set off *v* a reliefa; a porni
set out *v* a declara, a etala
set up *v* a înfiinţa, a instala
setback *n* piedică
setting *n* cadru, decor
settle *v* a rezolva; a stabili
settle down *v* a se instala
settle for *v*. a se împăca cu
settlement *n* aşezare; achitare
settler *n* colonist
setup *n* montare; sistem
seven *adj* şapte

seventeen *adj* şaptesprezece
seventh *adj* al şaptelea
seventy *adj* şaptezeci
sever *v* a despica
several *adj* mai mulţi
severance *n* separaţie
severe *adj* aspru; sever
severity *n* severitate
sew *v* a coase
sewage *n* canalizare
sewer *n* canal, cusător
sewing *n* cusut
sex *n* sex
sexuality *n* sexualitate
shabby *adj* ponosit, uzat
shack *n* colibă, baracă
shackle *n* înlănţuire
shade *n* umbră; răcoare
shadow *n* umbră
shady *adj* umbros, răcoros
shake *iv* a se cutremura
shaken *adj* zguduit
shaky *adj* şubred
shallow *adj* puţin adânc
sham *n* imitaţie, fals
shambles *n* abator
shame *v* a ruşina
shame *n* ruşine
shameful *adj* ruşinos
shameless *adj* neruşinat
shape *v* a modela, a forma
shape *n* formă, siluetă
share *v* a împărţi
share *n* porţie; cotă parte
shareholder *n* acţionar
shark *n* rechin
sharp *adj* ascuţit; abrupt
sharpen *v* a ascuţi
sharpener *n* ascuţitor
shatter *v* a sfărâma, a sparge
shattering *adj* strident, zdrobitor
shave *v* a bărbieri, a rade
she *pro* ea
shear *iv* a tunde oile
shed *iv* a vărsa
sheep *n* oaie
sheets *n* aşternuturi
shelf *n* raft
shell *n* coajă, carapace
shelter *v* a adăposti
shelter *n* adăpost
shelves *n* rafturi
shepherd *n* păstor
sherry *n* vin de Xeres
shield *v* a apăra
shield *n* scut

shift *n* schimb; schimbare
shift *v* a schimba
shine *iv* a străluci
shiny *adj* strălucitor
ship *n* vas, navă
shipment *n* încărcătură
shipwreck *n* naufragiu
shipyard *n* şantier naval
shirk *v* a evita
shirt *n* cămaşă
shiver *v* a tremura
shiver *n* tremur, fior
shock *v* a şoca
shock *n* şoc; lovitură
shocking *adj* şocant
shoddy *adj* grosolan
shoe *n* pantof
shoelace *n* şiret de pantof
shoepolish *n* luciu de pantofi
shoestore *n* magazin de pantofi
shoot *iv* a trage, a împuşca
shoot down *v* a împuşca
shop *v* a face cumpărături
shop *n* magazin
shoplifting *n* furt din magazine
shopping *n* cumpărături
shore *n* ţărm
short *adj* scurt; concis
shortage *n* lipsă, penurie
shortcoming *n* deficienţă
shortcut *n* scurtătură
shorten *v* a scurta
shorthand *n* stenografie
shortlived *adj* efemer, trecător
shortly *adv* curând, pe scurt
shorts *n* şort
shortsighted *adj* miop
shot *n* împuşcătură
shoulder *n* umăr
shout *v* a striga, a ţipa
shout *n* strigăt, ţipăt
shouting *n* strigare, ţipare
shove *v* a împinge
shove *n* împingere, ghiont
shovel *n* lopată
show *iv* a se arăta
show off *v* a face pe grozavul
show up *v* a apărea, a fi vizibil
showdown *n* explicaţie
shower *n* duş
shrapnel *n* şrapnel
shred *v* a fărâma
shred *n* zdreanţă, ruptură
shrewd *adj* isteţ, iute
shriek *v* a ţipa
shriek *n* ţipăt

shrimp *n* crevetă
shrine *n* chivot, altar
shrink *iv* a se strânge
shroud *n* linţoliu
shrouded *adj* învăluit
shrub *n* arbust, tufiş
shrug *v* a da din umeri
shudder *n* tremur, fior
shudder *v* a tremura
shuffle *v* a pune în grabă
shun *v* a evita
shut *iv* a se închide
shut off *v* a stinge
shut up *v* a fereca
shy *adj* timid
shyness *n* timiditate
sick *adj* bolnav, indispus
sicken *v* a fi bolnav
sickening *adj* dezgustător
sickle *n* seceră
sickness *n* boală
side *n* parte, latură
sideburns *n* perciuni
sidestep *v* a evita
sidewalk *n* trotuar
sideways *adv* lateral
siege *n* asediu
siege *v* a asedia
sift *v* a cerne
sigh *n* oftat, suspin
sigh *v* a spune oftând
sight *n* vedere
sign *v* a semna
sign *n* semn; indicaţie
signal *n* semnal
signature *n* semnătură
significance *n* importanţă
significant *adj* important
signify *v* a anunţa
silence *n* linişte, tăcere
silence *v* a reduce la tăcere
silent *adj* tăcut
silhouette *n* siluetă
silk *n* mătase
silly *adj* prost
silver *n* argint
silverplated *adj* argintat
silversmith *n* argintar
silverware *n* argintărie
similar *adj* similar
similarity *n* asemănare
simmer *v* a fierbe
simple *adj* simplu
simplicity *n* simplitate
simplify *v* a simplifica
simply *adv* pur şi simplu

simulate *v* a simula
simultaneous *adj* simultan
sin *v* a păcătui
sin *n* păcat
since *c* de când
since *pre* de la
since then *adv* de atunci
sincere *adj* sincer
sincerity *n* sinceritate
sinful *adj* păcătos
sing *iv* a cânta
singer *n* cântăreţ
single *n* singur
single *adj* singur; simplu
singular *adj* singular
sinister *adj* sinstru
sink *iv* a se scufunda
sink in *v* a pătrunde în
sinner *n* păcătos
sip *v* a sorbi
sip *n* sorbitură
sir *n* cavaler, domnule
siren *n* sirenă
sirloin *n* file de muşchi
sissy *adj* fătălău
sister *n* soră, maică
sister-in-law *n* cumnată
sit *iv* a sta jos, a şedea
site *n* poziţie, teren
sitting *n* şedere
situated *adj* situat
situation *n* situaţie
six *adj* şase
sixteen *adj* şaisprezece
sixth *adj* al şaselea
sixty *adj* şaizeci
sizable *adj* mărişor
size *n* mărime, dimensiune
size up *v* a aprecia
skate *v* a patina
skate *n* patină
skeleton *n* schelet
skeptic *adj* sceptic
sketch *v* a schiţa
sketch *n* schiţă
sketchy *adj* schiţat
ski *v* a schia
skill *n* îndemânare
skillful *adj* iscusit
skim *v* a lua crema
skin *v* a jupui
skin *n* piele
skinny *adj* slab
skip *v* a trece peste
skip *n* săritură
skirmish *n* încăierare

skirt *n* fustă
skull *n* craniu
sky *n* cer
skylight *n* lucarnă, luminator
skyscraper *n* zgârie-nori
slab *n* lespede
slack *adj* încet, leneş
slacken *v* a încetini, a slăbi
slacks *n* pantaloni largi
slam *v* a trânti, a bufni
slander *n* calomnie
slanted *adj* înclinat
slap *n* palmă, lovitură
slap *v* a pălmui
slash *n* lovitură
slash *v* a tăia, a răni
slate *n* placă, tăbliţă
slaughter *v* a tăia
slaughter *n* masacru
slave *n* rob
slavery *n* sclavie, robie
slay *iv* a ucide
sleazy *adj* soios, murdar
sleep *iv* a dormi
sleep *n* somn
sleeve *n* mânecă
sleeveless *adj* fără mâneci
sleigh *n* sanie
slender *adj* zvelt
slice *v* a tăia felii
slice *n* felie
slide *iv* a aluneca
slightly *adv* uşor, oarecum
slim *adj* subţirel; mic;
slip *v* a strecura
slip *n* alunecare
slipper *n* papuc
slippery *adj* alunecos
slit *iv* a tăia, a despica
slob *adj* nepriceput, nătâng
slogan *n* lozincă, slogan
slope *n* pantă
sloppy *adj* umed; neglijent
slot *n* deschizătură, şanţ
slow *adj* lent, încet
slow down *v* a încetini
slow motion *n* încetinitor
slowly *adv* încet
sluggish *adj* trândav, greoi
slum *n* mahala
slump *v* a se prăbuşi
slump *n* declin
slur *v* a mormăi
sly *adj* viclean, afurisit
smack *n* iz, plescăit
smack *v* a pocni, a plescăi

S

small *adj* mic, mărunt
small print *n* literă măruntă
smallpox *n* variolă
smart *adj* deştept
smash *v* a sfărâma
smear *n* pată, frotiu
smear *v* a păta; a unge
smell *iv* a mirosi, a avea iz
smelly *adj* mirositor
smile *v* a zâmbi
smile *n* zâmbet
smith *n* fierar, potcovar
smoke *v* a fuma, a afuma
smoked *adj* afumat
smoker *n* fumător
smoking gun *n* dovadă sigură
smooth *v* a netezi
smooth *adj* neted, lin
smoothly *adv* în mod lin
smoothness *n* netezime
smother *v* a înăbuşi, a stinge
smuggler *n* contrabandist
snail *n* melc
snake *n* şarpe
snapshot *n* instantaneu
snare *v* a prinde în capcană
snare *n* capcană, ispită
snatch *v* a apuca, a smulge
sneak *v* a şterpeli, a se furişa
sneeze *v* a strănuta
sneeze *n* strănut
sniff *v* a adulmeca
sniper *n* franctiror
snitch *v* a fura, a trăda
snooze *v* a aţipi
snore *v* a sforăi
snore *n* sforăit
snow *v* a ninge, a înzăpezi
snow *n* zăpadă, ninsoare
snowfall *n* ninsoare
snowflake *n* fulg de zăpadă
snub *v* a da peste nas
snub *n* ripostă
soak *v* a uda, a înmuia
soak in *v* a absorbi
soak up *v* a absorbi
soar *v* a se înălţa
sob *n* suspin
sober *adj* treaz, sobru
so-called *adj* aşa-numit
sociable *adj* sociabil
socialism *n* socialism
socialist *adj* socialist
socialize *v* a socializa
society *n* societate
sock *n* şosetă

sod *n* gazon, iarbă
sofa *n* canapea
soft *adj* moale, neted
soften *v* a muia
softly *adv* uşurel, domol
softness *n* moliciune
soggy *adj* ud leoarcă
soil *v* a murdări, a mânji
soil *n* sol, pământ
soiled *adj* murdar, mânjit
solace *n* consolare
solar *adj* solar
solder *v* a lipi
soldier *n* soldat
sold-out *adj* vândut
sole *n* talpă
sole *adj* singur, unic
solely *adv* numai
solemn *adj* solemn, grav
solicit *v* a solicita
solid *adj* solid
solidarity *n* solidaritate
solitary *adj* solitar
solitude *n* singurătate
soluble *adj* solubil
solution *n* soluţie, rezolvare
solve *v* a rezolva
solvent *adj* solvabil
somber *adj* sumbru
some *adj* nişte
somebody *pro* cineva
someday *adv* într-o zi
somehow *adv* cumva
someone *pro* cineva
something *pro* ceva
sometimes *adv* uneori
someway *adv* cumva, oarecum
somewhat *adv* oarecum
son *n* fiu
song *n* cântec
son-in-law *n* ginere
soon *adv* curând
soothe *v* a linişti, a împăca
sorcerer *n* vrăjitor
sorcery *n* vrăjitorie
sore *n* punct dureros
sore *adj* dureros
sorrow *n* regret, supărare
sorrowful *adj* nefericit, trist
sorry *adj* supărat
sort *n* fel, gen
sort out *v* a sorta
soul *n* suflet
sound *n* sunet; voce
sound *v* a suna din
sound out *v* a pronunţa

soup *n* supă
sour *adj* acru
source *n* sursă
south *n* sud
southeast *n* sud-est
southern *adj* sudic
southerner *n* locuitor din sud
southwest *n* sud-vest
souvenir *n* suvenir
sovereign *adj* suveran
sovereignty *n* suveranitate
soviet *adj* sovietic
sow *iv* a semăna
space *n* spaţiu
spacious *adj* spaţios
spade *n* cazma
Spain *n* Spania
span *v* a traversa
span *n* anvergură
Spaniard *n* spaniol
Spanish *adj* spaniol
spank *v* a bate
spanking *n* chelfăneală
spare *v* a cruţa
spare *adj* suplimentar
spare part *n* piesă de schimb
sparingly *adv* cu economie
spark *n* scânteie
spark off *v* a provoca
spark plug *n* bujie
sparkle *v* a scânteia, a licări
sparrow *n* vrabie
sparse *adj* rar, răsfirat
spasm *n* spasm
speak *iv* a vorbi
speaker *n* vorbitor
spear *n* suliţă
spearhead *v* vârf de suliţă
special *adj* special
specialize *v* a specializa
specialty *n* specialitate
species *n* specie
specific *adj* specific
specimen *n* specimen
speck *n* fir, fărâmiţă
spectacle *n* spectacol
spectator *n* spectator
speculate *v* a specula
speculation *n* speculaţie
speech *n* cuvântare
speechless *adj* mut, amuţit
speed *iv* a se grăbi
speed *n* viteză
speedily *adv* repede
speedy *adj* rapid, grabnic
spell *iv* a silabisi

spell *n* farmec, vrajă
spelling *n* citire literă cu literă
spend *iv* a cheltui
spending *n* cheltuială
sperm *n* spermă
sphere *n* sferă
spice *n* mirodenie
spicy *adj* picant
spider *n* păianjen
spiderweb *n* pânză de păianjen
spill *iv* a vărsa
spill *n* vărsare
spin *iv* a se învârti
spinster *n* fată bătrână
spirit *n* spirit
spiritual *adj* spiritual
spit *iv* a scuipa
spite *n* pică, duşmănie
spiteful *adj* duşmănos
splash *v* a stropi
splendid *adj* splendid
splendor *n* splendoare
splint *n* lopăţică
splinter *n* aşchie, schijă
splinter *v* a despica
split *n* separaţie, ruptură
split *iv* a se despica
split up *v* a se despărţi
spoil *v* a strica, a răsfăţa
spoils *n* profit
sponge *n* burete
sponsor *n* sponsor
spontaneity *n* spontaneitate
spontaneous *adj* spontan
spooky *adj* fantomatic
spool *n* mosor, rolfilm
spoon *n* lingură
sporadic *adj* sporadic
sport *n* sport
sportman *n* sportiv
sporty *adj* dichisit
spot *v* a păta, a recunoaşte
spot *n* pată; loc
spotless *adj* nepătat
spotlight *n* reflector
spouse *n* soţ, soţie
sprain *v* a luxa, a scrânti
sprawl *v* a întinde
spray *v* a pulveriza
spread *iv* a se întinde
spring *iv* a sări; a apărea
spring *n* primăvară; salt
springboard *n* trambulină
sprinkle *v* a stropi, a presăra
sprout *v* a produce
spruce up *v* a se aranja

spur *v* a îndemna
spur *n* pinten; îndemn
spy *v* a spiona
spy *n* spion
squalid *adj* sordid, murdar
squander *v* a risipi, a irosi
square *adj* pătrat
square *n* pătrat, piaţă
squash *v* a terciui, a zdrobi
squeak *v* a chiţăi
squeaky *adj* scârţâit, strident
squeamish *adj* fandosit, mofturos
squeeze *v* a strânge
squeeze in *v* a înghesui
squeeze up *v* a se înghesui
squid *n* calmar
squirrel *n* veveriţă
stab *v* a înjunghia
stab *n* înjunghiere
stability *n* stabilitate
stable *adj* stabil
stable *n* grajd
stack *n* teanc
staff *n* prăjină, personal
stage *n* scenă; estradă
stage *v* a pune în scenă
stagger *v* a speria, a zăpăci
staggering *adj* uluitor
stagnant *adj* stagnant
stagnate *v* a stagna
stagnation *n* stagnare
stain *v* a păta
stain *n* pată
stair *n* treaptă
staircase *n* scară a unei clădiri
stairs *n* scară a unei clădiri
stake *n* par; rug; miză
stake *v* a sprijini, a miza
stale *adj* stătut
stalemate *n* pat la şah
stalk *v* a urmări
stalk *n* tulpină, cotor
stall *n* grajd
stall *v* a adăposti
stammer *v* a rosti cu greu
stamp *v* a ştampila, a marca
stamp *n* ştampilă, timbru
stamp out *v* a distruge, a lichida
stampede *n* panică
stand *iv* a se ridica
stand *n* suport, stand
stand for *v* a reprezenta
stand out *v* a se distinge
standard *n* drapel; emblemă
standardize *v* a standardiza
standing *n* durată, poziţie

standpoint *n* punct de vedere
standstill *adj* oprit
staple *v* a capsa
staple *n* belciug, capsă
stapler *n* capsator
star *n* stea
starch *n* amidon
starchy *adj* amilaceu
stare *v* a privi
stark *adj* ţeapăn, curat
start *v* a începe, a porni
start *n* start, început
startle *v* a surprinde
startled *adj* surprins, speriat
starvation *n* foamete
starve *v* a înfometa
state *n* stare; situaţie; stat
state *v* a declara
statement *n* declaraţie
station *n* staţie, gară
stationary *adj* staţionar
stationery *n* papetărie
statistic *n* statistică
statue *n* statuie
status *n* statut; situaţie
statute *n* lege, statut
staunch *adj* fidel, neclintit
stay *v* a propti, a sta
stay *n* şedere, oprire
steady *adj* ferm; sigur
steak *n* friptură
steal *iv* a fura
stealthy *adj* furiş, tainic
steam *n* abur, vapori
steel *n* oţel
steep *adj* abrupt
stem *n* tulpină, origine
stem *v* a stăvili
stench *n* duhoare
step *n* pas; ritm
step down *v* a abdica
step out *v* a ieşi
step up *v* a progresa
stepbrother *n* frate vitreg
step-by-step *adv* pas cu pas
stepdaughter *n* fiică vitregă
stepfather *n* tată vitreg
stepladder *n* scară mobilă
stepmother *n* mamă vitregă
stepsister *n* soră vitregă
stepson *n* fiu vitreg
sterile *adj* steril
sterilize *v* a steriliza
stern *n* pupă, coadă
stern *adj* sever, aspru
sternly *adv* cu severitate

stew *n* tocană, ostropel
stewardess *n* stewardesă
stick *n* băţ, baston
stick *iv* a înfige, a băga
stick around *v* a sta prin preajmă
stick out *v* a ieşi în afară
stick to *v* a menţine
sticker *n* etichetă
sticky *adj* lipicios
stiff *adj* ţeapăn
stiffen *v* a înţepeni
stiffness *n* înţepenire
stifle *v* a înăbuşi
stifling *adj* sufocant
still *adj* liniştit, tihnit
still *adv* încă, totuşi
stimulant *n* stimulent
stimulate *v* a stimula
stimulus *n* stimulent
sting *iv* a fi înţepător
sting *n* înţepătură
stinging *adj* pişcător
stingy *adj* meschin
stink *iv* a duhni
stink *n* duhoare
stinking *adj* împuţit
stipulate *v* a stipula
stir *v* a agita; a învârti
stir up *v* a stârni
stitch *v* a însăila
stitch *n* însăilare, cusătură
stock *v* a stoca
stock *n* trunchi; butuc
stocking *n* ciorap lung
stockroom *n* depozit
stoic *adj* stoic
stomach *n* stomac
stone *n* piatră
stone *v* a bate cu pietre
stool *n* scaun
stop *v* a opri
stop *n* oprire, stop
stop by *v* a trece pe la
stop over *v* a face o escală
storage *n* depozitare
store *v* a aproviziona
store *n* depozit, magazin
stork *n* barză
storm *n* furtună
stormy *adj* furtunos
story *n* poveste
stove *n* sobă, plită
straight *adj* drept, direct
straighten out *v* a îndrepta
strain *v* a întinde, a strecura
strain *n* încordare, luxaţie

strained *adj* forţat, încordat
strainer *n* strecurătoare
strait *n* strâmtoare
stranded *adj* împotmolit
strange *adj* ciudat, straniu
stranger *n* străin
strangle *v* a strangula
strap *n* bretea
strategy *n* strategie
straw *n* pai
strawberry *n* căpşună
stray *adj* rătăcit
stray *v* a rătăci
stream *n* pârâu; curent
street *n* stradă
streetcar *n* tramvai
streetlight *n* felinar stradal
strength *n* forţă, tărie
strengthen *v* a întări
strenuous *adj* dificil
stress *n* stres; presiune
stressful *adj* stresant
stretch *n* întindere
stretch *v* a întinde
stretcher *n* targă
strict *adj* sever, rigid
stride *iv* a păşi
strife *n* ceartă, conflict
strike *n* grevă
strike *iv* a lovi; a intra
strike out *v* a se zbate
strike up *v* a începe să cânte
striking *adj* izbitor
string *n* sfoară; strună
stringent *adj* strict, obligatoriu
strip *n* dungă, şuviţă
strip *v* a dezbrăca
stripe *n* dungă
striped *adj* dungat, vărgat
strive *iv* a se strădui
stroke *n* lovitură; atac
stroll *v* a se plimba
strong *adj* puternic
structure *n* structură
struggle *v* a se zbate
struggle *n* luptă, efort
stub *n* cotor; ciot
stubborn *adj* încăpăţânat
student *n* student
study *v* a studia
stuff *n* material; ţesătură
stuff *v* a umple, a îndesa
stuffing *n* umplutură
stuffy *adj* îmbâcsit
stumble *v* a se împiedica
stun *v* a şoca, a ameţi

stunning *adj* grozav
stupendous *adj* uluitor, fantastic
stupid *adj* stupid
stupidity *n* prostie, stupiditate
sturdy *adj* viguros, robust
stutter *v* a se bâlbâi
style *n* stil, manieră
subdue *v* a supune
subdued *adj* supus
subject *v* a expune
subject *n* subiect; materie
sublime *adj* sublim
submerge *v* a inunda
submissive *adj* supus
submit *v* a supune
subpoena *v* a cita
subpoena *n* citaţie
subscribe *v* a subscrie
subscription *n* subscripţie
subsequent *adj* ulterior
subsidiary *adj* auxiliar
subsidize *v* a stipendia
subsidy *n* subsidiu
subsist *v* a se menţine
substance *n* substanţă
substandard *adj* subetalon
substantial *adj* substanţial
substitute *v* a înlocui
substitute *n* înlocuitor
subtitle *n* subtitlu
subtle *adj* subtil
subtract *v* a scădea
subtraction *n* scădere
suburb *n* suburbie
subway *n* metrou
succeed *v* a moşteni
success *n* succes
successful *adj* victorios
successor *n* succesor
succulent *adj* suculent
succumb *v* a ceda, a muri
such *adj* asemenea
suck *v* a suge
sucker *adj* sugaci, fraier
sudden *adj* brusc
suddenly *adv* deodată
sue *v* a da în judecată
suffer *v* a suferi
suffer from *v* a suferi de
suffering *n* suferinţă
sufficient *adj* suficient
suffocate *v* a sufoca
sugar *n* zahăr
suggest *v* a sugera
suggestion *n* sugestie
suggestive *adj* sugestiv

suicide *n* sinucidere
suit *n* costum, cerere
suitable *adj* potrivit
suitcase *n* valiză
sullen *adj* mohorât
sulphur *n* sulf
sum *n* sumă, total
sum up *v* a sumariza
summarize *v* a rezuma
summary *n* rezumat, sumar
summer *n* vară
summit *n* vârf, culme
summon *v* a convoca
sumptuous *adj* somptuos
sun *n* soare
sunblock *n* protecţie solară
sunburn *n* bronzare
Sunday *n* duminică
sundown *n* apusul soarelui
sunglasses *n* ochelari de soare
sunken *adj* scofâlcit, supt
sunny *adj* însorit
sunrise *n* răsăritul soarelui
sunset *n* apusul soarelui
superb *adj* superb
superfluous *adj* inutil
superior *adj* superior
superiority *n* superioritate
supermarket *n* supermarket
superpower *n* supraputere
supersede *v* a înlocui
superstition *n* superstiţie
supervise *v* a supraveghea
supervision *n* supraveghere
supper *n* cină
supple *adj* suplu
supplier *n* furnizor
supplies *n* provizii
supply *v* a furniza
support *v* a sprijini, a susţine
supporter *n* susţinător
suppose *v* a presupune
supposing *c* dar dacă
supposition *n* presupunere
suppress *v* a înăbuşi
supremacy *n* supremaţie
supreme *adj* suprem
surcharge *n* supraîncărcare
sure *adj* sigur
surely *adv* cu siguranţă
surf *v* a face surfing
surface *n* suprafaţă
surge *n* val, răbufnire
surgeon *n* chirurg
surgical *adv* chirurgical
surname *n* nume de familie

surpass *v* a întrece
surplus *n* surplus
surprise *v* a surprinde
surprise *n* surpriză
surrender *v* a preda, a ceda
surrender *n* capitulare
surround *v* a înconjura
surroundings *n* împrejurimi
surveillance *n* supraveghere
survey *n* a supraveghea
survival *n* supravieţuire
survive *v* a supravieţui
survivor *n* supravieţuitor
susceptible *adj* susceptibil
suspect *v* a suspecta
suspect *n* suspect
suspend *v* a suspenda
suspenders *n* bretele
suspense *n* aşteptare
suspension *n* suspendare
suspicion *n* suspiciune
suspicious *adj* suspicios
sustain *v* a susţine
sustenance *n* susţinere
swallow *v* a înghiţi
swamp *n* mlaştină
swamped *adj* mlăştinos
swan *n* lebădă
swap *v* a schimba
swap *n* schimb
swarm *n* roi
sway *v* a stăpâni
swear *iv* a jura, a înjura
sweat *n* transpiraţie
sweat *v* a transpira
sweater *n* truditor, pulover
Sweden *n* Suedia
Sweedish *adj* suedez
sweep *iv* a mătura
sweet *adj* dulce
sweeten *v* a îndulci
sweetheart *n* iubit, iubită
sweetness *n* dulceaţă
sweets *n* dulciuri
swell *iv* a se umfla
swelling *n* umflătură
swift *adj* rapid
swim *iv* a înota
swimmer *n* înotător
swimming *n* înot
swindle *v* a escroca
swindle *n* escrocherie
swindler *n* escroc
swing *iv* a se legăna
swing *n* legănare
Swiss *adj* elveţian

switch *v* a schimba
switch *n* comutator, macaz
switch off *v* a tăia, a întrerupe
switch on *v* a aprinde
Switzerland *n* Elveţia
swivel *v* a învârti
swollen *adj* umflat
sword *n* sabie
swordfish *n* peşte-sabie
syllable *n* silabă
symbol *n* simbol
symbolic *adj* simbolic
symmetry *n* simetrie
sympathize *v* a simpatiza
sympathy *n* simpatie
symphony *n* simfonie
symptom *n* simptom
synagogue *n* sinagogă
synchronize *v* a sincroniza
synod *n* sinod
synonym *n* sinonim
synthesis *n* sinteză
syphilis *n* sifilis
syringe *n* seringă
syrup *n* sirop
system *n* sistem
systematic *adj* sistematic

T

table *n* masă
tablecloth *n* faţă de masă
tablespoon *n* lingură
tablet *n* tabletă; bucată
tack *n* ţintă
tackle *v* a aborda, a deschide
tact *n* tact
tactful *adj* abil, plin de tact
tactical *adj* tactic
tactics *n* tactică
tag *n* etichetă
tail *n* coadă
tail *v* a urmări
tailor *n* croitor
tainted *adj* pătat, stricat
take *iv* a lua
take apart *v* a desfac
take away *v* a lua, a îndepărta
take back *v* a retrage
take in *v* a pofti în casă
take off *v* a pleca
take out *v* a extrage, a scoate
take over *v* a prelua
tale *n* poveste
talent *n* talent

S T

talk *v* a discuta
talkative *adj* flecar
tall *adj* înalt
tame *v* a îmblânzi
tangent *n* tangentă
tangerine *n* mandarină
tangible *adj* palpabil
tangle *n* încurcătură
tank *n* rezervor, tanc
tanned *adj* bronzat
tantamount to *adj* echivalent cu
tantrum *n* supărare
tap *n* robinet
tape *n* bandă
tape recorder *n* magnetofon
tapestry *n* tapet, tapiserie
tar *n* gudron
tarantula *n* tarantulă
tardy *adv* încet
target *n* ţintă; ţel; sarcină
tariff *n* tarif
tarnish *v* a întuneca
tart *n* tartă
tartar *n* tartru
task *n* sarcină
taste *v* a gusta; a simţi
taste *n* gust, preferinţă
tasteful *adj* gustos
tasteless *adj* fără gust
tasty *adj* gustos
tavern *n* cârciumă
tax *n* taxă
tea *n* ceai
teach *iv* a fi profesor
teacher *n* profesor
team *n* echipă
teapot *n* ceainic
tear *iv* a se rupe
tear *n* lacrimă
tearful *adj* scăldat în lacrimi
tease *v* a tachina
teaspoon *n* linguriţă
technical *adj* tehnic
technician *n* tehnician
technique *n* tehnică
technology *n* tehnologie
tedious *adj* plicticos
tedium *n* plictiseală
teenager *n* adolescent
teeth *n* dinţi
telegram *n* telegramă
telepathy *n* telepatie
telephone *n* telefon
telescope *n* telescop
televise *v* a televiza
television *n* televiziune

tell *iv* a spune, a povesti
teller *n* povestitor
temper *n* temperament
temperature *n* temperatură
tempest *n* furtună, vijelie
temple *n* templu
temporary *adj* temporar
tempt *v* a ispiti
temptation *n* ispită
tempting *adj* ispititor
ten *adj* zece
tenacity *n* tenacitate
tenant *n* chiriaş
tendency *n* tendinţă
tender *adj* moale; delicat
tenderness *n* delicateţe
tennis *n* tenis
tenor *n* tenor
tense *adj* încordat
tension *n* tensiune
tent *n* cort
tentacle *n* tentacul
tentative *adj* experimental
tenth *n* zecime
tenuous *adj* subtil, subţire
tepid *adj* călduţ
term *n* termen
terminate *v* a înceta
terminology *n* terminologie
termite *n* termită
terms *n* învoială
terrace *n* terasă
terrain *n* sol, teren
terrestrial *adj* terestru
terrible *adj* teribil
terrific *adj* teribil, straşnic
terrify *v* a înspăimânta
terrifying *adj* înspăimântător
territory *n* teritoriu
terror *n* teroare
terrorism *n* terorism
terrorist *n* terorist
terrorize *v* a teroriza
terse *adj* concis
test *v* a testa, a încerca
test *n* test, încercare
testament *n* testament
testify *v* a declara
testimony *n* mărturie
text *n* text
textbook *n* manual
texture *n* ţesătură
thank *v* a mulţumi
thankful *adj* recunoscător
thanks *n* mulţumiri
that *adj* acel, acea

thaw *v* a topi, a dezgheţa
thaw *n* dezgheţ
theater *n* teatru
theft *n* furt, hoţie
theme *n* temă, subiect
themselves *pro* înşişi
then *adv* atunci, apoi
theologian *n* teolog
theology *n* teologie
theory *n* teorie
therapy *n* terapie
there *adv* acolo
therefore *adv* deci, prin urmare
thermometer *n* termometru
thermostat *n* termostat
these *adj* aceşti
thesis *n* teză
they *pro* ei, ele
thick *adj* gros; dens
thicken *v* a îngroşa
thickness *n* grosime
thief *n* hoţ
thigh *n* coapsă, pulpă
thin *adj* subţire; slab; rar
thing *n* lucru, obiect
think *iv* a se gândi
thinly *adv* sumar, de-abia
third *adj* al treilea
thirst *v* a fi însetat
thirsty *adj* însetat
thirteen *adj* treisprezece
thirty *adj* treizeci
this *adj* acest
thorn *n* spin, ciulin
thorny *adj* ţepos
thorough *adj* complet, profund
those *adj* acei
though *c* deşi
thought *n* gând
thoughtful *adj* amabil
thousand *adj* mie
thread *v* a înşira pe aţă
thread *n* aţă, fir
threat *n* ameninţare
threaten *v* a ameninţa
three *adj* trei
thresh *v* a treiera; a îmblăti
threshold *n* prag; intrare
thrifty *adj* econom, prosper
thrill *v* a emoţiona
thrill *n* fior, emoţie
thrive *v* a prospera, a reuşi
throat *n* gât
throb *n* puls, vibraţie
throb *v* a pulsa, a vibra
thrombosis *n* tromboză

throne *n* tron
throng *n* mulţime
through *pre* prin
throw *iv* a arunca
throw away *v* a irosi
throw up *v* a vomita
thug *n* criminal
thumb *n* degetul mare
thumbtack *n* piuneză
thunder *n* tunet
thunderbolt *n* fulger
Thursday *n* joi
thus *adv* astfel, aşa
thwart *v* a contrazice
thyroid *n* tiroidă
tickle *v* a gâdila
tickle *n* gâdilat
ticklish *adj* gâdilos
tidal wave *n* val de reflux
tide *n* flux, maree
tidy *adj* ordonat
tie *v* a lega; a fixa
tie *n* legătură; funie
tiger *n* tigru
tight *adj* etanş
tighten *v* a închide, a strânge
tile *n* ţiglă; tei
till *adv* până, până ce
till *v* a cultiva
tilt *v* a înclina
timber *n* cherestea
time *n* timp
time *v* a potrivi la timp
timeless *adj* fără sfârşit, nedatat
timely *adj* potrivit
times *n* vremuri
timetable *n* program, orar
timid *adj* timid
timidity *n* timiditate
tin *n* tinichea, cositor
tiny *adj* mititel
tip *n* bacşiş; vârf
tiptoe *n* vârful picioarelor
tired *adj* obosit
tiredness *n* oboseală
tireless *adj* neobosit
tiresome *adj* obositor
tissue *n* ţesut, ţesătură
title *n* titlu
to *pre* la, pe
toad *n* broască râioasă
toast *v* a prăji; a toasta
toast *n* pâine prăjită, toast
toaster *n* prăjitor de pâine
tobacco *n* tutun
today *adv* azi, astăzi

toddler *n* copilaş, pici
toe *n* deget de la picior
together *adv* împreună
toil *v* a trudi
toilet *n* toaletă
token *n* semn, simbol
tolerable *adj* tolerabil
tolerance *n* toleranţă
tolerate *v* a tolera
toll *n* dangăt de clopot; bir
toll *v* a suna din clopot
tomato *n* roşie
tomb *n* mormânt, cavou
tombstone *n* piatră funerară
tomorrow *adv* mâine
ton *n* tonă
tone *n* ton, glas
tongs *n* cleşte
tongue *n* limbă
tonic *n* tonic
tonight *adv* diseară, la noapte
tonsil *n* amigdală
too *adv* de asemenea
tool *n* unealtă, instrument
tooth *n* dinte
toothache *n* durere de dinţi
toothpick *n* scobitoare
top *n* vârf, culme
topic *n* temă, chestiune
topple *v* a se bălăbăni
torch *n* torţă
torment *v* a chinui
torment *n* chin, durere
torrent *n* torent
torrid *adj* torid
torso *n* tors, trunchi
tortoise *n* broască ţestoasă
torture *v* a tortura
torture *n* tortură
toss *v* a clătina, a răsturna
total *adj* total
totalitarian *adj* totalitar
totality *n* totalitate, întreg
touch *n* atingere; tuşeu
touch *v* a atinge
touch on *v* a se referi la
touch up *v* a retuşa
touching *adj* emoţionant
tough *adj* tare, rezistent
toughen *v* a întări
tour *n* tur, turneu
tourism *n* turism
tourist *n* turist
tournament *n* turneu, competiţie
tow *v* a remorca
tow truck *n* camion cu remorcă

towards *pre* către, spre
towel *n* prosop
tower *n* turn
towering *adj* înalt, dominant
town *n* oraş
town hall *n* primărie
toxic *adj* toxic
toxin *n* toxină
toy *n* jucărie
trace *v* a trasa
track *n* urmă, pistă
track *v* a urmări
traction *n* tracţiune
tractor *n* tractor
trade *n* profesie, negoţ
trade *v* a schimba
trademark *n* marca fabricii
trader *n* comerciant
tradition *n* tradiţie
traffic *n* trafic, circulaţie
traffic *v* a trafica
tragedy *n* tragedie
tragic *adj* tragic
trail *v* a da de urmă
trail *n* urmă, potecă
trailer *n* remorcă, urmăritor
train *n* tren, trenă
train *v* a instrui
trainee *n* cel care este instruit
trainer *n* antrenor, instructor
training *n* instrucţie, instruire
trait *n* trăsătură
traitor *n* trădător
trajectory *n* traiectorie
tram *n* tramvai
trample *v* a călca în picioare
trance *n* transă
tranquility *n* linişte, calm
transaction *n* tranzacţie
transcend *v* a depăşi
transcribe *v* a transcrie
transfer *v* a transfera
transfer *n* transfer
transform *v* a transforma
transformation *n* transformare
transfusion *n* transfuzie
transient *adj* trecător, efemer
transit *n* a tranzita
transition *n* tranziţie
translate *v* a traduce
translator *n* traducător
transmit *v* a transmite
transparent *adj* transparent
transplant *v* a transplanta
transport *v* a transporta
trap *n* capcană, cursă

trash *n* gunoi
trash can *n* coş de gunoi
traumatic *adj* traumatic
traumatize *v* a traumatiza
travel *v* a călători
traveler *n* călător
tray *n* tavă, tablă
treacherous *adj* trăsător, înşelător
treachery *n* trădare
tread *iv* a călca, a păşi
treason *n* trădare
treasure *n* comoară
treasurer *n* trezorier
treat *v* a trata
treat *n* trataţie
treatment *n* tratament
treaty *n* tratat
tree *n* copac, arbore
tremble *v* a tremura
tremendous *adj* enorm
tremor *n* tremur
trench *n* tranşee, şanţ
trend *n* tendinţă, curent
trendy *adj* la modă, elegant
trespass *v* a încălca
trial *n* proces; necaz
triangle *n* triunghi
tribe *n* trib
tribulation *n* necaz, supărare
tribunal *n* tribunal
tribute *n* tribut
trick *v* a păcăli
trick *n* şmecherie; truc
trickle *v* a picura
tricky *adj* înşelător, complicat
trigger *v* a declanşa
trigger *n* trăgaci
trim *v* a aranja, a tunde
trimester *n* trimestru
trimmings *n* adaosuri, înflorituri
trip *n* călătorie; excursie
trip *v* a sări peste
triple *adj* triplu
tripod *n* trepied
triumph *n* triumf
triumphant *adj* triumfal
trivial *adj* neserios, frivol
trivialize *v* a banaliza
trolley *n* cărucior, troleu
troop *n* trupă, detaşament
trophy *n* trofeu
tropic *n* tropic
tropical *adj* tropical
trouble *n* necaz, încurcătură
trouble *v* a deranja
troublesome *adj* supărător

trousers *n* pantaloni lungi
trout *n* păstrăv
truce *n* armistiţiu
truck *n* camion
trucker *n* şofer de camion
trumped-up *adj* contrafăcut
trumpet *n* trompetă
trunk *n* trunchi; trup
trust *v* a crede
trust *n* încredere
truth *n* adevăr
truthful *adj* sincer, adevărat
try *v* a încerca
tub *n* cadă
tuberculosis *n* tuberculoză
Tuesday *n* marţi
tuition *n* taxă şcolară
tulip *n* lalea
tumble *v* a se răsturna
tummy *n* burtă
tumor *n* tumoare
tumult *n* tumult
tumultuous *adj* tumultuos
tuna *n* ton
tune *n* melodie
tune *v* a potrivi, a acorda
tunic *n* tunică
tunnel *n* tunel
turbine *n* turbină
turbulence *n* turbulenţă
turf *n* brazdă de iarbă
Turk *adj* turc
Turkey *n* Turcia
turmoil *n* tumult
turn *n* întoarcere
turn *v* a întoarce
turn back *v* a întoarce înapoi
turn down *v* a respinge
turn in *v* a băga înăuntru
turn off *v* a închide
turn on *v* a deschide
turn out *v* a stinge, a produce
turn over *v* a preda, a răsturna
turn up *v* a fi regăsit
turret *n* turnuleţ
turtle *n* broască ţestoasă
tusk *n* fildeş, colţ
tutor *n* profesor, meditator
tweezers *n* pensetă
twelfth *adj* al doisprezecelea
twelve *adj* doisprezece
twentieth *adj* al douăzecilea
twenty *adj* douăzeci
twice *adv* dublu
twilight *n* amurg, crepuscul
twin *n* frate geamăn

twinkle *v* a licări
twist *v* a răsuci, a învârti
twist *n* răsucire; ocol
twisted *adj* răsucit
twister *n* escroc, dificultate
two *adj* doi
tycoon *n* magnat
type *n* tip; persoană; tipar
type *v* a bate la maşină
typical *adj* tipic
tyranny *n* tiranie
tyrant *n* tiran

U

ugliness *n* urâţenie
ugly *adj* urât
ulcer *n* bubă, ulcer
ultimate *adj* final, ultim
ultimatum *n* ultimatum
ultrasound *n* ultrasunet
umbrella *n* umbrelă
umpire *n* arbitru
unable *adj* incapabil
unanimity *n* unanimitate
unarmed *adj* neînarmat
unassuming *adj* modest
unattached *adj* neataşat
unavoidable *adj* inevitabil
unaware *adj* surprins
unbearable *adj* insuportabil
unbeatable *adj* imbatabil
unbelievable *adj* de necrezut
unbiased *adj* nepărtinitor
unbroken *adj* întreg
unbutton *v* a descheia
uncertain *adj* nesigur
uncle *n* unchi
uncomfortable *adj* incomod
uncommon *adj* neobişnuit
unconscious *adj* inconştient
uncover *v* a descoperi
undecided *adj* indecis
undeniable *adj* de netăgăduit
under *pre* sub
undercover *adj* clandestin
underdog *n* supus
undergo *v* a păţi, a trece prin
underground *adj* subteran
underlie *v* a susţine
underline *v* a sublinia
underlying *adj* fundamental
undermine *v* a submina

underneath *pre* sub
underpass *n* pasaj subteran
understand *v* a înţelege
understandable *adj* de înţeles
understanding *n* înţelegere
undertake *v* a întreprinde
underwear *n* lenjerie intimă
underwrite *v* a gira
undeserved *adj* nemeritat
undesirable *adj* indezirabil
undisputed *adj* necontestat
undo *v* a desface
undress *v* a dezbrăca
undue *adj* nepotrivit
unearth *v* a dezgropa
uneasiness *n* tulburare
uneasy *adj* neliniştit
uneducated *adj* needucat
unemployed *adj* şomer
unemployment *n* şomaj
unending *adj* nesfârşit
unequal *adj* inegal
unequivocal *adj* neechivoc
uneven *adj* inegal
uneventful *adj* calm, tihnit
unexpected *adj* neaşteptat
unfailing *adj* constant
unfair *adj* necinstit, nejust
unfairly *adv* pe nedrept
unfairness *n* nedreptate
unfaithful *adj* necredincios
unfamiliar *adj* nefamiliar
unfasten *v* a deschide
unfavorable *adj* nefavorabil
unfit *adj* nepotrivit
unfold *v* a desfăşura
unforeseen *adj* neprevăzut
unforgettable *adj* de neuitat
unfounded *adj* nefondat
unfriendly *adj* neprietenos
unfurnished *adj* nemobilat
ungrateful *adj* nerecunoscător
unhappiness *n* nefericire
unhappy *adj* nefericit
unharmed *adj* nevătămat
unhealthy *adj* nesănătos
unheard-of *adj* nemaipomenit
unhurt *adj* nevătămat
unification *n* unificare
uniform *n* uniformă
uniformity *n* unformitate
unify *v* a unifica
unilateral *adj* unilateral
union *n* uniune
unique *adj* unic
unit *n* unitate

unite *v* a uni
unity *n* unitate
universal *adj* universal
universe *n* univers
university *n* universitate
unjust *adj* nedrept
unjustified *adj* neîndreptăţit
unknown *adj* necunoscut
unlawful *adj* ilegal
unleaded *adj* fără plumb
unleash *v* a lăsa liber
unless *c* dacă nu
unlikely *adj* improbabil
unlimited *adj* nelimitat
unload *v* a descărca
unlock *v* a descuia
unlucky *adj* nenorocos
unmarried *adj* necăsătorit
unmask *v* a demasca
unmistakable *adj* sigur, evident
unnecessary *adj* inutil, de prisos
unnoticed *adj* neobservat
unoccupied *adj* neocupat
unofficially *adv* neoficial
unpack *v* a despacheta
unpleasant *adj* neplăcut
unplug *v* a scoate din priză
unpopular *adj* nepopular
unpredictable *adj* imprevizibil
unprofitable *adj* nerentabil
unprotected *adj* neprotejat
unravel *v* a descurca
unreal *adj* ireal
unrealistic *adj* nerealist
unreasonable *adj* iraţional
unrelated *adj* fără legătură
unreliable *adj* neserios
unrest *n* nelinişte
unsafe *adj* nesigur
unselfish *adj* altruist
unspeakable *adj* indescriptibil
unstable *adj* instabil
unsteady *adj* inconstant
unsuccessful *adj* neizbutit
unsuitable *adj* nepotrivit
unsuspecting *adj* nebănuitor
unthinkable *adj* inimaginabil
untie *v* a dezlega
until *pre* până
untimely *adj* inoportun
untouchable *adj* de neatins
untrue *adj* neadevărat
unusual *adj* neobişnuit
unveil *v* a dezvălui
unwillingly *adv* fără voie
unwind *v* a dezveli

unwise *adj* nechibzuit
unwrap *v* a despacheta
upbringing *n* creştere
upcoming *adj* proxim
update *v* a aduce la zi
upgrade *v* a înălţa
upheaval *n* prefacere
uphill *adv* în sus
uphold *v* a susţine
upholstery *n* tapiţerie
upkeep *n* întreţinere
upon *pre* pe
upper *adj* superior, de sus
upright *adj* drept
uprising *n* răscoală
uproar *n* gălăgie, rumoare
uproot *v* a dezrădăcina
upset *v* a tulbura, a supăra
upside-down *adv* întors pe dos
upstairs *adv* sus pe scăr
uptight *adj* încordat, nervos
up-to-date *adj* la modă
upturn *n* sporire, progres
upwards *adv* în sus
urban *adj* urban
urge *n* îndemn
urge *v* a îndemna, a mâna
urgency *n* urgenţă
urgent *adj* urgent
urinate *v* a urina
urine *n* urină
urn *n* urnă
us *pro* pe noi, nouă
usage *n* utilizare
use *v* a folosi, a utiliza
use *n* folosire, utilizare
used to *adj* obişnuit cu
useful *adj* util
usefulness *n* utilitate
useless *adj* inutil
user *n* utilizator
usher *n* aprod, plasator
usual *adj* obişnuit
usurp *v* a uzurpa
utensil *n* unealtă
uterus *n* uter
utilize *v* a utiliza, a folosi
utmost *adj* extrem, maximum
utter *v* a rosti, a exprima

V

vacancy *n* loc liber
vacant *adj* neocupat, vacant
vacate *v* a elibera
vacation *n* vacanţă
vaccinate *v* a vaccina
vaccine *n* vaccin
vacillate *v* a şovăi, a oscila
vagrant *n* vagabond
vague *adj* vag
vain *adj* orgolios, de prisos
vainly *adv* zadarnic
valiant *adj* viteaz
valid *adj* valabil
validate *v* a valida
validity *n* valabilitate
valley *n* vale
valuable *adj* valoros
value *n* valoare
valve *n* valvă, supapă
vampire *n* vampir
van *n* dubă
vandal *n* vandal
vandalism *n* vandalism
vandalize *v* a vandaliza
vanguard *n* avangardă
vanish *v* a dispărea
vanity *n* vanitate
vanquish *v* a înfânge
vaporize *v* a evapora
variable *adj* variabil
varied *adj* variat; schimbător
variety *n* varietate
various *adj* divers
varnish *v* a vernisa
varnish *n* lac, smalţ
vary *v* a varia
vase *n* vază, vas
vast *adj* vast, mare
veal *n* carne de viţel
veer *v* a vira, a coti
vegetable *v* legumă
vegetarian *v* vegetarian
vegetation *n* vegetaţie
vehicle *n* vehicul
veil *n* văl, voal
vein *n* venă, nervură
velocity *n* viteză
velvet *n* catifea
venerate *v* a venera
vengeance *n* răzbunare
venom *n* venin
vent *n* ieşire, supapă
ventilate *v* a ventila

ventilation *n* ventilaţie
venture *v* a risca
venture *n* aventură, risc
verb *n* verb
verbally *adv* verbal
verbatim *adv* exact
verdict *n* verdict
verge *n* margine, limită
verification *n* verificare
verify *v* a verifica
versatile *adj* multilateral
verse *n* vers
versed *adj* versat
version *n* versiune
versus *pre* contra
vertebra *n* vertebră
very *adv* chiar, foarte
vessel *n* vas
vest *n* vestă
vestige *n* vestigiu
veteran *n* veteran
veterinarian *n* veterinar
veto *v* a interzice
viaduct *n* viaduct
vibrant *adj* vibrant
vibrate *v* a vibra
vibration *n* vibraţie
vice *n* viciu
vicinity *n* vecinătate
vicious *adj* vicios
victim *n* victimă
victimize *v* a persecuta
victor *n* învingător
victorious *adj* victorios
victory *n* victorie
view *n* vedere
view *v* a privi, a vedea
viewpoint *n* privelişte
vigil *n* veghe, priveghi
village *n* sat
villager *n* sătean
villain *n* ticălos
vindicate *v* a dovedi
vindictive *adj* răzbunător
vine *n* viţă de vie
vinegar *n* oţet
vineyard *n* podgorie
violate *v* a viola, a încălca
violence *n* violenţă
violent *adj* violent
violet *n* violet, violetă
violin *n* vioară
violinist *n* violonist
viper *n* viperă
virgin *n* fecioară
virginity *n* virginitate

virile *adj* viril
virility *n* virilitate
virtue *n* virtute
virtually *adv* realmente, efectiv
virtuous *adj* virtuos
virulent *adj* otrăvitor, mortal
virus *n* virus
visibility *n* vizibilitate
visible *adj* vizibil
vision *n* vedere, viziune
visit *n* vizită
visit *v* a vizita
visitor *n* vizitator
visual *adj* vizual
visualize *v* a vizualiza
vital *adj* vital
vitality *n* vitalitate
vitamin *n* vitamină
vivacious *adj* vivace
vivid *adj* vioi, viu
vocabulary *n* vocabular
vocation *n* vocaţie
vogue *n* vogă, modă
voice *n* voce
void *adj* gol; nul
volatile *adj* volatil
volcano *n* vulcan
volleyball *n* volei
voltage *n* voltaj
volume *n* volum; tom; cantitate
volunteer *n* voluntar
vomit *v* a vărsa, a vomita
vomit *n* vărsătură, vomare
vote *v* a vota
vote *n* vot, votare
voting *n* votare
vouch for *v* a garanta
voucher *n* chitanţă, bon
vow *v* a promite, a jura
vowel *n* vocală
voyage *n* croazieră
voyager *n* călător
vulgar *adj* vulgar
vulgarity *n* vulgaritate
vulnerable *adj* vulnerabil
vulture *n* vultur

W

wafer *n* biscuit, gofră
wag *v* a da din coadă
wage *n* salariu
wagon *n* vagon de marfă
wail *v* a boci, a plânge
wail *n* bocet
waist *n* talie, centură
wait *v* a aştepta
waiter *n* chelner
waiting *n* aşteptare
waitress *n* chelneriţă
waive *v* a renunţa la
wake up *iv* a se trezi
walk *v* a se plimba
walk *n* plimbare, mers
walkout *n* marş de grevă
wall *n* zid, perete
wallet *n* portofel
walnut *n* nucă
walrus *n* morsă
waltz *n* vals
wander *v* a cutreiera
wanderer *n* hoinar
wane *v* a scădea
want *v* a dori, a necesita
war *n* război
ward *n* protecţie, pază
warden *n* paznic
wardrobe *n* garderobă
warehouse *n* depozit
warfare *n* strategie
warm *adj* cald, călduros
warm up *v* a se încălzi
warmth *n* căldură
warn *v* a avertiza
warning *n* avertisment
warp *v* a întreţese
warped *adj* inadecvat
warrant *v* a garanta
warrant *n* autorizaţie
warranty *n* garanţie scrisă
warrior *n* războinic
warship *n* vas de luptă
wart *n* neg
wary *adj* precaut
wash *v* a spăla
washable *adj* lavabil
wasp *n* viespe
waste *v* a irosi, a risipi
waste *n* risipă
waste basket *n* coş de hârtii
wasteful *adj* risipitor
watch *n* pază, gardă

watch *v* a păzi
watch out *v* a avea grijă
watchful *adj* atent, precaut
watchmaker *n* ceasornicar
water *n* apă
water *v* a uda, a adăpa
water down *v* a subţia cu apă
waterfall *n* cascadă
waterheater *n* boiler
watermelon *n* pepene verde
waterproof *adj* impermeabil
watershed *n* cumpăna apelor
watertight *adj* etanş
watery *adj* apos
watt *n* watt
wave *n* val; unduire
waver *v* a şovăi
wavy *adj* ondulat
wax *n* ceară
way *n* drum; cale
way in *n* intrare
way out *n* ieşire
we *pro* noi
weak *adj* slab, firav
weaken *v* a slăbi
weakness *n* slăbiciune
wealth *n* avere
wealthy *adj* bogat
weapon *n* armă
wear *n* folosire; purtare
wear *iv* a se purta; a ţine
wear down *v* a uza; a roade
wear out *v* a uza; a istovi
weary *adj* obosit, istovit
weather *n* vreme, climă
weave *iv* a se ţese
web *n* plasă; ţesătură
web site *n* web site
wed *iv* a se căsători
wedding *n* nuntă
wedge *n* despicătură
Wednesday *n* miercuri
weed *n* buruiană
weed *v* a privi
week *n* săptămână
weekday *adj* zi de lucru
weekend *n* weekend
weekly *adv* săptămânal
weep *iv* a plânge
weigh *v* a cântări
weight *n* greutate, pondere
weird *adj* ciudat
welcome *v* a ura bun venit
welcome *n* bun venit
weld *v* a suda
welder *n* sudor

welfare *n* bunăstare
well *n* bine, situaţie bună
well-known *adj* bine-cunoscut
well-to-do *adj* înstărit, avut
west *n* vest
westbound *adv* mergând către vest
western *adj* vestic
westerner *adj* locuitor din vest
wet *adj* ud, umed
whale *n* balenă
wharf *n* debarcader, doc
what *adj* ce, care
whatever *adj* indiferent care
wheat *n* grâu
wheel *n* roată
wheelbarrow *n* roabă
wheelchair *n* scaun cu rotile
wheeze *v* a rosti cu greu
when *adv* când
whenever *adv* oricând
where *adv* unde, încotro
whereas *c* pe când
whereupon *c* la care
wherever *c* oriunde
whether *c* indiferent dacă
which *adj* care
while *c* în timp ce
whim *n* capriciu, poftă
whine *v* scâncet
whip *v* a biciui; a smulge
whip *n* bici, cravaşă
whirl *v* a lua pe sus
whirlpool *n* bulboană
whiskers *n* favoriţi, mustăţi
whisper *v* a şopti
whisper *n* şoaptă
whistle *v* a fluiera
whistle *n* fluier, fluierat
white *adj* alb
whiten *v* a albi
whittle *v* a ciopârţi
who *pro* cine
whoever *pro* oricine
whole *adj* întreg, complet
wholehearted *adj* din toată inima
wholesale *n* toptan
wholesome *adj* sănătos, folositor
whom *pro* pe cine
why *adv* de ce
wicked *adj* blestemat, rău
wickedness *n* răutate, ticăloşie
wide *adj* larg, întins
widely *adv* în mare măsură
widen *v* a lărgi
widespread *adj* răspândit
widow *n* văduvă

widower *n* văduv
width *n* întindere
wield *v* a mânui
wife *n* soţie
wig *n* perucă
wiggle *v* a răsuci
wild *adj* sălbatic
wild boar *n* porc mistreţ
wilderness *n* sălbăticie
wildlife *n* natură sălbatică
will *n* voinţă; testament
willfully *adv* intenţionat
willing *adj* doritor
willingly *adv* cu plăcere
willingness *n* bunăvoinţă
willow *n* salcie
wily *adj* viclean
wimp *adj* incapabil
win *iv* a câştiga
win back *v* a recâştiga
wind *n* vânt
wind *iv* a adulmeca
wind up *v* a încheia
winding *adj* şerpuitor
windmill *n* moară de vânt
window *n* fereastră
windpipe *n* beregată
windshield *n* parbriz
windy *adj* cu vânt, vântos
wine *n* vin
winery *n* cramă
wing *n* aripă
wink *n* clipit
wink *v* a clipi
winner *n* câştigător
winter *n* iarnă
wipe *v* a şterge
wipe out *v* a termina, a curăţa
wire *n* sârmă; fir; telegramă
wireless *adj* fără fir
wisdom *n* înţelepciune
wise *adj* înţelept
wish *v* a dori, a nădăjdui
wish *n* dorinţă
wit *n* inteligenţă
witch *n* vrăjitoare
witchcraft *n* vrăjitorie
with *pre* cu
withdraw *v* a retrage
withdrawal *n* retragere
withdrawn *adj* retras
wither *v* a se veşteji
withhold *iv* a reţine
within *pre* înăuntru
without *pre* fără
withstand *v* a se împotrivi la

witness *n* martor
witty *adj* spiritual, amuzant
wives *n* soţii
wizard *n* vrăjitor
wobble *v* a legăna, a clătina
woes *n* necazuri
wolf *n* lup
woman *n* femeie
womb *n* pântece
women *n* femei
wonder *v* a se întreba ceva
wonder *n* minune, mirare
wonderful *adj* minunat
wood *n* pădure
wooden *adj* de lemn
wool *n* lână
woolen *adj* de lână
word *n* cuvânt, vorbă
wording *n* formulare
work *n* muncă
work *v* a munci; a prelucra
workable *adj* practicabil
workbook *n* carte tehnică
worker *n* muncitor
workshop *n* atelier
world *n* lume, pământ
worldly *adj* lumesc
worldwide *adj* mondial
worm *n* vierme
worn-out *adj* istovit, uzat
worrisome *adj* tulburat
worry *v* a-şi face griji
worry *n* nelinişte, grijă
worse *adj* rău, situaţie proastă
worsen *v* a înrăutăţi
worship *n* veneraţie, cult
worst *adj* cel mai rău
worth *adj* în valoare de
worthless *adj* fără valoare
worthwhile *adj* care merită
worthy *adj* merituos
would-be *adj* aşa-zis, pretins
wound *n* rană
wound *v* a răni
wrap *v* a înfăşura
wrap up *v* a învălui, a înfofoli
wrapping *n* înveliş, ambalaj
wrath *n* mânie
wreath *n* ghirlandă
wreck *v* a distruge, a nărui
wreckage *n* rămăşiţe
wrench *n* smulgere, smucitură
wrestle *v* a se lupta
wrestler *n* luptător
wrestling *n* lupte
wretched *adj* nenorocit, mizerabil

wring *iv* a răsuci, a stoarce
wrinkle *v* a se zbârci
wrinkle *n* zbârcitură, rid
wrist *n* încheietura mâinii
write *iv* a scrie
write down *v* a nota
writer *n* scriitor
writhe *v* a se zvârcoli
writing *n* scris, scriere
written *adj* scris
wrong *adj* greşit, incorect

X-mas *n* Crăciun
X-ray *n* rază X, radiografie

yacht *n* iaht
yam *n* rădăcină de batat
yard *n* iard
yarn *n* fir tors
yawn *n* căscat
yawn *v* a căsca
year *n* an
yearly *adv* anual
yearn *v* a tânji
yeast *n* drojdie
yell *v* a ţipa
yellow *adj* galben
yes *adv* da
yesterday *adv* ieri
yet *c* totuşi
yield *v* a produce
yield *n* producţie
yoke *n* jug
yolk *n* gălbenuş
you *pro* tu
young *adj* tânăr
youngster *n* băiat, flăcău
your *adj* tău, ta, tăi, tale
yours *pro* al tău
yourself *pro* tu însuţi, te

youth *n* tinereţe
youthful *adj* tânăr, tineresc

Z

zap *v* a ucide
zeal *n* zel, entuziasm
zealous *adj* zelos, entuziast
zebra *n* zebră
zero *n* zero
zest *n* zel, interes
zinc *n* zinc
zip code *n* cod poştal
zipper *n* fermoar
zone *n* zonă, regiune
zoo *n* grădină zoologică
zoology *n* zoologie

English-Romanian

Bilingual Dictionaries, Inc.

Abbreviations

English - Romanian

a - article - articol
adj - adjective - adjectiv
adv - adverb - adverb
c - conjunction - conjuncţie
e - exclamation - interjecţie
f - feminine (noun) - substantiv feminin
m - masculine (noun) - substantiv masculin
n - neuter (noun) - substantiv neutru
pre - preposition - prepoziţie
pro - pronoun - pronume
v - verb - verb

A

abajur *n* lampshade
abandona *v* abandon
abate *m* abbot
abate *v* avert, digress
abator *n* shambles
abdica *v* abdicate
abdicare *f* abdication
abdomen *n* abdomen
aberaţie *f* aberration
abia *adv* barely, hardly
abil *adj* tactful, deft
abilitate *f* ability
abis *n* abyss
abisal *adj* abysmal
aboli *v* abolish
abordabil *adj* approachable
abrevia *v* abbreviate
abreviere *f* abbreviation
abroga *v* abrogate
abrupt *adj* steep
absent *adj* absent
absenţă *f* absence
absolut *adj* absolute
absolvi *v* graduate
absolvire *f* graduation
absorbant *adj* absorbent
absorbi *v* absorb, soak in
absorbit *adj* engrossed
abstinenţă *f* abstinence
abstract *adj* abstract
absurd *adj* absurd
abţine *v* abstain
abunda *v* abound
abundent *adj* plentiful
abundenţă *f* abundance
abur *m* fumes, steam
abuz *n* abuse
abuza *v* abuse
abuziv *adj* abusive
ac *n* needle
academic *adj* academic
academie *f* academy
accelera *v* accelerate
accelerator *n* accelerator
accent *n* accent
accepta *v* accept, admit
acceptabil *adj* acceptable
acceptare *f* acceptance
acces *n* access
accesibil *adj* accessible
accident *n* accident
accidental *adj* accidental
acei *adj* those

acel *adj* that
acelaşi *adj* same
acest *adj* this
aceşti *adj* these
achita *v* acquit
achitare *f* acquittal
achiziţie *f* acquisition
acid *m* acid
aciditate *f* acidity
aclama *v* acclaim
aclimatiza *v* acclimatize
acolo *adv* there
acomoda *v* accommodate
acompania *v* accompany
acoperi *v* cover
acoperire *f* coverup
acoperiş *n* roof
acord *n* agreement, accord, consent
acorda *v* award, grant
acordeon *n* accordion
acrobat *m* acrobat
acru *adj* sour
acru *m* acre
acţiona *v* act, do
acţionar *m* shareholder
acţiune *f* deed, action
activ *adj* active
activa *v* activate
activare *f* activation
activist *adj* militant
activitate *f* activity
actor *m* actor
actriţă *f* actress
actual *adj* actual
acum *adv* now
acumula *v* accumulate
acumulare *f* buildup
acurateţe *f* accuracy
acustic *adj* acoustic
acut *adj* acute
acuza *v* accuse
acuzat *m* defendant
acuzaţie *f* accusation
acvariu *n* aquarium
acvatic *adj* aquatic
adânc *adj* deep
adânci *v* deepen
adâncime *f* depth
adaosuri *n* trimmings
adăpost *n* shelter
adăposti *v* shelter
adapta *v* adapt
adaptabil *adj* adaptable
adaptare *f* adaptation
adaptor *n* adapter
adăuga *v* add

adăugare *f* addition
adecvat *adj* adequate
adera *v* adhere
adesea *adv* often
adevăr *n* truth
adeziv *adj* adhesive
adiacent *adj* adjacent
adică *adv* namely
adjectiv *n* adjective
administra *v* administer
admira *v* admire
admirabil *adj* admirable
admiraţie *f* admiration
admirativ *adj* complimentary
admirator *m* admirer
admite *v* admit
admitere *f* admission
admonesta *v* admonish
admonestare *f* admonition
adnota *v* annotate
adnotare *f* annotation
adolescent *m* adolescent
adolescenţă *f* adolescence
adopta *v* adopt
adopţie *f* adoption
adoptiv *adj* adoptive
adora *v* adore
adorabil *adj* adorable
adoraţie *f* adoration
adormit *adj* asleep
adresa *v* address
adresă *f* address
adresant *m* addressee
aduce *v* bring
aduce înapoi *v* bring back
aduce la zi *v* update
adulaţie *f* adulation
adulmeca *v* sniff; wind
adult *m* adult, grown-up
adulter *n* adultery
aduna *v* amass, gather, congregate
adunare *f* assembly
adverb *n* adverb
adversar *m* adversary
aer *n* air
aerisi *v* air
aerodrom *n* airfield
aeronavă *f* aircraft
aeroport *n* airport
afabil *adj* affable
afacere *f* deal, affair
afacerist *m* businessman
afară *adv* out, outside
afecta *v* affect
afecţiune *f* affection
afectuos *adj* affectionate

aferat *adv* busily
afilia *v* affiliate
afiliere *f* affiliation
afinitate *f* affinity
afirma *v* affirm, assert
afirmaţie *f* assertion
afirmativ *adj* affirmative
afiş *n* poster, placard
afla *v* find out
afluent *adj* affluent
afluenţă *f* affluence
aflux *n* influx
afrodisiac *adj* aphrodisiac
afront *n* affront
afuma *v* fumigate
afumat *adj* smoked
agăţa *v* cling
agendă *f* agenda
agent *m* agent, henchman
agenţie *f* agency
agil *adj* agile
agita *v* stir
agitat *adj* bustling
agitaţie *f* fuss
agitator *m* agitator
aglomera *v* agglomerate
aglomerat *adj* crowded
agnostic *m* agnostic
agonie *f* agony
agrafă *f* paperclip
agrava *v* aggravate
agravare *f* aggravation
agresiune *f* aggression
agresiv *adj* aggressive
agresor *m* aggressor
agricol *adj* agricultural
agricultură *f* agriculture, farming
a-i da fiori *v* creep
a-i păsa de *v* care about
aici *adv* here
aisberg *n* iceberg
aiura *v* rave
ajun *n* eve
ajunge *v* catch up, get
ajunge la *v* get down to
ajusta *v* adjust
ajustabil *adj* adjustable
ajutor *n* helper, aide
al *pre* of
al cincelea *adj* fifth
al douăzecilea *adj* twentieth
al lui *pro* his
al meu *pro* mine
al nostru *pro* ours
al nouălea *adj* ninth
al o sutălea *adj* hundredth

al optulea *adj* eighth
al patrulea *adj* fourth
al şaptelea *adj* seventh
al şaselea *adj* sixth
al tău *pro* yours
al treilea *adj* third
alăpta *v* nurse
alarma *v* alert
alarmă *f* alarm
alarmant *adj* alarming
alături *adv* abreast
alb *adj* white
albastru *adj* blue
albi *v* whiten
albină *f* bee
albuş *n* egg white
alcătui *v* compile
alcoolic *adj* alcoholic
alcoolism *n* alcoholism
alee *f* alley
alegaţie *f* allegation
alege *v* elect
alegere *f* choice, election
alegorie *f* allegory
alerga *v* run
alergător *m* runner
alergic *adj* allergic
alergie *f* allergy
alertă *f* alert
alfabet *n* alphabet
algebră *f* algebra
alia *v* ally
aliaj *n* alloy
alianţă *f* alliance
aliat *adj* allied
aliat *m* ally
alifie *f* ointment
aligator *m* alligator
alimenta *v* fuel
alimentare *f* nourishment
alimente *n* foodstuff
alina *v* alleviate
alinia *v* align, line up
aliniere *f* alignment
almanah *n* almanac
alo *e* hello
aloca *v* allocate
alocaţie *f* grant
alt *adj* other
altar *n* altar
altercaţie *f* altercation
alterna *v* alternate
alternativ *adj* alternate
alternativă *f* alternative
Alteţa *f* Highness
altfel *adv* otherwise

altitudine *f* altitude
altoi *n* graft
altoi *v* graft
altruist *adj* unselfish
aluat *n* dough
aluminiu *n* aluminum
alună *f* hazelnut
alună arahidă *f* peanut
aluneca *v* glide, slide
alunecare *f* slip
alunecos *adj* slippery
alunga *v* dispel
alungit *adj* oblong
aluniţă *f* mole
aluzie *f* allusion, innuendo
amabil *adj* amiable
amâna *v* adjourn, postpone
amânare *f* postponement
amândoi *adj* both
amaneta *v* pledge
amar *adj* bitter
amărăciune *f* bitterness
amărî *v* embitter
amator *adj* amateur
ambasadă *f* embassy
ambasador *m* ambassador
ambiguu *adj* ambiguous
ambiţie *f* ambition
ambiţios *adj* ambitious
ambivalent *adj* ambivalent
ambulanţă *f* ambulance
amenda *v* amend
amendă *f* fine
amendament *n* amendment
ameninţa *v* threaten
ameninţare *f* threat, menace
american *adj* American
amestec *n* blend, mixture
amesteca *v* blend, mix, mingle
amestecat *adj* mixed-up
amestecător *n* blender
ameţeală *f* dizziness
ameţi *v* daze
ameţit *adj* dizzy
amfibiu *adj* amphibious
amfiteatru *n* amphitheater
amiază *f* noon
amidon *n* starch
amigdală *f* tonsil
amilaceu *adj* starchy
aminti *v* remind
amintire *f* remembrance
amiral *m* admiral
amnezie *f* amnesia
amnistie *f* amnesty
amoniac *n* ammonia

amoral *adj* amoral
amorf *adj* amorphous
amorţeală *f* numbness
amorţi *v* deaden
amorţit *adj* numb
amortiza *v* amortize
amplifica *v* amplify
amplificator *n* amplifier
amplu *adj* ample
amprentă *f* fingerprint
amputa *v* amputate
amputare *f* amputation
amurg *n* twilight
amuza *v* amuse
amuzament *n* amusement
amuzant *adj* amusing
amvon *n* pulpit
an *m* year
an bisect *m* leap year
analiza *v* analyze
analiză *f* analysis
analogie *f* analogy
ananas *m* pineapple
anarhie *f* anarchy
anarhist *m* anarchist
anatomie *f* anatomy
anchetă *f* inquest
ancoră *f* anchor
anecdotă *f* anecdote
anemic *adj* anemic
anemie *f* anemia
anestezie *f* anesthesia
anexă *f* annex
anexiune *f* annexation
angaja *v* employ
angajament *n* engagement
angajare *f* employment
angajator *m* employer
angelic *adj* angelic
anghină *f* angina
anghinare *f* artichoke
Anglia *f* England
anglican *adj* Anglican
angrenaj *n* gear
anima *v* animate
animal *n* animal
animal de casă *n* pet
animaţie *f* animation
aniversare *f* anniversary
anonim *adj* anonymous
anonimat *n* anonymity
anormal *adj* abnormal
anormalitate *f* abnormality
anotimp *n* season
anşoa *n* anchovy
antecedent *n* antecedent

antenă *f* antenna
anterior *adj* former, prior
antibiotic *n* antibiotic
antic *adj* ancient
antichitate *f* antiquity
anticipa *v* anticipate
anticipare *f* anticipation
antidot *n* antidote
antilopă *f* antelope
antipatie *f* dislike
antipatiza *v* dislike
antrena *v* coach
antrenare *f* coaching
antrenor *m* coach, trainer
antreprenor *m* entrepreneur
antreu *n* entree
anual *adj* annual
anual *adv* yearly
anula *v* annul, cancel
anulare *f* cancellation, repeal
anunţ *n* announcement
anunţa *v* announce, notify
anxietate *f* anxiety
apă *f* water
apă de colonie *f* cologne
apăra *v* champion, defend, hit back
apărare *f* defense
apărătoare *f* fender
apărător *m* defender
apărea *v* show up, appear
aparent *adj* apparent
apariţie *f* apparition, appearance
apartament *n* apartment
aparţine *v* belong, pertain
apatie *f* apathy
apeduct *n* aqueduct
apel *n* appeal
apendice *n* appendix
apendicită *f* appendicitis
aperitiv *n* appetizer
apetit *n* appetite
aplauda *v* applaud
aplauze *f* applause
apleca *v* lean, bend down
aplica *v* apply, implement
aplicabil *adj* applicable
aplicant *m* applicant
aplicaţie *f* application
apocalips *n* apocalypse
apos *adj* watery
apostol *m* apostle
apostolic *adj* apostolic
apostrof *n* apostrophe
aprecia *v* appreciate
apreciere *f* appreciation
aprilie *m* April

aprinde *v* switch on, ignite, flare-up
aprindere *f* lighting
aprins *adj* hectic
aprins *adv* ablaze, alight
aproape *adv* almost, nearly
aproape de *pre* about, near
aproba *v* approve, sanction
aprobare *f* approval
aprod *m* usher
apropia de *v* approach
apropiat *adj* close
apropiere *f* proximity
aproviziona *v* store
aproximativ *adj* approximate
aproximativ *adv* about
aptitudine *f* aptitude
apuca *v* grab, snatch
apucare *f* clutch, grip
apune *v* set
ara *v* plow
arab *adj* Arabic
arabil *adj* arable
aramă *f* copper
aranja *v* arrange, spruce up
aranjament *n* arrangement
aranjare *f* adjustment
arăta *v* hold up, show
arbitra *v* arbitrate
arbitrar *adj* arbitrary
arbitrare *f* arbitration
arbitru *m* arbiter, referee
arbust *m* shrub
arc *n* arc
arcă *f* ark
arcadă *f* arch
arctic *adj* arctic
arde *v* burn, scorch
ardei gras *m* bell pepper
arenă *f* arena
arendaş *m* lessee
aresta *v* arrest
arestare *f* arrest
argilă *f* clay
argint *n* silver
argintar *m* silversmith
argintărie *f* silverware
argintat *adj* silverplated
argument *n* argument
arhaic *adj* archaic
arheologie *f* archaeology
arhiepiscop *m* archbishop
arhitect *m* architect
arhitectură *f* architecture
arhivă *f* archive
arid *adj* arid
aripă *f* wing

aripioară *f* fin
aristocrat *m* aristocrat
aristocraţie *f* aristocracy
aritmetică *f* arithmetic
armă *f* weapon
armă de foc *f* firearm
armament *n* armaments
armată *f* army
armistiţiu *n* truce, cease-fire
armonie *f* harmony
armoniza *v* harmonize
armură *f* armor
arogant *adj* arrogant
aroganţă *f* arrogance
aromatic *adj* aromatic
arsenal *n* arsenal
arsenic *n* arsenic
arsură *f* burn
arsură la stomac *f* heartburn
artă *f* art
arteră *f* artery
articol *n* article, item
articula *v* articulate
articulare *f* articulation
articulaţie *f* joint
artificial *adj* artificial
artilerie *f* artillery
artist *m* artist
artistic *adj* artistic
artrită *f* arthritis
arunca *v* hurl, throw
arunca o privire *v* glimpse
arzător *adj* ardent, fiery
as *m* ace
asalt *n* assault
asalta *v* assault
asambla *v* assemble
aşa-numit *adj* so-called
asasin *m* assassin
asasina *v* assassinate
asasinat *n* assassination
aşa-zis *adj* would-be
ascendenţă *f* ascendancy
ascetic *adj* ascetic
aşchie *f* chip, splinter
ascultător *m* listener
ascunde *v* conceal, hide
ascuns *adj* hidden, covert
ascunzătoare *f* hideaway
ascuţi *v* sharpen
ascuţit *adj* sharp, acute
ascuţitor *n* sharpener
aseară *adv* last night
asedia *v* siege, besiege
asediu *n* siege
asemănare *f* resemblance

asemenea *adj* such
aşezare *f* settlement
aşezat *adj* seated
asfalt *n* asphalt
asfinţit *n* sunset
asfixia *v* asphyxiate
asfixiere *f* asphyxiation
a-şi aminti *v* recollect
a-şi asuma *v* assume
a-şi bate joc *v* scoff
a-şi face de cap *v* riot
a-şi face griji *v* worry
asigura *v* assure, ensure, insure
asigurare *f* assurance
asimila *v* assimilate
asimilare *f* assimilation
asista *v* assist
asistenţă *f* assistance
asocia *v* associate
asociaţie *f* association
asortat *adj* assorted
aspect *n* aspect, looks
aspira *v* aspire
aspiraţie *f* aspiration
aspirină *f* aspirin
asprime *f* harshness
aspru *adj* harsh, rough
aştepta *v* await, expect
aşteptare *f* suspense, waiting
asterisc *f* asterisk
aşternut *n* bedding
aşternuturi *n* sheets
asteroid *m* asteroid
astfel *adv* hereby, thus
astmă *f* asthma
astmatic *adj* asthmatic
astrolog *m* astrologer
astrologie *f* astrology
astronaut *m* astronaut
astronom *m* astronomer
astronomic *adj* astronomic
astronomie *f* astronomy
astupa *v* plug
asuda *v* exude
asumare *f* assumption
asupri *v* oppress
asuprire *f* oppression
asurzi *v* deafen
asurzitor *adj* deafening
aţă *f* thread
atac *f* attack, hit
ataca *v* assail, attack
atacator *m* attacker
atârna *v* hang
ataşa *v* attach, affix
ataşament *n* attachment

ataşat *adj* attached
aţâţător *adj* rousing
ateism *n* atheism
atelier *n* workshop
atent *adj* attentive
atenţie *f* attention
atenua *v* attenuate
atenuant *adj* attenuating
atenuante *adj* extenuating
ateu *m* atheist
atinge *v* reach, attain
atingere *f* reach, touch
aţipeală *f* doze
aţipi *v* snooze, doze
atitudine *f* attitude
atlet *m* athlete
atletic *adj* athletic
atmosferă *f* atmosphere
atmosferic *adj* atmospheric
atom *m* atom
atomic *adj* atomic
atotputernic *adj* almighty
atracţie *f* attraction
atractiv *adj* attractive
atrăgător *adj* lovely
atrage *v* attract, draw
atribui *v* attribute
atroce *adj* atrocious
atrocitate *f* atrocity
atrofia *v* atrophy
atunci *adv* then
audibil *adj* audible
audienţă *f* audience
auditoriu *n* auditorium
august *m* August
aur *n* gold
auriu *adj* golden
auster *adj* austere
autentic *adj* authentic
autenticitate *f* authenticity
autentifica *v* authenticate
autobuz *n* bus
autograf *n* autograph
automat *adj* automatic
automobil *n* car, auto
autonom *adj* autonomous
autonomie *f* autonomy
autopsie *f* autopsy
autor *m* author
autoritar *adj* bossy
autoritarist *adj* authoritarian
autoritate *f* authority
autoriza *v* authorize
autorizaţie *f* authorization
autostop *n* hitchhike
autostradă *f* freeway

auxiliar *adj* auxiliary
auz *n* hearing
auzi *v* hear
avalanşă *f* avalanche
avangardă *f* vanguard
avanpremieră *f* preview
avans *n* advance
avansa *v* advance
avantaj *n* advantage
avantajos *adj* expedient
avar *adj* avaricious
avaria *v* harm
avariţie *f* avarice
avea *v* have
avea grijă *v* beware
avea o reverie *v* daydream
avea voie *v* may
aventură *f* adventure
avere *f* wealth
aversiune *f* aversion
avertisment *n* warning
avertiza *v* forewarn
aviaţie *f* aviation
aviator *m* aviator
avion *n* plane
avocat *m* attorney
avort *n* abortion
avorta *v* abort
ax *n* axle
axă *f* axis
axilă *f* armpit
axiomă *f* axiom
azi *adv* today
azil *n* asylum
azot *n* nitrogen

B

bac *n* ferry
bacşiş *n* tip
bacterie *f* bacteria
băga de seamă *v* heed
băga înăuntru *v* turn in
băgăcios *adj* nosy
bagaj *n* baggage
baghetă *f* baguette
băiat *m* youngster, boy
baie *f* bathroom
baioneta *f* bayonet
bălăbăni *v* topple
balama *f* hinge
balansa *v* balance
balanţă *f* balance

bâlbâi *v* stutter
balcon *n* balcony
bălegar *n* manure, dung
balenă *f* whale
balon *n* balloon
balot *n* bale
balsam *n* balm
balsamic *adj* balmy
baltag *n* hatchet
balustradă *f* handrail
bambus *m* bamboo
banalitate *f* banality
banaliza *v* trivialize
banană *f* banana
bancă *f* bank, bench
banchet *n* banquet
bancrută *f* bankruptcy
bandă *f* gang; tape, band
bandaj *n* bandage
bandaja *v* bandage
bandit *m* bandit, robber
bani *m* money
bani gheaţă *m* cash
baniţă *f* peck
bântui *v* haunt
bănuială *f* inkling
bănuitor *adj* distrustful
bara *v* bar
bară *f* bar
bară de metal *f* crowbar
baraj *n* barrage
barbă *f* beard
barbar *m* barbarian
barbarie *f* barbarism
bărbătesc *adj* manly
bărbaţi *m* men
bărbăţie *f* manliness
bărbie *f* chin
bărbier *m* barber
bărbieri *v* shave
bărbos *adj* bearded
barcă *f* boat
bârfă *f* gossip
bârfi *v* gossip, malign
baricadă *f* barricade
barieră *f* barrier
baril *m* barrel
barman *m* bartender
barometru *n* barometer
barză *f* stork
baschet *n* basketball
baseball *n* baseball
băşică *f* bladder
bastard *m* bastard
bastion *n* bulwark
baston *n* cane, baton

băţ *n* stick, bat
bătaia inimii *f* heartbeat
bătaie *f* beating
bătălie *f* battle
batalion *n* battalion
bate *v* spank, lash, beat
bate cu pietre *v* stone
bate în ţăruşi *v* pile
bate la maşină *v* type
baterie *f* battery
batistă *f* handkerchief
batjocori *v* mock
batjocură *f* mockery
bătrâior *adj* elderly
bătrâneţe *f* old age
bătut *adj* beaten
băutor *m* drinker
băutură *f* beverage
baza *v* base
bază *f* base, basis
bază de date *f* database
baza pe *v* reckon on
bâzâi *v* buzz
bâzâit *n* buzz
bazar *n* bazaar
bazin *n* basin
bea *v* drink
beat *adj* drunk
belciug *n* staple
Belgia *f* Belgium
belgian *adj* Belgian
beligerant *adj* belligerent
beneficiar *m* beneficiary
beneficiu *n* benefit
benign *adj* benign
berbec *m* ram
bere *f* beer
beregată *f* windpipe
beretă *f* beret
bestial *adj* bestial
bestialitate *f* bestiality
bestie *f* beast
beţie *f* drunkenness
beton *n* concrete
biblic *adj* biblical
biblie *f* bible
bibliografie *f* bibliography
bibliotecă *f* library
bibliotecar *m* librarian
bici *n* scourge, whip
bicicletă *f* bicycle
biciui *v* flog, whip
bigamie *f* bigamy
bigot *adj* bigot
bigotism *n* bigotry
bijuterie *f* jewel

bijutier *m* jeweler
bilanţ *n* account
biliard *n* billiards
bilingv *adj* bilingual
bilunar *adj* bimonthly
bine *adv* alright
bine *n* well
bine-cunoscut *adj* well-known
binecuvânta *v* bless
binecuvântare *f* blessing
binecuvântat *adj* blessed
binefăcător *m* benefactor
binevoitor *adj* benevolent
binoclu *n* binoculars
biografie *f* biography
bioligie *f* biology
biologic *adj* biological
bir *n* toll
birocrat *m* bureaucrat
birocraţie *f* bureaucracy
birou *n* office, bureau
biscuit *m* biscuit
biserică *f* church
bivol *m* buffalo
bizar *adj* bizarre
bizon *m* bison
bizui pe *v* recline, rely on
blană *f* fur
blând *adv* gingerly
blând *adj* kind, bland
blasfemie *f* blasphemy
blestema *v* damn, curse
blestemat *adj* wicked
bleumarin *adj* navy blue
bloc *n* block
bloca *v* blockade, clog
blocadă *f* blockade
blocaj *n* blockage
blond *adj* blond
blufa *v* bluff
blugi *m* jeans
bluză *f* blouse
boală *f* ailment, illness, disease
bob *n* grain
boboc *m* bud
bocet *n* wail
boci *v* mourn, wail
bogat *adj* wealthy
bogăţie *f* affluence
boicota *v* boycott
boiler *n* waterheater
bol *n* bowl
bolnav *adj* ailing, sick
bolovan *m* boulder
bombă *f* bomb
bombarda *v* bomb

bombardament *n* bombing
bonă *f* babysitter
bonus *n* bonus
borcan *n* jar
bordel *n* brothel
bosumflat *adj* grouchy
botanică *f* botany
botez *n* baptism, christening
boteza *v* baptize
botniţă *f* muzzle
bou *m* ox
bovine *f* oxen
box *n* boxing
boxer *m* boxer
brânză *f* cheese
braţ *n* arm
brăţară *f* bracelet
brazdă *f* furrow
brazdă de iarbă *f* turf
bretea *f* strap
bretele *f* suspenders
brichetă *f* lighter
brici *n* razor
brigadă *f* brigade
Britania *f* Britain
briză *f* breeze
broască *f* frog
broască râioasă *f* toad
broască ţestoasă *f* turtle
broda *v* embroider
broderie *f* embroidery
bronşită *f* bronchitis
bronz *n* bronze
bronzare *f* sunburn
bronzat *adj* tanned
broşă *f* pin
broşură *f* brochure
brunet *adj* brunette
brusc *adj* sudden, brusque
brusc *adv* abruptly
brut *adj* brute
brutal *adj* brutal
brutalitate *f* brutality
brutaliza *v* brutalize
brutar *m* baker
brutărie *f* bakery
bubui *v* boom
bucălat *adj* chubby
bucată *f* chunk, piece
bucătar *m* cook
bucătar şef *m* chef
bucătărie *f* kitchen
bucăţică *f* scrap, morsel
buclă *f* curl
bucura *v* rejoice
bucurie *f* joy

bucuros *adj* glad
budincă *f* pudding
bufet *n* cafeteria
bufniţă *f* owl
bufon *m* goof
buget *n* budget
bujie *f* spark plug
bulă *f* bubble
bulb *m* bulb
bulboană *f* whirlpool
buletin *n* bulletin
buletin de ştiri *n* newscast
buletin de vot *n* ballot
bulevard *n* boulevard
bumbac *n* cotton
bun *adj* good
bun *n* asset
bun venit *n* welcome
bunăstare *f* welfare
bunătate *f* goodness
bunăvoinţă *f* willingness
buncăr *n* bunker
bunic *m* grandfather
bunică *f* grandmother
bunici *m* grandparents
bunicuţă *f* granny
bunuri *n* goods
burete *m* sponge
burghez *adj* bourgeois
buric *n* belly button
burniţa *v* drizzle
burniţă *f* drizzle
bursă *f* scholarship
burtă *f* tummy, belly
buruiană *f* weed
busolă *f* compass
bust *n* bust
butoiaş *n* keg
butonieră *f* buttonhole
butuc *m* log
buză *f* lip
buzunar *n* pocket

C

ca *pre* like
cabană *f* chalet
cablu *n* cable
cacao *f* cocoa
cadă *f* bathtub
cadavru *n* corpse
cădea *v* fall, tumble
cădere *f* downfall

C

căderea nopţii *f* nightfall
cadran *n* dial
cadru *n* framework
cafea *f* coffee
caier *n* fleece
caiet *n* notebook
câine *m* dog
caisă *f* apricot
cal *m* horse
cal de bătaie *m* laughing stock
cal înşeuat *m* mount
calamitate *f* calamity
călări *v* ride
călător *m* traveler
călători *v* travel
călătorie *f* journey
călăuză *f* guide
călăuzi *v* guide
călăuzire *f* guidance
călca *v* tread
călca rufe *v* iron
călcâi *n* heel
calcar *n* limestone
calcul *n* calculation
calcula *v* calculate
calcula greşit *v* miscalculate
calculator *n* calculator
cald *adj* warm
căldură *f* heat, warmth
călduţ *adj* lukewarm
cale *f* path
cale ferată *f* railroad
calendar *n* calendar
calibra *v* calibrate
calibru *n* caliber
califica *v* qualify
calitate *f* quality
calm *n* composure, calm
calm *adj* quiet, calm
calma *v* chill out
calmar *m* squid
calomnie *f* calumny
calorie *f* calorie, monk
călugăr *m* friar
călugăriţă *f* nun
căluş *n* gag
calvar *n* martyrdom
cămară *f* pantry
camarad *m* buddy
cămaşă *f* shirt
cămătar *m* pawnbroker
cameră *f* chamber, room
cameră de zi *f* living room
cămilă *f* camel
camion *n* truck
câmp *n* field

C

câmp de mine *n* minefield
campa *v* camp
campanie *f* campaign
câmpie *f* plain
campion *m* champ, champion
camufla *v* camouflage
camuflaj *n* camouflage
cană *f* mug
canal *n* canal, channel
canaliza *v* drain
canalizare *f* drainage
canapea *f* sofa, couch
canar *m* canary
cancelar *m* chancellor
cancer *n* cancer
canceros *adj* cancerous
când *adv* when
candelabru *n* chandelier
candidat *m* candidate
candidatură *f* candidacy
candoare *f* candor
cândva *adv* once
cangrenă *f* gangrene
cangur *m* kangaroo
canibal *m* cannibal
canion *n* canyon
canistră *f* canister
canoe *f* canoe
canoniza *v* canonize
cânta *v* sing
cântar *n* scale
cântăreţ *m* singer
cântări *v* weigh
cântec *n* chant, song
cantină *f* canteen
cantitate *f* amount
cantonament *n* quarters
cap *n* cape
capabil *adj* able, capable
capac *n* lid
capacitate *f* capacity
căpăstru *n* bridle
capăt *n* dead end
căpăta *v* acquire
capcană *f* pitfall, trap, snare
capelă *f* chapel
capelă funerară *f* mortuary
capelan *m* chaplain
căpetenie *f* ringleader
capital *n* capital
capitalism *n* capitalism
capitaliza *v* capitalize
căpitan *m* captain
capitol *n* chapter
capitula *v* capitulate
capitulare *f* surrender

capodoperă *f* masterpiece
caporal *m* corporal
capră *f* goat
capricios *adj* moody
capriciu *n* whim
capsa *v* staple
capsator *n* stapler
capsulă *f* capsule
căpşună *f* strawberry
captiva *v* captivate
captivant *adj* enthralling
captivitate *f* captivity
captura *v* capture
captură *f* capture
căptuşeală *f* lining
căptuşi *v* pad
căra *v* carry
carabină *f* rifle
caracatiţă *f* octopus
caracter *n* character
caracteristic *adj* characteristic
cărămidă *f* brick
carat *n* carat
caravană *f* caravan
carboniza *v* char
cărbune *m* coal
cărbune de lemn *m* charcoal
carburator *n* carburetor
carcasă *f* carcass
cârciumă *f* saloon
card *n* card
cardiac *adj* cardiac
cardiologie *f* cardiology
care *adj* which
care atârnă *adj* baggy
care creşte *adj* increasing
care împiedică *adj* impending
care intră *adj* incoming
care merită *adj* worthwhile
care rămâne *adj* remaining
care te înfioară *adj* creepy
caricatură *f* caricature
carieră *f* career
carieră de piatră *f* quarry
carismă *f* charisma
carismatic *adj* charismatic
caritabil *adj* charitable
caritate *f* charity
cârjă *f* crutch
cârje *f* crook
cârlig *n* hook
carlingă *f* cockpit
cârmă *f* helm, rudder
carnagiu *n* carnage
carnal *adj* carnal
cârnat *m* sausage

carne *f* meat, flesh
carne de pasăre *f* poultry
carne de porc *f* pork
carne de vacă *f* beef
carne de viţel *f* veal
carnet de cecuri *n* checkbook
cârpă *f* cloth, rag
carpetă *f* rug
cârpi *v* patch
carte *f* book
carte tehnică *f* workbook
cartier general *n* headquarters
cartof *m* potato
cartofi prăjiţi *m* fries
carton *n* cardboard
cartuş *n* cartridge
cărucior *n* cart
casă *f* home, house
casă de bilete *f* box office
căsători *v* marry, wed
căsătorie *f* marriage
căsătorit *adj* married
cască *f* helmet
căsca *v* yawn
cascadă *f* waterfall
căscat *n* yawn
caserolă *f* casserole
casier *m* cashier
cast *adj* chaste
castă *f* caste
castană *f* chestnut
castel *n* castle
căşti *f* headphones
câştig *n* gain
câştiga *v* gain, win
câştigător *m* winner
castitate *f* chastity
castor *m* beaver
castravete *m* cucumber
căsuţă *f* cottage
cât *n* quotient
cataclism *n* cataclysm
catacombă *f* catacomb
catalog *n* catalog
cataloga *v* catalog
catâr *m* mule
căţăra *v* mount
cataractă *f* cataract
cataramă *f* buckle
căţărare *f* climbing
catarg *n* mast
catarg de steag *n* flagpole
catastrofă *f* catastrophe
catedrală *f* cathedral
categorie *f* category
catehism *n* catechism

căţeluş *m* puppy
catifea *f* velvet
catolic *adj* catholic
catolicism *n* Catholicism
către *pre* towards
cătun *n* hamlet
cătuşe *f* handcuffs
cauciuc *n* rubber
căuta *v* look for, seek
căutare *f* quest
cauţiune *f* bail
cauza *v* cause
cauză *f* cause
cavaler *m* knight, sir
cavalerie *f* cavalry
cavernă *f* cavern
cavitate *f* cavity
caz *n* case
cazarmă *f* barracks
cazino *n* casino
cazma *f* spade
ce *adj* what
ceai *n* tea
ceainic *n* teapot, kettle
ceapă *f* onion
ceară *f* wax
ceartă *f* strife, quarrel
ceas *n* clock
ceaşcă *f* cup
ceasornicar *m* watchmaker
ceaţă *f* mist, fog
ceaţă uşoară *f* haze, fog
cec de plată *n* paycheck
ceda *v* concede
cel mai bun *adj* best
cel mai mult *adj* most
cel mai puţin *adj* least
cel mai rău *adj* worst
cel mai recent *adj* latest
celebra *v* celebrate
celebritate *f* celebrity
celibat *n* celibacy
celibatar *m* bachelor
celular *n* cellphone
cent *m* cent
centenar *n* centenary
centimetru *n* centimeter
centra *v* center
central *adj* central
centraliza *v* centralize
centru *n* center, hub
centrul oraşului *n* downtown
cenuşă *f* cinder, ash
cenuşiu *adj* gray
cenzura *v* censure
cenzură *f* censorship

cer *n* sky
ceramică *f* ceramic
cerb *m* deer
cerc *n* circle
cercel *m* earring
cerceta *v* look into, search
cercetare *f* search
cercetaş *m* scout
cere *v* request, require
cereală *f* cereal
cerebral *adj* cerebral
ceremonie *f* ceremony
cerere *f* demand, request
ceresc *adj* celestial
cerinţă *f* requirement
cerne *v* sift
cerneală *f* ink
cerşetor *m* beggar
cerşi *v* beg
certa *v* argue, quarrel
certăreţ *adj* quarrelsome
certifica *v* certify
certificat *n* certificate
cerul gurii *n* palate
cerumen *n* earwax
cetăţean *m* citizen
cetăţenesc *adj* civil
cetăţenie *f* citizenship
ceţos *adj* foggy, misty
ceva *pro* something
cheag *n* clot
cheie *f* key
chel *adj* bald
chelfăneală *f* spanking
chelner *m* waiter
chelneriţă *f* waitress
cheltui *v* spend
cheltuială *f* expenditure
chema *v* summon, call
chemare *f* calling, call
cherestea *f* timber
chestiona *v* inquire
chestionar *f* questionnaire
chiar *adv* very
chiar dacă *c* even if
chiar mai *c* even more
chibrit *n* match
chibzui *v* ponder
chicoti *v* chuckle, giggle
chiftea *f* meatball
chilipir *n* bargaining
chiloţi *m* briefs
chimic *adj* chemical
chimie *f* chemistry
chimist *m* chemist
chin *n* affliction, anguish

chinui *v* torment, afflict
chinuitor *adj* agonizing, distressing
chioşc *n* kiosk
chioşc de ziare *n* newsstand
chiparos *m* cypress
chipeş *adj* good-looking
chipurile *adv* allegedly
chiriaş *m* tenant
chirie *f* rent
chirurg *m* surgeon
chirurgical *adv* surgical
chist *n* cyst
chiţăi *v* squeak
chitanţă *f* receipt
chitară *f* guitar
chivot *n* shrine
cianat *m* cyanide
cicălitor *adj* nagging
cicatrice *f* scar
ciclist *m* cyclist
ciclon *n* cyclone
ciclu *n* cycle
cidru *n* cider
cifră *f* figure
cilindru *m* cylinder
ciment *n* cement
cimitir *n* cemetery
cimpanzeu *m* chimpanzee
cină *f* dinner, supper
cinci *adj* five
cincisprezece *adj* fifteen
cincizeci *adj* fifty
cine *pro* who
cinematograf *n* cinema
cineva *pro* somebody, someone
cinic *adj* cynic
cinism *n* cynicism
cinste *f* honesty
cinstit *adj* honest
cioară *f* crow
cioc *n* bill
cioc de pasăre *n* beak
ciocan *n* hammer
ciocni *v* clash, collide
ciocni de *v* run into
ciocnire *f* clash, collision
ciocolată *f* chocolate
ciomăgi *v* bludgeon, club
ciopli *v* carve
ciorap lung *m* stocking
ciorchine *m* cluster
circ *n* circus
circuit *n* circuit
circula *v* circulate
circular *adj* circular
circulaţie *f* circulation

C

circumcide *v* circumcise
circumcizie *f* circumcision
circumstanţă *f* circumstance
circumstanţial *adj* circumstancial
cireaşă *f* cherry
cisternă *f* cistern
cita *v* subpoena, quote
citat *n* quotation
citaţie *f* subpoena
citi *v* read
cititor *m* reader
ciudă *f* grudge
ciudat *adj* strange, weird
ciudăţenie *f* oddity
ciuguli *v* nibble
ciumă *f* plague, pest
ciunti *v* curtail
ciuntire *f* bluntness
ciupercă *f* mushroom
ciupi *v* pinch, nip
ciupit *n* pinch
civic *adj* civic
civiliza *v* civilize
civilizaţie *f* civilization
clădi *v* build
clădire *f* building
clan *n* clan
clandestin *adj* clandestine
clar *adj* clear, lucid
clarificare *f* clarification
clarinet *n* clarinet
claritate *f* clearness
clasă *f* class
clasic *adj* classic
clasifica *v* classify
clăti *v* rinse
clătina *v* toss
clauză *f* clause
claviatură *f* keyboard
claviculă *f* collarbone
claxona *v* honk
clemă *f* clamp
clemenţă *f* clemency
cler *n* clergy
clerical *adj* clerical
cleşte *m* pincers, tongs, pliers
client *m* client, customer
clientelă *f* clientele
climat *n* climate
climateric *adj* climatic
clinică *f* clinic
clinti *v* budge
clipă *f* instant
clipi *v* blink, wink
clipit *n* wink
clona *v* clone

clonare *f* cloning
clopot *n* bell
clopotniţă *f* belfry
clovn *m* clown
club *n* club
coabita *v* cohabit
coace *v* bake, mellow
coadă *f* queue
coafor *m* hairdresser
coafură *f* hairdo
coagula *v* coagulate
coagulare *f* coagulation
coajă *f* peel, shell
coajă de nucă *f* nut-shell
coaliţie *f* coalition
coapsă *f* thigh
coase *v* sew
coastă *f* coast
coastă de deal *f* hillside
coborâre *f* descent
coborî *v* debase, descend
cocaină *f* cocaine
cocoaşă *f* hunch
cocor *m* crane
cocoş *m* cock, rooster
cocoşat *m* hunchback
cocteil *n* cocktail
cocurent *m* contestant
cod *n* cod, code
cod poştal *n* zip code
codifica *v* codify
coeficient *m* coefficient
coerent *adj* coherent
coexista *v* coexist
coeziune *f* cohesion
cofeină *f* caffeine
coincide *v* coincide
coincidenţă *f* coincidence
coji *v* peel
colabora *v* collaborate
colaborare *f* collaboration
colaborator *m* collaborator
colateral *adj* collateral
colecta *v* collect
colecţie *f* collection
colector *m* collector
coleg *m* colleague
coleg de clasă *m* classmate
colegiu *n* college
colesterol *n* cholesterol
colete *n* parcel post
colibă *f* hut, shack, cabin
colică *f* colic
colier *n* necklace
colindă *f* carol
colivie *f* cage

coloană *f* column
colonel *m* colonel
colonial *adj* colonial
colonie *f* colony
colonist *m* settler
coloniza *v* colonize
colonizare *f* colonization
colora *v* color
colorat *adj* colorful
colosal *adj* colossal
colţ *n* corner
comă *f* coma
comanda *v* command
comandament *n* commandment
comandant *m* commander
combatant *m* combatant
combate *v* combat
combina *v* combine
combinaţie *f* combination
combustibil *m* fuel
combustie *f* combustion
comediant *m* comedian
comedie *f* comedy
comemora *v* commemorate
comenta *v* comment
comentariu *n* comment
comercial *adj* commercial
comerciant *m* trader
comerţ *n* commerce
comestibil *adj* edible
cometă *f* comet
comfort *n* comfort
comfortabil *adj* comfortable
comic *adj* humorous
comision *n* commission
comite *v* commit, perpetrate
comitet *n* committee
comoară *f* treasure
comodităţi *f* amenities
compact *adj* compact
companie *f* company
companion *m* companion
compara *v* compare
comparabil *adj* comparable
comparaţie *f* comparison
comparativ *adj* comparative
compartiment *n* compartment
compasiune *f* compassion
compatibil *adj* compatible
compatriot *m* compatriot
compendiu *n* compendium
compensa *v* compensate
compensaţie *f* compensation
competent *adj* competent
competenţă *f* competence
competiţie *f* competition

competitiv *adj* competitive
competitor *m* competitor
complement *n* complement
complet *adj* complete
complet *adv* entirely
completare *f* completion
complexitate *f* complexity
complica *v* complicate
complicat *adj* complex
complicaţie *f* complication
complice *m* accomplice
complicitate *f* complicity
compliment *n* compliment
complimente *n* regards
complotist *m* conspirator
componentă *f* component
comportament *n* behavior
comportare *f* demeanor
compoziţie *f* composition
compozitor *m* composer
comprima *v* compress
comprimare *f* compression
compromis *n* compromise
compromite *v* compromise
compune *v* compose
compus *m* compound
computer *n* computer
comun *adj* common
comunica *v* communicate
comunicare *f* communication
comunism *n* communism
comunist *adj* communist
comunitate *f* community
comuniune *f* communion
comuta *v* commute
comutator *n* switch
con *n* cone
conac *n* mansion
concedia *v* dismiss
concentra *v* concentrate, focus on
concentrare *f* concentration
concentric *adj* concentric
concepe *v* conceive
concept *n* concept
concepţie *f* outlook
concert *n* concert
concesie *f* concession
concesiune *f* lease
conciliant *adj* conciliatory
concis *adj* concise
concizie *f* brevity
concluzie *f* conclusion
concomitent *adj* concurrent
concret *adj* concrete
concura *v* compete
concurs *n* contest

C

condamna *v* condemn, convict
condamnare *f* condemnation
condensa *v* condense
condensare *f* condensation
condescinde *v* condescend
condiment *n* seasoning
condiţie *f* condition
condiţional *adj* conditional
condoleanţe *f* condolences
condominiu *n* condo
conducător *m* leader, ruler
conduce *v* drive, manage
conducere *f* leadership
conduită *f* conduct
conecta *v* connect
conexiune *f* connection
confecţii *f* garment
conferi *v* confer
conferinţă *f* conference
confident *m* confidant
confidenţial *adj* confidential
confirma *v* confirm
confirmare *f* confirmation
confisca *v* confiscate
confiscare *f* confiscation, seizure
conflict *n* conflict
conform cu *pre* according to
conformist *adj* conformist
conformitate *f* conformity
confrunta *v* confront
confruntare *f* confrontation
confunda *v* confound
confundabil *adj* confusing
confuzie *f* confusion
congestie *f* congestion
congestionat *adj* congested
congregaţie *f* congregation
congres *n* congress
coniac *n* brandy
conjuga *v* conjugate
conjugal *adj* conjugal
conjuncţie *f* conjunction
conjunctură *f* junction
conopidă *f* cauliflower
consacra *v* consecrate
consecinţă *f* consequence
consecutiv *adj* consecutive
consecvenţă *f* consistency
consemnare *f* consignment
consens *n* consensus
conserva *v* conserve
conservă *f* can
conservare *f* conservation
conservat *adj* canned
conservator *adj* conservative
considera *v* consider

considerabil *adj* considerable
consideraţie *f* consideration
consilier *m* adviser
consiliu *n* council
consistent *adj* consistent
consoană *f* consonant
consola *v* console
consolă *f* bracket
consolare *f* consolation
consolator *m* comforter
consolida *v* consolidate
conspira *v* conspire
conspiraţie *f* conspiracy
consta în *v* consist
constant *adj* constant
constanţă *f* constancy
constelaţie *f* constellation
consternare *f* consternation
conştient *adj* aware, conscious
conştienţă *f* conciousness
conştiinţă *f* conscience
constipa *v* constipate
constipat *adj* constipated
constipaţie *f* constipation
constitui *v* constitute
constituţie *f* constitution
constrânge *v* constrain
constrângere *f* coercion
construcţie *f* construction
constructiv *adj* constructive
constructor *m* builder
construi *v* construct
consul *m* consul
consulat *n* consulate
consulta *v* consult
consultaţie *f* consultation
consuma *v* consume
consumaţie *f* consumption
consumator *m* consumer
cont *n* account
contabil *m* accountant
contabilitate *f* bookkeeping
contact *n* contact
contagios *adj* contagious
contamina *v* contaminate
contaminare *f* contamination
conteiner *n* container
contempla *v* contemplate
contemporar *adj* contemporary
contesă *f* countess
context *n* context
conţine *v* contain
continent *n* continent
continental *adj* continental
continua *v* continue
continuare *f* continuation

C

continuitate *f* continuity
conţinut *n* contents
continuu *adj* continuous
contra *pre* against, versus
contrabandă *f* contraband
contrabandist *m* smuggler
contracara *v* counteract
contract *n* contract
contracta *v* contract
contracţie *f* contraction
contradicţie *f* contradiction
contradictoriu *adj* conflicting
contrafăcut *adj* trumped-up
contrar *adj* adverse
contrariul *n* opposite
contrast *n* contrast
contrazice *v* contradict
contribuabil *m* contributor
contribui *v* contribute
contribuţie *f* contribution
control *n* control
controla *v* control, check
controversă *f* controversy
controversat *adj* controversial
contur *n* contour, outline
contuzie *f* bruise
convalescent *adj* convalescent
convenabil *adj* convenient
convenienţă *f* convenience
convenţie *f* convention
convenţional *adj* conventional
conversa *v* converse, chat
conversaţie *f* conversation
converti *v* convert
convertit *m* convert
convingător *adj* convincing
convinge *v* convince
convingere *f* conviction
convoca *v* convene
convoi *n* convoy
convulsie *f* convulsion
coopera *v* cooperate
cooperare *f* cooperation
cooperatist *adj* cooperative
coordona *v* coordinate
coordonare *f* coordination
coordonator *m* coordinator
copac *m* tree
copertă *f* cover
copia *v* copy
copie *f* copy
copil *m* child
copil mic *m* infant
copilărie *f* childhood
copilăros *adj* childish
copilaş *m* baby, toddler

copist *m* copier
copită *f* hoof
copleşi *v* overwhelm
copleşitor *adj* awesome
copt *adj* mellow, ripe
cor *n* choir, chorus
corabie *f* sail
corb *m* raven
cordial *adj* cordial
cordon *n* cordon
corect *adj* correct, fair, justify
corecta *v* correct
corecţie *f* correction
corectitudine *f* fairness
coresponda *v* mail
corespondent *m* correspondent
corespunde *v* correspond
corespunzător *adj* corresponding
coridă *f* bull fight
coridor *n* corridor
corn *n* horn
cornet *n* cornet
coroană *f* crown
coronar *adj* coronary
corp *n* body
corpolent *adj* burly
corporal *adj* corporal
corporaţie *f* corporation
corpuscul *m* corpuscle
cort *n* tent
cortină *f* curtain
corupe *v* corrupt
corupt *adj* corrupt
corupţie *f* bribery
coş *n* pimple
coş de gunoi *n* trash can
coş de hârtii *n* waste basket
cosi *v* mow
cosiţă *f* braid
coşmar *n* nightmare
cosmetic *n* cosmetic
cosmic *adj* cosmic
cosmonaut *m* cosmonaut
cost *n* cost
costa *v* cost
costisitor *adj* costly
costum *n* costume, suit
costumier *m* dresser
cot *n* elbow
coti *v* curve, bend
cotor *n* stub
covor *n* carpet
crab *m* crab
Crăciun *n* Christmas, X-mas
cramă *f* winery
crampă *f* cramp

C

craniu *n* skull
crăpa *v* crack
crăpătură *f* crack
cras *adj* crass
crater *n* crater
cravată *f* necktie
crea *v* create
creastă *f* ridge, crest
creaţie *f* creation
creativ *adj* creative
creativitate *f* creativity
creator *m* creator
creatură *f* creature
crede *v* believe
credibil *adj* believable
credibilitate *f* credibility
credincios *m* believer
credinţă *f* belief
credit *n* credit
creditor *m* creditor
creier *n* brain
creion *n* pencil
cremă de ouă *f* custard
crematoriu *n* crematorium
cremos *adj* creamy
crepuscul *n* dusk
cresta *v* dent
creşte *v* grow, increase
creştere *f* growth
creştin *adj* christian
creştinism *n* Christianity
cretă *f* chalk
cretin *adj* moron
crevetă *f* shrimp
crez *n* creed
crimă *f* crime, felony
criminal *adj* criminal, heinous
criminal *m* thug, felon
cristal *n* crystal
criteriu *n* criterion
critic *adj* critical
critica *v* criticize
critică *f* criticism
criză *f* crisis
croazieră *f* voyage
crocant *adj* crispy, crunchy
crocodil *m* crocodile
croitor *m* tailor
cronic *adj* chronic
cronică *f* chronicle
cronologie *f* chronology
cruce *f* cross
cruciadă *f* crusade
crucial *adj* crucial
cruciat *m* crusader
crucifica *v* crucify

crucificare *f* crucifixion
crucifix *n* crucifix
crud *adj* crude, raw
crustă *f* crust
cruţa *v* spare
cruzime *f* cruelty
cu *pre* with
cu acurateţe *adv* neatly
cu condiţia *c* providing that
cu desăvârşire *adv* fully
cu destinaţia *adj* bound for
cu economie *adv* sparingly
cu faţa la *pre* facing
cu furie *adv* furiously
cu hopuri *adj* bumpy
cu laşitate *adv* cowardly
cu mândrie *adv* proudly
cu plăcere *adv* willingly
cu privire la *pre* regarding
cu severitate *adv* sternly
cu siguranţă *adv* surely
cu toate acestea *c* nonetheless
cu zgârcenie *adv* grudgingly
cub *n* cube
cub de gheaţă *n* ice cube
cubic *adj* cubic
cuceri *v* conquer
cucerire *f* conquest
cuceritor *m* conqueror
cufunda *v* duck; immerse
cui de osie *n* linchpin
cuib *n* nest
culege *v* pick
culme *f* apex
culmina *v* culminate
culoar *n* aisle, hallway
culoare *f* color
cult *n* cult
cultiva *v* cultivate
cultivare *f* cultivation
cultură *f* culture
cultural *adj* cultural
cum *adv* how
cum cuvine *adv* nicely
cumnat *m* brother-in-law
cumnată *f* sister-in-law
cumpăna apelor *f* watershed
cumpăra *v* buy, purchase
cumpărare *f* purchase
cumpărător *m* buyer
cumpărături *f* shopping
cumplit *adj* dire
cumva *adv* somehow
cunoaştere *f* knowledge
cunoştinţă *f* acquaintance
cupă plină *f* bumper

cuplu *n* couple
cupon *n* coupon
cuprinde *v* comprise
cuprindere *f* coverage
cuprins de dor *adj* lonesome
cuprinzător *adj* comprehensive
cuprinzător *adv* inclusive
cuptor *n* oven
curaj *n* courage, bravery
curajos *adj* brave, bold
curând *adv* soon, shortly
curat *adj* neat, clean
curăţa *v* clean, clear
curăţenie *f* cleanliness
curăţi *v* purge
curăţitor *m* cleaner
curba *v* flex
curbă *f* curve
curcubeu *n* rainbow, bow
curea *f* belt
curent *adj* current
curent *n* flow
curge *v* flow
curier *m* courier
curios *adj* curious
curiozitate *f* curiosity
curs *n* course
cursă *f* race
curta *v* court
curte *f* court, courtship
curte interioară *f* patio
curtea casei *f* courtyard
curtenitor *adj* courteous
curtoazie *f* courtesy
cusătoreasă *f* seamstress
cusătură *f* seam
cuşcă de câine *f* kennel
cuşetă *f* berth
custode *m* custodian
cusut *n* sewing
cută *f* pleat
cuter *n* cutter
cutie *f* box, bin
cutie poştală *f* mailbox
cuţit *n* knife
cuţitar *m* hoodlum
cutreiera *v* scour
cutremur *n* earthquake
cutremura *v* quake, shake
cuvânt *n* word
cuvântare *f* speech
cuvertură *f* bedspread

D

da *adv* yes
da *v* give
da bătut *v* drop out
da de necaz *v* mess up
da de urmă *v* trail
da din coadă *v* wag
da din umeri *v* shrug
da greş *v* backfire
da în foc *v* boil over
da la o parte *v* brush aside
da o formă *v* formalize
da peste *v* bump into
dacă *c* if
dacă nu *c* unless
daltă *f* chisel
damnaţiune *f* damnation
Danemarca *f* Denmak
dans *n* dance, dancing
dansa *v* dance
dantelă *f* lace
dantură *f* dentures
dar *c* but
dar *n* gift
dar dacă *c* supposing
dărâma *v* demolish
dărâmat *adj* dilapidated
dărâmături *f* rubble
data *v* date
dată *f* date
date *f* data
datină *f* custom
datora *v* owe
datorat *adj* due
datornic *m* debtor
dăunător *adj* detrimental
dazamăgit *adj* disenchanted
de asemenea *adv* also, too
de atunci *adv* since then
de bază *adj* grassroots
de când *c* since
de ce *adv* why
de chiţibuşar *adj* nitpicking
de coastă *adj* coastal
de curând *adv* newly
de fapt *adv* actually
de fiecare *adv* apiece
de înţeles *adj* understandable
de la *pre* since
de lână *adj* woolen
de lemn *adj* wooden
de modă veche *adj* old-fashioned
de nădejde *adj* dependable
de neatins *adj* untouchable

D

de necrezut *adj* unbelievable
de neiertat *adj* inexcusable
de netăgăduit *adj* undeniable
de neuitat *adj* unforgettable
de-a lungul *pre* along
de-abia *adv* thinly
deal *n* hill
deasupra *pre* above
debarca *v* disembark
debarcader *n* wharf
debarcare *f* landing
debit *n* debit, outlet
debut *n* debut
decadă *f* decade
decădea *v* decay
decadenţă *f* decadence
decapita *v* behead
decedat *adj* deceased
decembrie *m* December
decent *adj* decent
decenţă *f* decency
decepţie *f* deception
deces *n* demise
deci *adv* therefore
decide *v* decide
decima *v* decimate
decisiv *adj* decisive
decizie *f* decision
declanşa *v* trigger
declara *v* declare
declaraţie *f* declaration
declin *n* slump, decline
declinare *f* declension
decofeinizat *adj* decaff
decola *v* lift off
decolare *f* lift-off
decolora *v* fade
decolorat *adj* faded
deconecta *v* disconnect
decongela *v* defrost
decont *n* discount
deconta *v* discount
decor *n* décor
decora *v* decorate
decorativ *adj* decorative
decret *n* decree
decreta *v* decree
dedica *v* dedicate
dedicaţie *f* dedication
deduce *v* deduce
deductibil *adj* deductible
deducţie *f* deduction
defăima *v* defame
defect *n* defect
defecta *v* malfunction
defecţiune *f* defection

D

deficient *adj* defective
deficienţă *f* deficiency
deficit *n* deficit
defini *v* define
definiţie *f* definition
definitiv *adj* definitive
deforma *v* deform, distort
deformare *f* distortion
degajat *adj* casual
degenera *v* degenerate
degenerare *f* degeneration
degenerat *adj* degenerate
degerat *adj* frostbitten
degerătură *f* frostbite
deget *n* digit
deget de la mână *n* finger
deget de la picior *n* toe
degetul mare *n* thumb
deghiza *v* disguise
deghizare *f* disguise
degrada *v* degrade
degradare *f* degradation
degradat *adj* degrading
degustare *f* foretaste
deja *adv* already
delapida *v* embezzle
delega *v* delegate
delegare *f* delegation
delegat *m* delegate
delfin *m* dolphin
delibera *v* deliberate
delicat *adj* delicate
delicateţe *f* delicacy
delicios *adj* delicious
delicvent *adj* delinquent
delicvenţă *f* delinquency
deluros *adj* hilly
demasca *v* unmask, expose
demisie *f* resignation
demite *v* depose
demnitar *m* dignitary
demnitate *f* dignity
demobiliza *v* disband
democratic *adj* democratic
democraţie *f* democracy
demodat *adj* obsolete
demola *v* pull down
demolare *f* demolition
demon *m* devil
demonstra *v* demonstrate
demonstrativ *adj* demonstrative
demonta *v* dismantle
demoraliza *v* demoralize
denigra *v* denigrate
dens *adj* dense
densitate *f* density

D

dentar *adj* dental
dentist *m* dentist
denunţa *v* denounce
deodată *adv* suddenly
deodorant *n* deodorant
deoparte *adv* off
departament *n* department
departe *adv* far, away
depăşi *v* exceed
depăşit *adj* outdated
dependent *adj* dependent
dependenţă *f* dependence
depinde *v* depend
deplânge *v* deplore
deplasa *v* displace
deplorabil *adj* deplorable
deporta *v* deport
deportare *f* deportation
depozit *n* deposit, store
depozitare *f* storage
depravare *f* depravity
depravat *adj* depraved
deprecia *v* depreciate
depreciere *f* depreciation
depresiune *f* depression
deprima *v* depress
deprimant *adj* depressing
deprimat *adj* downcast
deraia *v* derail
deraiare *f* derailment
deranj *n* intrusion
deranja *v* intrude, trouble
deranjat *adj* deranged
derivat *adj* derivative
descalifica *v* disqualify
descărca *v* unload, dump
descărcare *f* discharge
descendent *m* descendant
descheia *v* unbutton
deschide *v* open, turn on, break open
deschide larg *v* open up
deschidere *f* opening
deschis *adj* outspoken
deschizătură *f* loophole
descifra *v* figure out
descompus *adj* putrid
descoperi *v* discover
descoperire *f* discovery
descreştere *f* decrease
descrie *v* describe
descriere *f* description
descriptiv *adj* descriptive
descuia *v* unlock
descuiat *adj* open-minded
desculţ *adj* barefoot
descuraja *v* discourage

descurajare *f* deterrence
descurajator *adj* discouraging
descurca *v* unravel
desemna *v* designate
desen *n* design, drawing
desen animat *n* cartoon
desenator *m* draftsman
desert *n* dessert
desface *v* take apart, undo
desfăşura *v* deploy, unfold
desfăşurare *f* deployment
desfigura *v* disfigure
deshidrata *v* dehydrate
deşi *c* although
despacheta *v* unpack
despărţi *v* divide, come apart
despărţire *f* parting
despărţitură *f* partition
despica *v* sever, splinter
despicătură *f* wedge
despotic *adj* despotic
deştept *adj* clever, smart
destin *n* destiny
destinaţie *f* destination
destinde *v* recreate
destrăbălat *adj* dissolute
destul *adv* enough
detalia *v* itemize
detaliu *n* detail
detaşa *v* detach
detaşabil *adj* detachable
detecta *v* detect
detectiv *m* detective
detector *n* detector
detergent *m* detergent
deteriora *v* deteriorate
deteriorare *f* deterioration
determina *v* determine
determinare *f* determination
determinat *adj* singleminded
detesta *v* abhor, detest, resent
detestabil *adj* detestable
deţine *v* detain
detona *v* detonate
detonare *f* detonation
detonator *n* detonator
detriment *n* detriment
deturna *v* hijack
deturnare *f* hijack
devaloriza *v* devalue
devalorizare *f* devaluation
devasta *v* devastate
devastare *f* devastation
devastator *adj* devastating
deveni *v* become
deviere *f* deviation

D

devora *v* devour
devotament *n* devotion
devreme *adv* early
dezacord *n* discord
dezagreabil *adj* distasteful
dezamăgi *v* disappoint
dezamăgire *f* disappointment
dezamăgit *adj* disappointing
dezaproba *v* disapprove
dezaprobare *f* disapproval
dezarma *v* disarm
dezarmament *f* disarmament
dezastru *n* disaster
dezastruos *adj* disastrous
dezavantaj *n* disadvantage
dezbate *v* debate
dezbatere *f* debate
dezbateri *f* proceedings
dezbinare *f* disruption, schism
dezbrăca *v* undress
dezechilibru *n* imbalance
dezerta *v* desert
dezertor *m* deserter
dezgheţ *n* thaw
dezgropa *v* unearth
dezgust *n* disgust
dezgustător *adj* disgusting
deziluzie *f* disillusion
dezinfecta *v* disinfect
dezinfectant *n* disinfectant
dezintegra *v* disintegrate
dezintegrare *f* disintegration
dezinteresat *adj* disinterested
dezirabil *adj* desirable
dezivnovăţi *v* exonerate
dezlega *v* loose
dezmoşteni *v* disinherit
deznădăjduit *adj* desperate
deznădejde *f* despair
dezolare *f* desolation
dezonoare *f* dishonor
dezonora *v* disgrace
dezonorabil *adj* dishonorable
dezordine *f* disorder
dezorganizat *adj* disorganized
dezorientat *adj* disoriented
dezrădăcina *v* uproot
dezumfla *v* deflate
dezvălui *v* disclose, reveal, unveil
dezveli *v* unwind
dezvolta *v* develop
dezvoltare *f* development
diabet *n* diabetes
diabetic *adj* diabetic
diabolic *adj* diabolical
diacon *m* deacon

diagnostic *n* diagnosis
diagnostica *v* diagnose
diagramă *f* diagram
dialect *n* dialect
dialog *n* dialogue
diamant *n* diamond
diamantin *adj* adamant
diametru *n* diameter
diaree *f* diarrhea
dichisit *adj* sporty
dicta *v* dictate
dictator *m* dictator
dictatorial *adj* dictatorial
dictatură *f* dictatorship
dicţionar *n* dictionary
dietă *f* diet
diferenţă *f* difference
diferi *v* differ
diferit *adj* different
dificil *adj* difficult
dificultate *f* difficulty
diformitate *f* deformity
diftong *m* diphthong
difuza *v* diffuse
dig *n* pier
digera *v* digest
digestie *f* digestion
digestiv *adj* digestive
dilemă *f* dilemma
dilua *v* dilute
dime *n* dime
dimensiune *f* dimension
dimineaţă *f* morning
diminua *v* diminish
din *pre* from
din nou *adv* afresh
din oră în oră *adv* hourly
din partea *adv* behalf (on)
din pricina *pre* because of
din toată inima *adj* wholehearted
dinamic *adj* dynamic
dinamită *f* dynamite
dinapoi *adj* rear
dinastie *f* dynasty
dincolo *adv* beyond
dinozaur *m* dinosaur
dinte *m* tooth
dinţi *m* teeth
dioceză *f* diocese
diplomă *f* diploma
diplomat *m* diplomat
diplomatic *adj* diplomatic
diplomaţie *f* diplomacy
direct *adj* direct
direcţie *f* direction
direcţiona *v* direct

director *m* director
dirijor *m* conductor
disc *n* disk
disciplină *f* discipline
discipol *m* disciple
discomfort *n* discomfort
discordant *adj* discordant
discredita *v* discredit
discrepanţă *f* discrepancy
discret *adj* discreet
discreţie *f* discretion
discrimina *v* discriminate
discriminare *f* discrimination
discuta *v* discuss, dispute
discutabil *adj* debatable
discuţie *f* discussion
diseară *adv* tonight
disident *adj* dissident
disloca *v* dislocate
disonant *adj* dissonant
dispărea *v* disappear
dispariţie *f* disappearance
dispărut *adj* missing
dispensare *f* dispensation
disperat *adj* hopeless
dispersa *v* disperse
dispersare *f* dispersal
disponibil *adj* available
disponibilitate *f* availability
dispoziţie *f* mood
dispozitiv *n* appliance
dispreţ *n* disdain
dispreţui *v* despise
dispreţuitor *adj* scornful
dispune *v* dispose
dispută *f* dispute
distant *adj* distant
distanţă *f* distance
distanţa în mile *f* mileage
distila *v* distill
distinct *adj* distinct
distincţie *f* distinction
distinctiv *adj* distinctive
distinge *v* distinguish, stand out
distra *v* entertain
distracţie *f* pastime, fun
distractiv *adj* entertaining
distrage *v* distract, divert
distragere *f* distraction
distrat *adj* absent
distribui *v* distribute
distribuţie *f* distribution
district *n* county, district
distructiv *adj* destructive
distrugător *n* destroyer
distruge *v* destroy, wreck

D

distrugere *f* destruction, ravage
disuada *v* dissuade
divers *adj* various
diversifica *v* diversify
diversitate *f* diversity
diversiune *f* diversion
dividend *n* dividend
divin *adj* divine
divinitate *f* divinity
divizibil *adj* divisible
diviziune *f* division
divorţ *n* divorce
divorţa *v* divorce
divulga *v* divulge
dizgraţie *f* disgrace
dizolva *v* dissolve
dizolvare *f* dissolution
doamnă *f* lady
doc *n* dock
docil *adj* docile
docilitate *f* docility
doctor *m* doctor
doctorie *f* drug
doctrină *f* doctrine
document *n* document
documentar *n* documentary
documentare *f* documentation
dogmatic *adj* dogmatic
doi *adj* two
doisprezece *adj* twelve
dolar *m* buck, dollar
doliu *n* mourning
dom *n* dome
domestic *adj* domestic
domestici *v* domesticate
domina *v* dominate
dominant *adj* towering
dominare *f* domination
dominaţie *f* dominion
domni *v* reign
domnie *f* reign
domnul *m* mister
dona *v* donate
donaţie *f* donation
donator *m* donor
dop *n* cork, plug
dor *n* longing
dori *v* desire, wish
dorinţă *f* desire, wish
doritor *adj* eager, willing
dormi *v* sleep
dormitor *n* bedroom
dormitor comun *n* dormitory
dosar *n* dossier, file
douăzeci *adj* twenty
dovadă *f* proof

dovadă sigură *f* smoking gun
dovedi *v* attest, prove
dovedi fals *v* disprove
dovedit *adj* proven
dovleac *m* pumpkin
dozaj *n* dosage
drag *adj* dear
dragoste *f* love
drăguţ *adj* nice, pretty
dramatic *adj* dramatic
dramatiza *v* dramatize
drapaj *n* drape
drapel *n* standard
drastic *adj* drastic
dreapta *f* right
drept *adv* right
drept *adj* erect, upright
drept de autor *n* copyright
dreptunghi *n* rectangle
dreptunghiular *adj* rectangular
dres *n* pantyhose
dric *n* hearse
droga *v* drug, dope
drojdie *f* yeast
drum *n* road, way
dual *adj* dual
dubă *f* van
dubios *adj* dubious
dubla *v* double
dublu *adj* double
dublu *adv* twice
duce *m* duke
duce *v* lead, conduct
duce la *adj* conducive
ducesă *f* duchess
dudui *v* rumble
duduit *n* rumble
duel *n* duel
duhni *v* stink
duhoare *f* stench, stink
duhovnic *m* confessor
dulap *n* cabinet
dulce *adj* sweet
dulceaţă *f* sweetness, conserve
dulciuri *n* candy, sweets
duminică *f* Sunday
Dumnezeu *m* God
dungă *f* stripe
dungat *adj* striped
după *pre* after
după aceea *adv* afterwards
după amiază *f* afternoon
duplicare *f* duplication
dura *v* last
durabil *adj* durable
durată *f* duration

durea *v* hurt
durere *f* ache, pain
durere de cap *f* headache
durere de dinţi *f* toothache
durere de urechi *f* earache
dureros *adj* hurtful, painful
duritate *f* hardness
duş *n* shower
duşman *m* foe
duşmănie *f* animosity
duşmănos *adj* spiteful
duzină *f* dozen

E

ea *pro* she
echilibru *n* equilibrium
echipa *v* equip
echipă *f* team
echipaj *n* crew
echipament *n* equipment
echivalent *adj* equivalent
echivalent cu *adj* tantamount to
eclipsa *v* overshadow
eclipsă *f* eclipse
ecluză *f* floodgate
ecologie *f* ecology
econom *adj* thrifty
economic *adj* economical
economie *f* economy
economii *f* savings
economisi *v* economize
ecou *n* echo
ecran *n* screen
ecraniza *v* screen
ecuaţie *f* equation
ecuator *n* equator
ediţie *f* edition
editor *m* publisher
educa *v* educate
educaţional *adj* educational
efect *n* effect
efectiv *adj* effective
efectivitate *f* effectiveness
efemer *adj* shortlived
effort *n* effort
eficient *adj* efficient
eficienţă *f* efficiency
efigie *f* effigy
efuziv *adj* effusive
egal *adj* equal
egala *v* equate
egalitate *f* equality

E

egoism *n* selfishness
egoist *adj* selfish
ei *pro* they, he
elabora *v* make up
elastic *adj* elastic, resilient
electric *adj* electric
electrician *m* electrician
electricitate *f* electricity
electriza *v* electrify
electrocuta *v* electrocute
electronic *adj* electronic
elefant *m* elephant
elegant *adj* elegant
eleganţă *f* elegance
element *n* element
elementar *adj* elementary
eleşteu *n* pond
elev *m* pupil
elevator *n* elevator
elibera *v* free, liberate, break free
eliberare *f* liberation
elicopter *n* helicopter
eligibil *adj* eligible
elimina *v* eliminate
elocvenţă *f* eloquence
Elveţia *f* Switzerland
elveţian *adj* Swiss
emana *v* emanate
emancipa *v* emancipate
emblemă *f* emblem
embrion *m* embryo
emfază *f* emphasis
emigra *v* emigrate
emigrant *m* emigrant
emisferă *f* hemisphere
emisiune *f* broadcast
emite *v* emit
emitere *f* emission
emoţie *f* excitement
emoţiona *v* excite, thrill
emoţional *adj* emotional
emoţionant *adj* touching
enciclopedie *f* encyclopedia
enclavă *f* enclave
energic *adj* energetic
energie *f* energy
enerva *v* annoy
enervant *adj* annoying
englezesc *adj* British
enigmă *f* puzzle
enoriaş *m* parishioner
enorm *adj* enormous
entuziasm *n* enthusiasm
entuziasma *v* enthuse
entuziast *adj* elated
enumera *v* enumerate

epidemie *f* epidemic
epilepsie *f* epilepsy
episcop *m* bishop
episod *n* episode
epistolă *f* epistle
epitaf *n* epitaph
epocă *f* age, epoch
epuiza *v* exhaust, give out
epuizant *adj* exhausting
eră *f* era
eradica *v* eradicate
ereditar *adj* hereditary
eretic *adj* heretic
erezie *f* heresy
ermetic *adj* hermetic
eroic *adj* heroic
eroină *f* heroin
eroism *n* heroism
erou *m* hero
erupe *v* erupt
erupţie *f* eruption, rash
eşarfă *f* scarf
escapadă *f* escapade
escava *v* excavate
escortă *f* escort
escroc *m* swindler
escroca *v* defraud
escrocherie *f* swindle
eşec *n* failure
esenţă *f* essence
esenţial *adj* essential
eseu *n* essay
esofag *n* esophagus
est *n* east
estetic *adj* aesthetic
estic *adj* eastern
estima *v* estimate
estimare *f* estimation
estuar *n* estuary
eşua *v* fail
etala *v* flaunt
etanş *adj* tight
etern *adj* everlasting
eternitate *f* eternity
etichetă *f* tag, sticker
eu *pro* I
euforie *f* euphoria
Europa *f* Europe
european *adj* European
evacua *v* evacuate
evada *v* escape
evalua *v* appraise, evaluate
evaluare *f* appraisal
evanghelie *f* gospel
evantai *n* fan
evapora *v* evaporate

E

evaziv *adj* evasive
eveniment *n* event
eventual *adj* contingent
eventualitate *f* contingency
evident *adj* obvious, patent
evita *v* avoid, shun, dodge
evitabil *adj* avoidable
evitare *f* avoidance
evoca *v* evoke
evolua *v* evolve
evoluţie *f* evolution
evreiesc *adj* Jewish
evreu *m* Jew
exact *adj* accurate, exact
exact *adv* literally, verbatim
exagera *v* exaggerate
exagerat *adj* overdone
examina *v* examine
examinare *f* examination
exaspera *v* exasperate
excela *v* excel
excelent *adj* excellent
excelenţă *f* excellence
excentric *adj* eccentric
excepţie *f* exception
excepţional *adj* exceptional
exces *n* excess
excesiv *adj* excessive
exclama *v* exclaim
exclude *v* exclude
excursie *f* excursion
executa *v* execute
executiv *n* executive
exemplar *adj* exemplary
exemplifica *v* exemplify
exemplu *n* example
exercitare *f* exertion
exerciţiu *n* exercise
exersa *v* exercise
exersare *adj* practising
exil *n* banishment
exila *v* exile, banish
exista *v* be, exist
existenţă *f* existence
exod *n* exodus
exorbitant *adj* exorbitant
exorcist *m* exorcist
exotic *adj* exotic
expansiune *f* expansion
expedia *v* dispatch
expediţie *f* expedition
expeditor *m* sender
experienţă *f* experience
experiment *n* experiment
experimental *adj* tentative
expert *adj* expert

expira *v* expire
expirare *f* expiration
explica *v* explain
explicabil *adj* accountable
explicaţie *f* showdown
explicit *adj* explicit
explicit *adv* expressly
exploata *v* exploit
exploatare *f* explotation
exploda *v* explode
explora *v* explore
explorator *m* explorer
explozie *f* explosion
exploziv *adj* explosive
exporta *v* export
expoziţie *f* display
expres *adj* express
expresie *f* expression
exprima *v* express
expropria *v* expropriate
expulza *v* expel
expulzare *f* expulsion
expune *v* display, exhibit
expus *adj* exposed
extaz *n* ecstasy
extensiune *f* extension
exterior *adj* exterior, outer
extermina *v* exterminate
extern *adj* foreign, external
extinde *v* extend, broaden, escalate
extrăda *v* extradite
extrădare *f* extradition
extrage *v* extract, take out
extras *n* excerpt
extravagant *adj* extravagant
extravaganţă *f* extravagance
extrem *adj* extreme
extrem *adv* exceedingly
extremist *adj* extremist
extremităţi *f* extremities
extrovertit *adj* extroverted
exulta *v* exult
ezita *v* hesitate
ezitant *adj* hesitant
ezitare *f* hesitation

F

F

fabrica *v* manufacture
fabrică *f* factory
fabrică de bere *f* brewery
fabricaţie *f* make
fabulă *f* fable
fabulos *adj* fabulous
face *v* make
face apel *v* appeal
face bucăţele *v* scrap
face curăţenie *v* cleanse
face faţă *v* cope
face gălăgie *v* clamor
face o escală *v* stop over
face pe şeful *v* boss around
face plinul *v* refuel
face posibil *v* enable
face recurs *v* recourse
face să tacă *v* gag
face surfing *v* surf
face troc *v* barter
factor *m* factor
factură *f* invoice
facultate *f* faculty
făcut în casă *adj* homemade
faimă *f* fame
faimos *adj* famous
făină *f* flour
falcă *f* jaw
falimenta *v* bankrupt
falit *adj* bankrupt, broke
fals *adj* fake, phoney
falsifica *v* falsify, fake
falsificare *f* forgery
falsificat *adj* counterfeit
familiar *adj* familiar
familie *f* family
fân *n* hay
fanatic *adj* fanatic
fandosit *adj* squeamish
fântână *f* fountain
fantastic *adj* fantastic
fantezie *f* fantasy
fantomă *f* ghost
fantomatic *adj* spooky
fapt *n* fact
faptă *f* feat
far *n* lighthouse
fără *pre* except, without
fără adăpost *adj* homeless
fără copii *adj* childless
fără cusătură *adj* seamless
fără efort *adv* lightly
fără fir *adj* cordless, wireless

fără fund *adj* bottomless
fără gust *adj* tasteless
fără legătură *adj* unrelated
fără mâneci *adj* sleeveless
fără oprire *adv* nonstop
fără plumb *adj* unleaded
fără sămânţă *adj* seedless
fără sens *adj* meaningless
fără serviciu *adj* jobless
fără ţintă *adj* aimless
fără valoare *adj* worthless
fără voie *adv* unwillingly
fărâma *v* shred
fărâmiţa *v* crumble
farfurie *f* dish, plate
farfurioară *f* saucer
farmacie *f* pharmacy
farmacist *m* pharmacist
farmec *n* allure
farsă *f* farce
fascina *v* fascinate
fasole *f* bean
fasole mare *f* kidney bean
făt *m* fetus
fată *f* girl, gal
faţă *f* front, face
fată bătrână *f* spinster
faţă de masă *f* tablecloth
faţă de pernă *f* pillowcase
fată în casă *f* maid
faţadă *f* frontage
fatal *adj* fatal, fateful
fătălău *adj* sissy
faţetă *f* facet
favoare *f* favor
favorabil *adj* favorable
favorit *adj* favorite
favoriţi *m* whiskers
fază *f* phase
fazan *m* pheasant
febră *f* fever
febril *adj* feverish
februarie *m* February
fecioară *f* maiden
federal *adj* federal
fel *n* sort
felicita *v* congratulate
felicitări *f* congratulations
felie *f* slice
felinar *n* lantern
felinar stradal *n* streetlight
femei *f* women
femeie *f* woman
femelă *f* female
feminin *adj* feminine
fenomen *n* phenomenon

ferăstrău *n* saw
fereastră *f* window
fereca *v* shut up
feri *v* fend
fericire *f* happiness
fericit *adj* happy
ferm *adj* firm, steady
fermă *f* farm
fermă de lapte *f* dairy farm
fermecător *adj* charming
ferment *m* ferment
fermenta *v* ferment
fermier *m* farmer
fermitate *f* firmness
fermoar *n* zipper
feroce *adj* ferocious
ferocitate *f* ferocity
fertil *adj* fertile
fertilitate *f* fertility
fertiliza *v* fertilize
festiv *adj* festive
festivitate *f* festivity
fi bolnav *v* sicken
fi bosumflat *v* grouch
fi codoş *v* pander
fi dator să *v* ought to
fi de acord *v* agree, concur
fi furios *v* rampage
fi în conflict *v* conflict
fi în dezacord *v* dissent
fi în litigiu *v* litigate
fi incompetent *v* malpractice
fi informat *v* know
fi însetat *v* thirst
fi înţepător *v* sting
fi la înălţime *v* live up
fi lipsit de *v* lack
fi născut *v* be born
fi profesor *v* teach
fi regăsit *v* turn up
fibră *f* fiber
ficat *m* liver
ficţiune *f* fiction
fictiv *adj* fictitious
fidel *adj* staunch
fidelitate *f* fidelity
fiecare *adj* each, every
fier *n* iron
fierar *m* blacksmith
fierbe *v* boil, simmer
fierbinte *adj* fervent
fiere *f* bile
fiică *f* daughter
fiică vitregă *f* stepdaughter
fiinţă *f* being
fiinţă umană *f* human being

fildeş *m* ivory, tusk
file de muşchi *n* sirloin
filială *f* branch office
film *n* film, movie
filozof *m* philosopher
filozofie *f* philosophy
filtra *v* filter
filtru *n* filter
fin *adv* fine
final *adj* final
finaliza *v* finalize
financiar *adj* financial
finanţa *v* finance
Finlanda *f* Finland
finlandez *adj* Finnish
fiord *n* fjord
fir *n* speck
fir tors *n* yarn
firav *adj* frail
firimitură *f* crumb, bit
firmă *f* firm
fitil *n* fuse
fiu *m* son
fiu vitreg *m* stepson
fixa *v* fasten, fix
fizică *f* physics
flacără *f* flame
flăcău *m* lad
flămând *adj* hungry
flanc *n* flank
flata *v* flatter
flatare *f* flattery
flaut *n* flute
flecar *adj* talkative
flexibil *adj* flexible
flirta *v* flirt
floare *f* flower
floricele *f* popcorn
flotă *f* fleet
fluctua *v* fluctuate
fluent *adv* fluently
fluid *n* fluid
fluier *n* whistle
fluiera *v* hiss, whistle
flutura *v* flutter
fluture *m* butterfly
fluviu *n* river
flux *n* tide
foame *f* hunger
foamete *f* starvation
foarfecă *f* scissors
foarte *adv* highly, quite
foarte mult *adv* lot
fobie *f* phobia
foc *n* fire, bonfire
foc concentric *n* crossfire

foc de tabără *n* campfire
focă *f* seal
folosi *v* avail, use
folosire *f* disposal
folositor *adj* beneficial
fond *n* fund
fond salarial *n* payroll
forja *v* forge
formă *f* form, shape
formal *adj* formal
formalism *n* red tape
formalitate *f* formality
formare *f* formation
format *n* format
formidabil *adj* formidable
formulă *f* formula
formulare *f* wording
fort *n* fort
forţa *v* force
forţă *f* strength, force
fortăreaţă *f* fortress
forţat *adj* strained
fortifica *v* fortify
fortificat *adj* entrenched
fosfor *n* phosphorus
fosilă *f* fossil
fost *adj* outgoing
fotbal *n* football
fotocopie *f* photocopy
fotograf *m* photographer
fotografia *v* photograph
fotografie *f* photography
fotoliu *n* armchair
fracţie *f* fraction
fractură *f* fracture
fragil *adj* breakable
fragment *n* fragment
frâna *v* brake
frână *f* brake
francheţe *f* frankness
franciză *f* franchise
franctiror *m* sniper
franjuri *n* fringe
Franţa *f* France
franţuzesc *adj* French
frate *m* brother
frate geamăn *m* twin
frate vitreg *m* stepbrother
fraternitate *f* fraternity
frăţesc *adj* brotherly
frăţie *f* brotherhood
frăţie de sânge *f* brethren
frâu *n* rein, curb
fraudă *f* fraud
freca *v* rub
freca cu peria *v* scrape, scrub

frecare *f* friction
frecvent *adj* frequent
frecventa *v* frequent
frecvenţă *f* frequency
fregată *f* frigate
frenetic *adj* frenzied
frenezie *f* frenzy
frică *f* fear
frig *n* coldness
frige *v* roast
frige la grătar *v* grill
frigid *adj* frigid
frigider *n* freezer
fript *adj* charbroiled
friptură *f* roast, steak
frişcă *f* cream
frivol *adj* frivolous
frontal *adj* front
frontieră *f* frontier, border
fruct *n* fruit
fructe de mare *n* seafood
frugal *adj* frugal
frugalitate *f* frugality
frumos *adj* beautiful
frumuseţe *f* beauty
frunte *f* forehead
frunză *f* leaf
frustrare *f* frustration
fugi *v* run away
fugi de *v* flee
fugitiv *m* fugitive
fular *n* muffler
fulger *n* lightning
fulgerare *f* flash
fulgi de ovăz *m* oatmeal
fuma *v* smoke
fumător *m* smoker
funcţie *f* function
funcţionar *m* clerk
fund *n* bottom
fundal *n* background
fundamental *adj* basic
fundaţie *f* foundation
funie *f* rope, cord
fura *v* snitch, steal
furcă *f* pitchfork
furculiţă *f* fork
furie *f* furor, fury, rage
furios *adj* furious, irate
furiş *adj* stealthy
furnal *n* furnace
furnică *f* ant
furniza *v* supply, provide
furnizor *m* supplier
fursec *n* cookie
furt *n* larceny, theft

furtun *n* hose
furtună *f* tempest, storm
furtunos *adj* stormy
fustă *f* skirt
fustă mini *f* miniskirt
fuziona *v* merge
fuziune *f* fusion, merger

G

gâdila *v* tickle
gâdilat *n* tickle
gâdilos *adj* ticklish
gâfâi *v* gasp
găină *f* hen
gaj *n* pledge
gălăgie *f* uproar
galaxie *f* galaxy
galben *adj* yellow
gălbeneală *f* paleness
gălbenuş *n* yolk
găleată *f* bucket, pail
galerie *f* gallery
galon *n* gallon
galopa *v* gallop
galvaniza *v* galvanize
gând *n* thought
gândac *m* beetle, bug
gândi *v* think
gangster *m* gangster
gânguri *v* crow
garaj *n* garage
garanta *v* guarantee
garanţie *f* guarantee
gard *n* fence
garderobă *f* wardrobe
gardian *m* guardian
gargarisi *v* gargle
garnisi *v* garnish
garnitură *f* garnish
garnizoană *f* garrison
garoafă *f* carnation
gâscă *f* goose
găsi *v* find
gâşte *f* geese
gastric *adj* gastric
gât *n* throat, neck
gât de sticlă *n* bottleneck
găti *v* cook
gătit *n* cooking
gaură *f* hole
gaz *n* gas
gazdă *f* host

găzdui *v* lodge
găzduire *f* lodging
gazolină *f* gasoline
gazon *n* sod
geamandură *f* buoy
geamăt *n* groan, moan
geană *f* eyelash
gelos *adj* jealous
gelozie *f* jealousy
gem *n* jam
geme *v* groan, moan
gen *n* gender
genă *f* gene
genera *v* generate
general *m* general
generaliza *v* generalize
generaţie *f* generation
generator *n* generator
generic *adj* generic
generos *adj* lavish
generozitate *f* generosity
genetic *adj* genetic
genial *adj* genial
geniu *n* genius
genocid *n* genocide
gentil *adj* gentle
gentleman *m* gentleman
genunchi *m* knee
geografie *f* geography
geologie *f* geology
geometrie *f* geometry
ger *n* frost
german *adj* German
Germania *f* Germany
germen *m* germ
geros *adj* frosty
gerunziu *n* gerund
gest *n* gesture
gestaţie *f* gestation
gesticula *v* gesticulate
gheară *f* claw
gheată *f* boot
gheaţă *f* ice
gheizer *n* geyser
ghemui *v* crouch
gherilă *f* guerrilla
gheţar *m* glacier
ghiceală *f* guess
ghici *v* guess
ghicitoare *f* riddle
ghid *n* guidebook
ghiftuire *f* glut
ghilotină *f* guillotine
ghimbir *m* ginger
ghindă *f* acorn
ghirlandă *f* garland, wreath

ghiveci *n* flowerpot
gigantic *adj* gigantic
gimnaziu *n* gymnasium
ginecologie *f* gynecology
ginere *m* son-in-law
gingie *f* gum
gira *v* endorse
girafă *f* giraffe
girant *m* guarantor
glacial *adj* freezing, icy
gladiator *m* gladiator
glandă *f* gland
glaspapir *n* sandpaper
gleznă *f* ankle
gloată *f* mob
glob *n* globe
globulă *f* globule
glonţ *n* bullet
glorie *f* glory
glorifica *v* glorify
glorios *adj* glorious
glosar *n* glossary
glucoză *f* glucose
glugă *f* hood
glumă *f* joke
glumi *v* joke
gofră *f* wafer
gol *adj* empty, naked
golf *n* bay, gulf
goli *v* deplete, empty
goliciune *f* emptiness
goni *v* chase away
gorilă *f* gorilla
gospodărie *f* household
gospodină *f* housekeeper
grabă *f* haste
grăbi *v* hurry, hurry up, hasten
grăbit *adj* hasty
grad *n* degree
grădină *f* garden
grădinar *m* gardener
gradual *adj* gradual
grafic *adj* graphic
grajd *n* stable, stall
gram *n* gram
gramatică *f* grammar
granit *n* granite
graniţă *f* boundary
grăpat *adj* harrowing
gras *adj* corpulent, fat, fatty
grăsime *f* fat
grătar *n* broiler, grill
graţie *f* grace
gratifica *v* gratify
graţios *adj* graceful
gratuitate *f* gratuity

grâu *m* wheat
grav *adj* grave
grav *adv* gravely
grava *v* engrave
graviditate *f* pregnancy
gravita *v* gravitate
gravitate *f* gravity
gravură *f* engraving
greaţă *f* nausea
greblă *f* rake
grecesc *adj* Greek
Grecia *f* Greece
grefier *m* recorder
gregar *adj* gregarious
greiere *m* cricket
grenadă *f* grenade
greoi *adj* dull
grepfrut *n* grapefruit
greşeală *f* error, blunder
greşi *v* err, mistake
greşit *adj* mistaken
greu *adj* heavy, hard
greutate *f* weight
grevă *f* strike
gri *adj* grayish
grijă *f* caution, concern
grijuliu *adj* careful
grimasă *f* grimace
grindă *f* beam
grindină *f* hail
gripă *f* flu, influenza
groapă *f* pit
groaznic *adj* gruelling
gros *adj* thick
grosime *f* thickness
grosolan *adj* gross
grotă *f* grotto
grotesc *adj* grotesque
grozav *adj* stunning
grup *n* group, batch
gudron *n* tar
guler *n* collar
gumă *f* eraser
gunoi *n* garbage
gură *f* mouth
gură de furtun *f* nozzle
gust *n* taste
gusta *v* savor, taste
gustos *adj* tasteful, tasty
gută *f* gout
guvern *n* government
guverna *v* govern
guvernantă *f* nanny
guvernator *m* governor

H

haină *f* coat
haine *f* clothes
hăituială *f* chase
halạt *n* gown
halat de baie *n* bathrobe
halbă *f* pint
halucina *v* hallucinate
hamac *n* hammock
hamal *m* porter
hamburger *m* hamburger
han *n* inn
handicap *n* handicap
hanger *n* dagger
haos *n* chaos
haotic *adj* chaotic
harpă *f* harp
harpon *n* harpoon
hartă *f* map, chart
hârtie *f* paper
hărţui *v* harass, hassle
hărţuire *f* harassment
haşiş *n* hashish
hazardat *adj* hazardous
hemoragie *f* hemorrhage
hernie *f* hernia
hidos *adj* hideous
hidraulic *adj* hydraulic
hidrogen *n* hydrogen
hienă *f* hyena
hilar *adj* hilarious
hipnotiza *v* hypnotize
hipnoză *f* hypnosis
hirotonisi *v* ordain
hirotonisire *f* ordination
hoinar *m* wanderer
hol *n* lobby
holeră *f* cholera
holocaust *n* holocaust
homar *m* lobster
hop *n* hitch
hormon *m* hormone
hoţ *m* thief
hotărâre *f* resolution
hotărât *adj* definite
hotel *n* hotel
hrană *f* nutrition
hrăni *v* nourish, nurture
hrănitor *adj* nutritious
huligan *m* hooligan

I

iad *n* hell
iaht *n* yacht
ianuarie *m* January
iapă *f* mare
iar *adv* afresh
iarăşi *adv* again
iarbă *f* grass, herb
iard *m* yard
iarnă *f* winter
iasomie *f* jasmine
icoană *f* icon
ideal *adj* ideal
idee *f* idea
identic *adj* identical
identifica *v* identify
identitate *f* identity
ideologie *f* ideology
idilă *f* affair
idiot *m* idiot
idol *m* idol
idolatrie *f* idolatry
ied *m* kid
ieftin *adj* inexpensive
iepure *m* rabbit
iepure de câmp *m* hare
ierarhie *f* hierarchy
ieri *adv* yesterday
ierta *v* forgive, pardon
iertare *f* forgiveness
iesle *f* manger
ieşi *v* come out, go out
ieşi în afară *v* protrude
ieşire *f* exit, way out
igienă *f* hygiene
ignora *v* ignore
ignorant *adj* ignorant
ignoranţă *f* ignorance
ilegal *adj* unlawful
ilicit *adj* illicit
ilogic *adj* illogical
ilumina *v* illuminate
ilustra *v* illustrate
ilustraţie *f* illustration
ilustru *adj* illustrious
iluzie *f* delusion
imaculat *adj* immaculate
imagina *v* imagine
imaginaţie *f* imagination
imagine *f* image
imatur *adj* immature
imaturitate *f* immaturity
imbatabil *adj* unbeatable
imediat *adv* instantly

imens *adj* immense
imensitate *f* immensity
imigra *v* immigrate
imigrant *m* immigrant
imigraţie *f* immigration
iminent *adj* imminent
imita *v* imitate
imitaţie *f* imitation
imn *n* anthem
imn religios *n* hymn
imobil *adj* immobile
imobiliza *v* immobilize
imoral *adj* immoral
imoralitate *f* immorality
imortal *adj* immortal
imortalitate *f* immortality
impact *n* impact
imparţial *adj* impartial
impecabil *adj* flawless
imperfecţiune *f* imperfection
imperial *adj* imperial
imperialism *n* imperialism
imperiu *n* empire
impermeabil *adj* waterproof
impersonal *adj* impersonal
impertinent *adj* impertinent
impertinenţă *f* impertinence
impetuos *adj* impetuous
implacabil *adj* implacable
implanta *v* implant
implica *v* involve, imply
implicare *f* involvement
implicat *adj* involved
implicaţie *f* implication
implicit *adj* implicit
implora *v* implore, entreat
import *n* importation
importa *v* import
important *adj* significant
importanţă *f* importance
imposibil *adj* impossible
impotent *adj* impotent
impracticabil *adj* impractical
imprecis *adj* imprecise
impresionant *adj* impressive
imprevizibil *adj* unpredictable
imprim *v* impress
imprimantă *f* printer
imprimat *adj* ingrained
imprimerie *f* printing
improbabil *adj* unlikely
improviza *v* improvise
impuls *n* impulse
impulsiv *adj* impulsive
impunător *adj* imposing
impune *v* impose

impunere *f* imposition
impunitate *f* impunity
impur *adj* impure
imuabil *adj* immutable
imun *adj* immune
imunitate *f* immunity
imuniza *v* immunize
inaccesibil *adj* inaccessible
inadaptabil *adj* misfit
inadecvat *adj* warped
inadmisibil *adj* inadmissible
inamic *m* enemy
inapt *adj* disabled
inaugura *v* inaugurate
inaugurare *f* inauguration
incapabil *adj* unable
incapacitate *f* inability
incendia *v* fire
incendiator *m* arsonist
inch *m* inch
inchiziţie *f* inquisition
incident *n* incident
incinera *v* cremate
incintă *f* premises
incitare *f* incitement
incizie *f* incision
include *v* include
incoerent *adj* incoherent
incomod *adj* awkward
incompatibil *adj* incompatible
incompetent *adj* incompetent
incomplet *adj* incomplete
inconsistent *adj* inconsistent
inconstant *adj* unsteady
inconştient *adj* unconscious
incontinenţă *f* incontinence
incorect *adj* incorrect
incorigibil *adj* incorrigible
incredibil *adj* incredible
incult *adj* illiterate
incurabil *adj* incurable
incursiune *f* raid
indecenţă *f* indecency
indecis *adj* undecided
indefinit *adj* indefinite
independent *adj* independent
independenţă *f* independence
indescriptibil *adj* unspeakable
indezirabil *adj* undesirable
indica *v* indicate
indicator *n* marker
indicaţie *f* indication
indice *m* index
indiferent *adj* indifferent
indiferent care *adj* whatever
indiferent dacă *c* whether

indiferent de *adv* regardless
indiferenţă *f* indifference
indigestie *f* indigestion
indirect *adj* indirect
indiscret *adj* indiscreet
indiscreţie *f* indiscretion
indispensabil *adj* indispensable
indispus *adj* indisposed
indisputabil *adj* indisputable
individ *m* fellow
indivizibil *adj* indivisible
indulgent *adj* indulgent
industrie *f* industry
ineficace *adj* ineffective
ineficient *adj* inefficient
inegal *adj* uneven, unequal
inegalitate *f* inequality
inel *n* ring
inevitabil *adj* inevitable
inexact *adj* inaccurate
inexplicabil *adj* inexplicable
infailibil *adj* infallible
infam *adj* infamous
infanterie *f* infantry
infecta *v* infect
infecţie *f* infection
inferior *adj* inferior
infestat *adj* infested
infideliatate *f* infidelity
infiltra *v* infiltrate
infiltrare *f* infiltration
infinit *adj* infinite
infirmerie *f* infirmary
infirmieră *f* nurse
inflamabil *adj* flammable
inflamare *f* inflammation
inflaţie *f* inflation
influenţă *f* influence
informa *v* inform
informator *m* informer
informaţie *f* information
infracţiune *f* infraction
infuzie *f* infusion
ingeniozitate *f* ingenuity
ingera *v* ingest
inginer *m* engineer
ingredient *n* ingredient
inhala *v* inhale
inhiba *v* inhibit
inimaginabil *adj* unthinkable
inimă *f* heart
iniţia *v* initiate
iniţial *adj* initial
iniţiale *f* initials
iniţiativă *f* initiative
injecta *v* inject

injecţie *f* injection
inocent *adj* innocent
inocenţă *f* innocence
inofensiv *adj* harmless
inoportun *adj* untimely
inovaţie *f* innovation
inoxidabil *adj* ruthless
inscripţie *f* inscription
insectă *f* insect
insensibil *adj* insensitive
inseparabil *adj* inseparable
insera *v* insert
inserare *f* insertion
insignă *f* badge
insinua *v* insinuate
insinuare *f* insinuation
insipid *adj* insipid
insista *v* insist
insistent *adj* pushy
insistenţă *f* insistence
insolaţie *f* heatstroke
insolenţă *f* rudeness
insolubil *adj* insoluble
insomnie *f* insomnia
inspecta *v* inspect
inspector *m* inspector
inspecţie *f* inspection
inspira *v* inspire
inspiraţie *f* inspiration
instabil *adj* unstable
instabilitate *f* instability
instala *v* install, settle down
instalare *f* installation
instalator *m* plumber
instantaneu *n* snapshot
instiga *v* instigate
instinct *n* instinct
institui *v* institute
instituţie *f* institution
instructor *m* instructor
instrucţie *f* training
instrui *v* instruct, train
insuficient *adj* insufficient
insulă *f* island
insulta *v* affront, insult
insultă *f* insult
insuportabil *adj* unbearable
insurecţie *f* insurrection
insurgenţă *f* insurgency
integra *v* integrate
integrare *f* integration
integritate *f* integrity
inteligent *adj* intelligent
inteligenţă *f* wit
intens *adj* intense
intensifica *v* intensify

intensitate *f* intensity
intenţie *f* intention
intenţiona *v* intend
intenţionat *adj* deliberate
intenţionat *adv* willfully
intercepta *v* intercept
interdicţie *f* ban
interes *n* interest
interesa *v* concern
interesant *adj* interesting
interesat *adj* interested
interior *adj* inner, interior
interludiu *n* interlude
intermediar *m* intermediary
intern *adj* inland
interna *v* intern
interoga *v* quiz
interpret *m* interpreter
interpreta *v* interpret
interpretare *f* interpretation
intersecta *v* intersect
intersecţie *f* crossroads
interval *n* interval
interveni *v* intervene
intervenţie *f* intervention
interviu *n* interview
interzice *v* prohibit, forbid
interzicere *f* prohibition
intestin *n* intestine
intestine *n* bowels
intestinul gros *n* colon
intim *adj* intimate
intimida *v* intimidate
intimitate *f* intimacy
intoleranţă *f* intolerance
intra *v* come in, go in
intra în *v* enter
intrare *f* entrance
intravenos *adj* intravenous
intrigant *adj* intriguing
intrigă *f* intrigue
intrinsec *adj* intrinsic
introduce *v* introduce
introducere *f* introduction
introvertit *adj* introvert
intrus *m* intruder
intuiţie *f* intuition
inuman *adj* inhuman
inunda *v* flood, inundate
inundare *f* flooding
inutil *adj* useless
invada *v* invade
invadator *m* invader
invalid *m* invalid, cripple
invazie *f* invasion
inventa *v* invent

I

inventar *n* inventory
invenţie *f* invention
invers *adv* conversely
investi *v* invest
investiga *v* investigate
investigaţie *f* investigation
investitor *m* investor
investiţie *f* investment
invidia *v* envy
invidie *f* envy
invidios *adj* envious
invincibil *adj* invincible
invita *v* invite
invitaţie *f* invitation
invizibil *adj* invisible
invoca *v* invoke
iod *n* iodine
ipocrit *adj* hypocrite
ipocrizie *f* hypocrisy
ipotecă *f* mortgage
ipoteză *f* hypothesis
iraţional *adj* irrational
ireal *adj* unreal
irefutabil *adj* irrefutable
ireversibil *adj* irreversible
irezistibil *adj* irresistible
iriga *v* irrigate
irigaţie *f* irrigation
irita *v* irritate
iritant *adj* irritating
Irlanda *f* Ireland
irlandez *adj* Irish
ironic *adj* ironic
ironie *f* irony
irosi *v* waste, lavish
iscusit *adj* skillful
islamic *adj* Islamic
ispăşi *v* atone, expiate
ispăşire *f* expiation
ispită *f* temptation
ispiti *v* tempt
ispititor *adj* enticing
ispravă *f* exploit
isteric *adj* hysterical
isterie *f* hysteria
isteţ *adj* astute, shrewd
istoric *m* historian
istorie *f* history
istovi *v* wear out
istovire *f* exhaustion
istovit *adj* worn-out
Italia *f* Italy
italian *adj* Italian
itinerar *n* itinerary
iubi *v* love
iubit *adj* beloved

iubit *m* lover, sweetheart
iubitor *adj* loving
iudaism *n* Judaism
iulie *m* July
iunie *m* June
ivi *v* loom
iz *n* smack
izbitor *adj* striking
izbucni *v* burst
izbucnire *f* outbreak
izgoni *v* oust, evict
izgonire *f* dismissal
izola *v* insulate, seal off
izolare *f* isolation

Î

îmbarca *v* embark, board
îmbălsăma *v* embalm
îmbătat *adj* intoxicated
îmbătrânit *adj* decrepit
îmbâcsit *adj* stuffy
îmbina *v* join
îmblănit *adj* furry
îmblânzi *v* mitigate, relent
îmbogăţi *v* enrich
îmbrăca *v* clothe, dress
îmbrăcare *f* dressing
îmbrăcăminte *f* clothing
îmbrăţişa *v* embrace
îmbrăţişare *f* embrace
îmbunătăţi *v* improve
îmbunătăţire *f* improvement
îmbutelia *v* bottle
împacheta *v* pack
împăca *v* reconcile, get along
împăca cu *v* settle for
împărat *m* emperor
împărăteasă *f* empress
împărţi *v* share
împiedica *v* hinder, prevent; stumble
împiedicare *f* impediment
împinge *v* push, shove
împingere *f* shove
împleti *v* knit
împlini *v* fulfill
împlinire *f* fulfillment
împodobi *v* adorn
împotmoli *v* bog down
împotmolit *adj* stranded
împotriva *pre* against
împotrivi *v* oppose
împotrivi la *v* withstand

împovăra *v* burden
împovărător *adj* burdensome
împrăştia *v* scatter
împrejurimi *f* surroundings
împreună *adv* together
împrospăta *v* freshen
împrumut *n* loan
împrumuta *v* borrow
împuşca *v* gun down
împuşcătură *f* gunshot
împuţit *adj* stinking
în *pre* in, inside
în aer liber *adv* outdoor
în afară de *adv* aside from
în altă parte *adv* elsewhere
în apropiere *adj* nearby
în avans *adv* beforehand
în comun *adv* jointly
în derivă *adv* adrift
în diagonală *adj* diagonal
în faţă *pre* ahead
în glumă *adv* jokingly
în grabă *adv* hastily
în impas *adj* deadlock
în întregime *adv* completely
în jos *adv* downhill
în jur de *pre* close to
în jurul *pre* around
în linii mari *adv* broadly
în mijlocul *pre* amid
în mod clar *adv* plainly
în mod curent *adv* currently
în mod evident *adv* obviously
în mod firesc *adv* naturally
în mod formal *adv* formally
în mod lin *adv* smoothly
în mod obişnuit *adv* ordinarily
în mod public *adv* publicly
în mod reciproc *adv* mutually
în plus *adj* plus
în plus *adv* else
în prealabil *adv* previously
în primul rând *adv* primarily
în regulă *adv* okay
în schimb *adv* instead
în secret *adv* secretly
în sfârşit *adv* lastly
în silă *adv* reluctantly
în spatele *pre* behind
în special *adv* mainly
în străinătate *adv* overseas
în surplus *adj* overweight
în sus *adv* upwards
în timp ce *c* while
în timpul *pre* during
în ultima vreme *adv* lately

în valoare de *adj* worth
în viitor *adv* hereafter
în zilele noastre *adv* nowadays
înainta *v* proceed
înaintaş *m* precursor
înainte *adv* forward; before
înainte *pre* before
înalt *adj* tall, high
înapoi *adv* back
înapoia *v* give back, return
înarma *v* arm
înarmat *adj* armed
înăbuşi *v* smother, quell, stifle
înălbi *v* bleach
înălbitor *m* bleach
înălţa *v* exalt, upgrade, soar
înălţime *f* height
înăuntru *pre* within
înăuntru *adv* indoor
încadra *v* frame
încarcera *v* incarcerate
încă *adv* still
încăierare *f* skirmish
încălca *v* trespass
încălcare *f* breach
încălţăminte *f* footwear
încălzi *v* heat, warm-up
încălzire *f* heating
încăpăţânare *f* obstinacy
încăpăţânat *adj* stubborn
încărca *v* load
încărcat *adj* laden, loaded
încărcătură *f* cargo
încătuşa *v* handcuff
încâlci *v* embroil
încânta *v* charm, delight
încântare *f* delight
încântător *adj* delightful
incendiere *n* arson
începător *m* beginner
începe *v* start, begin
început *n* beginning
încercare *f* attempt
încercui *v* encircle
încet *adv* slowly
încet *adj* slack
înceta *v* break up, desist, cease
înceta să *v* lay off
încetini *v* slow down
încetinitor *adj* lingering
înceţoşa *v* blur, dim
înceţoşat *adj* blurred
închega *v* curdle
încheia *v* finish, conclude
încheiere *f* closure
închide *v* close, lock, shut

închiria *v* hire, lease
închis *adj* closed
închisoare *f* prison
încins *adj* red-hot
înclina *v* incline
înclinat *adj* slanted
înclinaţie *f* inclination
încolţi *v* germinate
înconjura *v* beset, surround
încordare *f* strain
încordat *adj* uptight
încorona *v* crown
încoronare *f* coronation
încorporat *adj* built-in
încredere *f* trust, faith
încredinţa *v* entrust
încreţi *v* wrinkle
încrezător *adj* confident
încrezut *adj* conceited
încrucişa *v* criss-cross
încrunta *v* frown
încrustat *adj* inlaid
încuraja *v* encourage
încurca *v* confuse
încurcat *adj* puzzling
încurcătură *f* mess, muddle
încuviinţa *v* assent, nod
îndată ce *c* once
îndatorat *adv* in depth
îndatorire *f* duty
îndeaproape *adv* closely
îndemânare *f* know-how
îndemânatic *adj* handy
îndemn *n* urge
îndemna *v* goad, spur
îndepărta *v* remove, rid of, pull out
îndepărtare *f* removal
îndepărtat *adj* faraway
îndeplini *v* achieve, perform
îndeplinire *f* achievement
îndoctrina *v* indoctrinate
îndoi *v* redouble, bow, fold
îndoială *f* doubt
îndoielnic *adj* questionable
îndoitură *f* downturn
îndopa *v* cram
îndrazni *v* dare
îndrăzneală *f* audacity
îndrăzneţ *adj* daring
îndrepta *v* straighten out
îndreptăţi *v* justify
îndulci *v* sweeten
îndupleca *v* coax
îndura *v* endure
îndurare *f* mercy
îndurător *adj* merciful

îneca *v* choke, drown
înfăşura *v* wrap
înfânge *v* vanquish
înfige *v* stick
înfiinţa *v* set up
înfiorător *adj* appalling
înflori *v* blossom, flourish
înflorire *f* heyday
înfofoli *v* muffle
înfometa *v* starve
înfometat *adj* emaciated
înfrâna *v* refrain, rein
înfrângere *f* defeat
înfricoşat *adj* daunting
înfrumuseţa *v* beautify
înfuleca *v* gobble
înfuria *v* infuriate
îngăduinţă *f* leniency
îngăduitor *adj* lenient
îngăima *v* falter
îngâmfat *adj* cocky
îngenunchea *v* kneel
îngenunchia *v* genuflect
înger *m* angel
înghesui *v* squeeze in, squeeze up
îngheţa *v* chill, freeze
îngheţat *adj* frozen
îngheţată *f* ice cream
înghionti *v* prod
înghiţi *v* gulp, swallow
înghiţire *f* intake
înghiţitură *f* gulp
îngrădire *f* enclosure
îngrămădi *v* heap, crowd, mob
îngrăşa *v* fatten
îngriji *v* look after, attend
îngriji de *v* care for
îngrijitor *m* caretaker
îngropa *v* bury
îngroşa *v* thicken
îngrozi *v* appall, horrify
îngrozitor *adj* horrendous
îngust *adj* narrow
înjumătăţi *v* halve
înjunghia *v* stab
înjunghiere *f* stab
înjura *v* cuss
înlănţui *v* chain
înlănţuire *f* shackle
înlătura *v* discard
înlocui *v* substitute
înlocuire *f* replacement
înlocuitor *m* substitute
înmormântare *f* burial
înmulţi *v* multiply
înnăscut *adj* innate

înnebunit *adj* distraught
înnobila *v* dignify
înnorat *adj* cloudy
înot *n* swimming
înota *v* swim
înotător *m* swimmer
înrăutăţi *v* worsen
înregistra *v* register, check in
înregistrare *f* registration
înrola *v* enlist, enroll
înrolare *f* enrollment
înroşi *v* redden
înrudire *f* kinship
înrudit *adj* akin
însăila *v* stitch
însăilare *f* stitch
însărcinată *adj* pregnant
însăşi *pro* herself
însângerat *adj* gory
însemna *v* earmark
însetat *adj* thirsty
însorit *adj* sunny
însoţire *f* attendance
însoţitor *m* follower
înspăimânta *v* dismay, terrify
înspăimântat *adj* dreaded
înstărit *adj* well-to-do
înstrăinat *adj* estranged
înşela *v* deceive, delude
înşelăciune *f* deceit
înşelător *adj* tricky
înşelătorie *f* fallacy
înşfăcare *f* gripe
înşira pe aţă *v* thread
înşişi *pro* themselves
înşuruba *v* screw
întări *v* harden, toughen
întăriri *f* reinforcements
întâlni *v* encounter, meet
întâlnire *f* meeting
întâmpina *v* greet
întâmpla *v* happen
întâmplare *f* happening
întâmplător *adj* coincidental
întârzia *v* delay
întârziat *adj* belated
întârziere *f* delay
întemeietor *m* founder
întemniţa *v* imprison
întinde *v* stretch, sprawl, spread
întindere *f* stretch, width
întineri *v* rejuvenate
întins *adj* outstretched
întoarce *v* turn, go back
întoarcere *f* return
întors pe dos *adv* inside out

întotdeauna *adv* always
într-adevăr *adv* indeed, really
între *pre* among, between
între timp *adv* meantime
întreba *v* interrogate
întreba ceva *v* wonder
întrebare *f* question
întrece *v* outdo, surpass
întredeschis *adj* ajar
întreg *adj* whole
întremare *f* refreshment
întreprinde *v* undertake
întrerupe *v* interrupt, cut off, break off
întrerupere *f* interruption
întreţese *v* warp
întreţinere *f* upkeep
întrista *v* sadden
întristare *f* chagrin
într-o zi *adv* someday
întrucât *c* inasmuch as
întrupa *v* embody
întuneca *v* tarnish; darken
întunecat *adj* dark
întunecos *adj* gloomy, murky
întuneric *n* darkness
înţelege *v* understand
înţelege greşit *v* misunderstand
înţelegere *f* understanding
înţelepciune *f* wisdom
înţelept *adj* judicious
înţeles *n* meaning
înţepa *v* prick
înţepătură *f* puncture
înţepeni *v* stiffen
înţepenire *f* stiffness
învălmăşeală *f* hustle
învălmăşi *v* huddle
învălui *v* envelop, wrap up
învăluit *adj* shrouded
învăţa *v* learn
învăţat *adj* learned
învăţat *m* scholar
învăţătură *f* learning
învârti *v* revolve, spin
învecina *v* adjoin
învecina cu *v* border on
învecinat *adj* adjoining
înveliş *n* wrapping
înveseli *v* cheer, cheer up
învia *v* revive
înviere *f* resurrection
învineţi *v* bruise
învingător *m* victor
învinge *v* defeat
învinovăţi *v* blame
învins *adj* prostrate

Î

învins *m* loser
înviorant *adj* exhilarating
învoială *f* terms
înzestrat *adj* gifted

J

jachetă *f* jacket
jaf *n* robbery, holdup
jaguar *m* jaguar
jantă *f* rim
japonez *adj* Japanese
Japonia *f* Japan
jartieră *f* garter
jefui *v* rob, mug
jefuitor *m* hijacker
jeratic *n* embers
jerseu *n* jersey
jgheab *n* gutter
joc *n* game, play
joi *f* Thursday
jongler *m* juggler
jos *adv* down
jos *adj* low
jovial *adj* jovial
juca *v* play
jucărie *f* toy
jucător *m* player
jucăuş *adj* playful
judeca greşit *v* misjudge
judecată *f* judgment
judecător *m* judge
jug *n* yoke
jumătate *f* half
junghi *n* pang
junglă *f* jungle
jupui *v* skin
jura *v* swear
jurământ *n* oath
juraţi *m* jury
jurist *m* lawyer
jurnal *n* diary
jurnalist *m* journalist
just *adj* just
justifica *v* warrant
justiţie *f* justice
juvenil *adj* juvenile

K

karate *n* karate
kilogram *n* kilogram
kilometru *m* kilometer
kilowatt *m* kilowatt

L

la *pre* at, to
la bord *adv* aboard
la care *c* whereupon
la început *adv* initially
la întâmplare *adv* randomly
la modă *adj* fashionable
la o parte *adv* aside
la parter *adv* downstairs
la revedere *n* farewell
la sută *adv* percent
labă *f* paw
laba piciorului *f* foot
labirint *n* labyrinth, maze
laborator *n* lab
lac *n* varnish, lake
lacăt *n* padlock, lock
lăcătuş *m* locksmith
lacom *adj* greedy
lacom *m* glutton
lăcomie *f* greed
lacrimă *f* tear
lăcustă *f* locust
ladă *f* chest
lagună *f* lagoon
lalea *f* tulip
lamă *f* blade
lămâie *f* lemon
lamentare *f* lament
lampă *f* lamp
lână *f* wool
lâncezi *v* languish
lângă *pre* by
lansa *v* launch
lansa pe apă *v* float
lansare *f* launch
lanţ *n* chain
lapte *n* milk
lăptos *adj* milky
larg *adj* wide, broad
lărgi *v* enlarge
laringe *n* larynx
laş *m* coward
lăsa de o parte *v* put away

lăsa liber *v* unleash
lăsa moştenire *v* bequeath
lăsa pe spate *v* lean back
lăsa să iasă *v* let out
lăsa să plece *v* let go
laser *n* laser
laşitate *f* cowardice
laţ *n* noose
lateral *adj* lateral
lateral *adv* sideways
lăţime *f* breadth
latitudine *f* latitude
lătra *v* bark
lătrat *n* bark
laudă *f* praise
lăuda *v* praise
lăuda cu *v* boast
lavabil *adj* washable
laxativ *adj* laxative
leagăn *n* cradle
lebădă *f* swan
lebădoi *m* cob
lecţie *f* lesson
lectură *f* reading
lefter *adj* penniless
leg *adj* lawful
lega *v* tie, bind
lega la ochi *v* blindfold
legal *adj* legal
legalitate *f* legality
legaliza *v* legalize
legăna *v* dangle, wobble, swing
legănare *f* swing
legat la ochi *m* blindfold
legătură *f* liaison
lege *f* law, statute
legendă *f* legend
leghe *f* league
legifera *v* legislate
legislaţie *f* legislation
legislator *m* lawmaker
legislatură *f* legislature
legitim *adj* legitimate
legiune *f* legion
legumă *f* vegetable
lemne *n* lumber
lemne de foc *n* firewood
lene *f* laziness
leneş *adj* lazy
lenjerie *f* lingerie
lenjerie intimă *f* underwear
lent *adj* slow
lentilă *f* lens
leoaică *f* lioness
leopard *m* leopard
lepră *f* leprosy

L

lepros *m* leper
lesă *f* leash
leşin *n* faint
leşina *v* pass out, faint
lespede *f* slab
letal *adj* lethal
leu *m* lion
leucemie *f* leukemia
liber *adj* loose, free
libertate *f* freedom
librar *m* bookseller
librărie *f* bookstore
licări *v* gleam, twinkle
licărire *f* flicker, gleam
lichid *n* liquid
lichida *v* liquidate
lichidare *f* liquidation
lichior *n* liqueur
licita *v* bid
licitaţie *f* auction
ligament *n* ligament
limbă *f* tongue, language
limita *v* confine
limită *f* limit
limonadă *f* lemonade
limpede *adj* clear-cut, plain
lingav *adj* choosy
linge *v* lick
lingou *n* ingot
lingură *f* spoon
linguriţă *f* teaspoon
linie *f* line
linie aeriană *f* airline
linie de coastă *f* coastline
linie de frontieră *adj* borderline
linie de ghidare *f* guidelines
linişte *f* quietness
linişti *v* appease, calm down
linişţire *f* sedation
liniştit *adj* still
liniuţă *f* hyphen
linşa *v* lynch
linte *f* lentil
linţoliu *n* shroud
linx *m* lynx
lipi *v* glue, paste, adhere
lipici *n* glue
lipicios *adj* sticky
lipitoare *f* leech
lipsă *f* lack, shortage
lipsă de unitate *f* disunity
lipsit de *adj* devoid
lipsit de apărare *adj* defenseless
lipsit de griji *adj* carefree
lirică *f* poetry
lista *v* list

listă *f* backlog, list
listă electorală *f* poll
litanie *f* litany
literă *f* letter
literă măruntă *f* small print
literal *adj* literal
literat *adj* literate
literatură *f* literature
litieră *f* litter
litigiu *n* litigation
litoral *adj* seaside
litru *m* liter, litre
liturghie *f* liturgy
livadă *f* orchard
livid *adj* livid
livră *f* pound
lizibil *adj* legible
loc *n* lieu, place
loc liber *n* vacancy
local *adj* local
localiza *v* localize
localizat *adj* located
locatar *m* inmate
locaţie *f* location
locotenent *m* lieutenant
locui *v* reside, dwell
locuibil *adj* habitable
locuinţă *f* dwelling
locuitor *m* inhabitant
logic *adj* logical
logică *f* logic
logodi *v* engage
logodit *adj* engaged
logodnic *m* fiancé
loial *adj* loyal
longitudine *f* longitude
lopată *f* shovel
lopăţică *f* splint
lord *m* lord
loterie *f* lottery
loţiune *f* lotion
lovi *v* hit, batter
lovi cu ciocul *v* peck
lovitură *f* blow, knock
lovitură de stat *f* coup
lozincă *f* slogan
lozul cel mare *n* jackpot
lua *v* take away
lua crema *v* skim
lua pe sus *v* whirl
lubrifiere *f* lubrication
lucarnă *f* skylight
lucios *adj* glossy
luciu *n* gloss
luciu de pantofi *n* shoepolish
lucrat manual *adj* handmade

lucruri *n* belongings
lugubru *adj* bleak
lui *adj* his
lumânare *f* candle
lume *f* people, world
lumesc *adj* worldly
lumina *v* enlighten, brighten
lumină *f* light, beacon
luminos *adj* luminous
lună *f* moon
lună de miere *f* honeymoon
lunar *adv* monthly
lunecos *adj* elusive
lung *adj* long
lungi *v* lengthen
lungime *f* length
luni *f* Monday
lup *m* wolf
lupta *v* battle, fight
luptă *f* combat, fight
luptător *m* fighter
lupte *f* wrestling
lustru *n* polish
lustrui *v* polish
lux *n* luxury
luxa *v* sprain
luxos *adj* luxurious
luxuriant *adj* lush

M

mac *m* poppy
măcelar *m* butcher
măcelărie *f* butchery
machiaj *n* makeup
măduvă *f* bone marrow
măgar *m* donkey
magazin *n* shop
magic *adj* magical
magician *m* magician
magie *f* magic
magistrat *m* magistrate
magnat *m* tycoon
magnet *m* magnet
magnetic *adj* magnetic
magnetism *n* magnetism
magnetofon *n* tape recorder
magnitudine *f* magnitude
mahal *m* slum
mai *m* May
mai ales *adv* chiefly, mostly
mai bun *adj* better
mai degrabă *adv* rather
mai departe *adv* farther, further
mai jos *adv* below
mai mult *adj* more

mai mulţi *adj* several
mai puţin *adj* fewer, less
mai târziu *adv* later
maiestate *f* majesty
maiestuos *adj* majestic
maimuţă *f* ape, monkey
mâine *adv* tomorrow
maistru *m* foreman
major *adj* major
majordom *m* butler
majoritate *f* majority
majusculă *f* capital letter
malarie *f* malaria
malnutriţie *f* malnutrition
maltrata *v* maul
maltratare *f* mistreatment
mamă *f* mom, mother
mamă vitregă *f* stepmother
mămică *f* mummy
mamifer *n* mammal
mamut *m* mammoth
mână *f* hand
mână de lucru *f* manpower
manager *m* manager
mănăstire *f* monastery, convent
mănăstiresc *adj* monastic
mânca *v* dine, eat, feed
mâncare *f* food
mâncărime *f* itchiness
mandarină *f* tangerine
mandat *n* mandate
mandat poştal *n* money order
mândrie *f* pride
mândru *adj* proud
mânecă *f* sleeve
manechin *n* dummy
mâner rotund *n* knob
manevră *f* maneuver
mângâia *v* caress, fondle
mângâiere *f* caress, pat
maniac *adj* maniac
mânie *f* wrath
maniere *f* manners
manierism *n* mannerism
manifest *n* leaflet
manifesta *v* manifest
manipula *v* manipulate
manivelă *f* crank
mansardă *f* attic
manşetă *f* cuff
mantie *f* cloak
manual *adj* manual
manual *n* handbook
mânui *v* operate
mănunchi *n* bunch
mănuşă *f* glove

manuscris *n* manuscript
mânz *m* colt
măr *n* apple
mârâi *v* growl
marca *v* mark, score
marcă *f* brand
marca fabricii *f* trademark
marchiză *f* awning
mare *adj* big, great
mare *f* sea
mareşal *m* marshal
măreţ *adj* magnificent
măreţie *f* greatness
marfă *f* merchandise
margaretă *f* daisy
marginal *adj* marginal
margine *f* margin, brink
mări *v* magnify
mărime *f* size
marin *adj* marine
marina *v* marinate
marină *f* navy
marinar *m* sailor
mărinimie *f* bounty
marionetă *f* puppet
mărire *f* enlargement
mărişor *adj* sizable
marmură *f* marble
maron *adj* brown
marş *n* march
marş de grevă *n* walkout
mărşălui *v* march
Marte *m* Mars
marţi *f* Tuesday
martie *m* March
martir *m* martyr
martor *m* witness
martor ocular *m* eyewitness
mărturie *f* testimony
mărturisi *v* confess, confide
mărturisire *f* confession
mărturisit *adj* avowed
marxist *adj* marxist
masa *v* massage
masă *f* table
masă de oameni *f* meal
masacru *n* massacre
masaj *n* massage
mască *f* mask
mascul *m* male
masculin *adj* masculine
măsea *f* molar
maseza *f* masseuse
maşină *f* machine
masiv *adj* massive
măslină *f* olive

masochism *n* masochism
masor *m* masseur
măsura *v* gauge
măsură *f* measurement
maţ *n* gut
mătănii *f* rosary
mătase *f* silk
matematică *f* math
material *n* material
materialism *n* materialism
materie *f* matter
matern *adj* maternal
maternitate *f* maternity
matlasa *v* quit
mătreaţă *f* dandruff
matur *adj* mature
mătura *v* sweep
mătură *f* broom
maturitate *f* maturity
matuşă *f* aunt
maxim *adj* maximum
maximă *f* maxim
mazăre *f* green bean
mâzgăli *v* scribble
mecanic *m* mechanic
mecanism *n* mechanism
mecaniza *v* mechanize
medalie *f* medal
medalion *n* medallion
media *v* mediate
mediator *m* mediator
medicaţie *f* medication
medicină *f* medicine
medicinal *adj* medicinal
medie *f* average
medieval *adj* medieval
mediocritate *f* mediocrity
mediocru *adj* mediocre
medita *v* meditate
meditaţie *f* meditation
mediu *n* environment
megafon *n* loudspeaker
melancolie *f* melancholy
melc *m* snail
melodic *adj* melodic
melodie *f* melody, tune
membrană *f* membrane
membru *m* member, limb
memento *n* reminder
memora *v* memorize
memorabil *adj* memorable
memorandum *n* memo
memorie *f* memory
memorii *f* memoirs
meningită *f* meningitis
meniu *n* menu

M

menopauză *f* menopause
mentă *f* mint
mental *adj* mental
mentalitate *f* mentality
menţine *v* maintain, keep up, subsist
menţiona *v* mention
menţiune *f* mention
mercur *n* mercury
merge *v* go
merge în sus *v* go up
merge înainte *v* go ahead
merit *n* merit
merita *v* deserve
merituos *adj* deserving
meşă *f* hairpiece
mesager *m* messenger
mesaj *n* message
meschin *adj* stingy
Mesia *m* Messiah
mesteca *v* chew
meşteşugar *m* craftsman
metaforă *f* metaphor
metal *n* metal
metalic *adj* metallic
meteor *m* meteor
meticulos *adj* meticulous
metodă *f* method
metodic *adj* methodical
metric *adj* metric
metropolă *f* metropolis
metrou *n* subway
metru *m* meter
meu *adj* my
mexican *adj* Mexican
mic *adj* small, petty
mic dejun *n* breakfast
micime *f* pettiness
microb *m* microbe
microfon *n* microphone
microscop *n* microscope
microundă *f* microwave
micşora *v* lessen, downsize, dwindle
mie *adj* thousand
miel *m* lamb
miercuri *f* Wednesday
miere *f* honey
miez *n* core
miezul nopţii *n* midnight
miezul verii *n* midsummer
migdală *f* almond
migra *v* migrate
migrenă *f* migraine
mijloc *n* middle
milă *f* mile
mileniu *n* millennium
miliard *n* billion

miliardar *m* billionaire
miligram *n* milligram
milimetru *m* millimeter
milion *n* million
milionar *m* millionaire
milos *adj* compassionate
mima *v* mime
mină *f* mine
mincinos *adj* deceitful
minciună *f* falsehood, lie
miner *m* miner
mineral *n* mineral
minereu *n* ore
minge *f* ball
miniatură *f* miniature
minim *n* minimum
minimaliza *v* minimize
minion *adj* petite
minister *n* ministry
ministru *m* minister
minor *adj* minor
minoritate *f* minority
mintal *adv* mentally
minte *f* mind
minţi *v* lie
minunat *adj* gorgeous
minune *f* wonder
minus *adj* minus
minut *n* minute
miop *adj* nearsighted
miracol *n* miracle
miraculos *adj* miraculous
miraj *n* mirage
mire *m* bridegroom
mirean *m* layman
mireasă *f* bride
mirodenie *f* spice
miros *n* odor
mirosi *v* smell
mirositor *adj* smelly
mişca *v* move
mişcare *f* motion, move
misionar *m* missionary
misiune *f* mission
mister *n* mystery
misterios *adj* mysterious
mistic *adj* mystic
mistifica *v* mystify
mit *n* myth
mită *f* bribe, kickback
mititel *adj* tiny
mitralieră *f* machine gun
mitui *v* bribe
mixer *n* mixer
mizerabil *adj* despicable
mizerie *f* misery

mlaştină *f* swamp, bog
mlăştinos *adj* swamped
moale *adj* soft, tender
moară *f* mill
moară de vânt *f* windmill
moarte *f* death
moaşă *f* midwife
mobil *adj* mobile
mobila *v* furnish
mobilă *f* furniture
mobilier *n* furnishings
mobiliza *v* mobilize
mod *n* manner, mode
model *n* model, pattern
modela *v* shape
moderat *adj* moderate
moderaţie *f* moderation
modern *adj* modern
moderniza *v* modernize
modest *adj* modest
modestie *f* modesty
modifica *v* modify
modul *n* module
mohorât *adj* sullen
moleculă *f* molecule
molfăi *v* munch
moliciune *f* softness
molie *f* moth
molipsitor *adj* infectious
moloz *n* debris
momeală *f* enticement
moment *n* moment
momi *v* entice, lure
monarh *m* monarch
monarhie *f* monarchy
mondial *adj* worldwide
monedă *f* currency, coin
monogamie *f* monogamy
monolog *n* monologue
monopol *n* monopoly
monopoliza *v* monopolize
monoton *adj* monotonous
monotonie *f* monotony
monstru *m* monster
monstruos *adj* monstrous
montare *f* setup
monument *n* monument
monumental *adj* monumental
moral *adj* moral, ethical
morală *f* ethics, morality
morcov *m* carrot
morfină *f* morphine
mormăi *v* grumble
morman *n* heap
mormânt *n* grave, tomb
morsă *f* walrus

mort *adj* dead, lifeless
mortal *adj* deadly
mortalitate *f* mortality
moschee *f* mosque
moşie *f* estate
moşier *m* landlord
mosor *n* spool, reel
moşteni *v* inherit
moştenire *f* inheritance
moştenitoare *f* heiress
moştenitor *m* heir
mostră *f* sample
motel *n* motel
motiv *n* motive
motiva *v* motivate
moto *n* motto
motocicletă *f* motorcycle
motor *n* engine, motor
mozaic *n* mosaic
mucegai *n* mildew, mold
mucegăi *v* mold
mucegăit *adj* mouldy
muchie *f* edge
mucozitate *f* mucus
muia *v* soften
mult *adv* much
mulţi *adj* many
multilateral *adj* versatile
mulţime *f* multitude
mulţime de *adj* lots
multiplicare *f* multiplication
multiplu *adj* multiple
mulţumi *v* content
mulţumiri *f* thanks
mulţumit *adj* content
muncă *f* work, labor
munci *v* work
muncitor *m* worker
muniţie *f* ammunition
muniţii *f* munitions
munte *m* mountain
muntos *adj* mountainous
mură *f* blackberry
murdar *adj* dirty, filthy
murdări *v* pollute, soil
murdărie *f* grime, filth
muri *v* die
muribund *adj* dying
murmur *n* murmur
muşca *v* bite
muşcătură *f* nip, bite
muşchi *m* moss, muscle
muştar *n* mustard
mustaţă *f* mustache
musulman *adj* Muslim
mut *adj* mute, dumb

muta *v* dislodge; move out
mutare *f* relocation
mutila *v* cripple, maim
muzeu *n* museum
muzică *f* music
muzician *m* musician

N

naiv *adj* naïve, gullible
naos *n* nave
nară *f* nostril
narcotic *n* narcotic
nărui *v* raze
nas *n* nose
născoci *v* fabricate
născocire *f* concoction
născut *adj* born
naşte *v* breed
naştere *f* birth
nasture *m* button
nătâng *adj* dummy
naţional *adj* national
naţionaliate *f* nationality
naţionaliza *v* nationalize
naţiune *f* nation
nativ *adj* native
natură *f* nature
natural *adj* natural
naufragiat *m* castaway
naufragiu *n* shipwreck
năvăli în *v* burst into
naviga *v* navigate
navigaţie *f* navigation
navlosi *v* charter
navlosire *f* charter
năzui la *v* long for
ne *pro* ourselves
neadevărat *adj* untrue
neam *n* ancestry
neaşteptat *adj* unexpected
neataşat *adj* unattached
neatent *adj* oblivious
neatins *adj* intact
nebănuitor *adj* unsuspecting
nebun *adj* crazy, insane
nebun *m* madman
nebunesc *adj* frantic
nebuneşte *adv* madly
nebunie *f* madness
necăji *v* afflict, molest, grieve
necăsătorit *adj* unmarried
necaz *n* distress, grief

necazuri *n* woes
necesar *adj* necessary
necesita *v* necessitate
necesitate *f* necessity
nechibzuit *adj* unwise
necinste *f* dishonesty
necinstit *adj* dishonest
neciteţ *adj* illegible
neclar *adj* hazy
neclintit *adj* inflexible
necontestat *adj* undisputed
necredincios *adj* unfaithful
necredinţă *f* disloyalty
necruţător *adj* relentless
necunoscut *adj* unknown
nedatat *adj* timeless
nedrept *adj* unjust
nedreptate *f* injustice
nedureros *adj* painless
neechivoc *adj* unequivocal
needucat *adj* uneducated
nefamiliar *adj* unfamiliar
nefavorabil *adj* unfavorable
nefericire *f* unhappiness
nefericit *adj* unhappy
nefertil *adj* infertile
nefolosire *f* disuse
nefondat *adj* unfounded
nefumător *m* nonsmoker
neg *m* wart
nega *v* deny
negare *f* denial
negativ *adj* negative
neglija *v* neglect
neglijare *f* neglect
neglijent *adj* careless
neglijenţă *f* negligence
negocia *v* negotiate
negociere *f* negotiation
negru *adj* black
negustor *m* merchant
nehotărâre *f* indecision
nehotărât *adj* indecisive
neimportant *adj* insignificant
neînarmat *adj* unarmed
neîncetat *adj* incessant
neîncetat *adv* ceaselessly
neîncredere *f* disbelief
neîncrezător *adl* doubtful
neîndreptăţit *adj* unjustified
neîndurător *adj* heartless
neîntemeiat *adj* groundless
neîntrerupt *adj* ongoing
neizbutit *adj* unsuccessful
nejust *adj* unfair
nelegitim *adj* illegitimate

nelegiuire *f* misdemeanor
nelimitat *adj* unlimited
nelinişte *f* unrest, worry
neliniştit *adj* uneasy
nemăsurat *adj* incalculable
nemeritat *adj* undeserved
nemişcat *adj* motionless
nemobilat *adj* unfurnished
nemulţumire *f* displeasure
nemulţumit *adj* dissatisfied
nenorocire *f* adversity
nenorocit *adj* miserable
nenorocos *adj* unlucky
nenumărat *adj* countless
neobişnuit *adj* unusual
neobosit *adj* tireless
neobservat *adj* unnoticed
neocupat *adj* vacant
neoficial *adv* unofficially
nepărtinitor *adj* unbiased
nepăsător *adj* reckless
nepătat *adj* spotless
neplăcut *adj* unpleasant
nepoliteţe *f* disrespect
nepoliticos *adj* impolite
nepopular *adj* unpopular
nepot de bunic *m* grandson
nepot de unchi *m* nephew
nepotrivire *f* disparity
nepotrivit *adj* improper
nepretenţios *adj* down-to-earth
nepreţuit *adj* invaluable
neprevăzut *adj* unforeseen
nepriceput *adj* inexperienced
neprietenos *adj* unfriendly
neprotejat *adj* unprotected
neputincios *adj* helpless
nerăbdare *f* eagerness, impatience
nerăbdător *adj* impatient, jumpy
nerealist *adj* unrealistic
neregular *adj* irregular
nerelevant *adj* irrelevant
nerentabil *adj* unprofitable
neruşinat *adj* shameless
nerv *m* nerve
nervos *adj* nervous
nesănătos *adj* unhealthy
nesăţios *adj* insatiable
neserios *adj* unreliable
nesfârşit *adj* endless
nesigur *adj* uncertain
nesiguranţă *f* insecurity
nesincer *adj* insincere
nesinceritate *f* insincerity
nesocoti *v* disregard
nestăpânit *adj* addictive

nestatornic *adj* restless
nestemată *f* gem
nesuferit *adj* obnoxious
nesupunere *f* disobedience
nesupus *adj* disobedient
neted *adj* even, smooth
netezi *v* smooth
netezime *f* smoothness
neutraliza *v* neutralize
neutru *adj* neutral
nevătămat *adj* unhurt
nevinovat *adj* blameless
nevoiaş *adj* needy
nevoie *f* need
nevrotic *adj* neurotic
nicăieri *adv* nowhere
nichel *n* nickel
nici *adv* neither
nici *c* nor
nici unul *adj* neither
niciodată *adv* never
nicotină *f* nicotine
nicovală *f* anvil
nimeni *pro* nobody
nimic *n* nothing
nimici *v* annihilate
nimicire *f* annihilation
ninge *v* snow
ninsoare *f* snowfall
nisip *n* sand
nişte *adj* some
nitui *v* clinch, rivet
nituit *adj* riveting
nivel *n* level
nivela *v* level
noapte *f* night
nobil *adj* noble
nobil *m* nobleman
nobleţe *f* nobility
nocturn *adj* nocturnal
nod *n* knot
noi *pro* we
noiembrie *m* November
nomad *m* migrant
nonsens *n* nonsense
nor *m* cloud
noră *f* daughter-in-law
nord *n* north
nord-est *n* northeast
nordic *adj* northern
normă *f* norm
normal *adj* normal
normal *adv* normally
normaliza *v* normalize
noroc *n* luck, fortune
norocos *adj* fortunate, lucky

noroi *n* mud
noroios *adj* muddy
Norvegia *f* Norway
norvegian *adj* Norwegian
nostalgic *adj* homesick
nostalgie *f* nostalgia
nostim *adj* cute, funny
nostru *adj* our
nota *v* write down, note
notă de subsol *f* footnote
notar *m* notary
notaţie *f* notation
notificare *f* notification
noţiune *f* notion
notoriu *adj* notorious
nou *adj* new
nouă *adj* nine
nouă *pro* us
nouăsprezece *adj* nineteen
nouăzeci *adj* ninety
nou-născut *m* newborn
nou-nouţ *adj* brand-new
noutate *f* novelty
nou-venit *m* newcomer
novice *m* novice
nu *adv* not
nu ajunge *v* run out
nu asculta *v* disobey
nuanţă *f* nuance
nucă *f* walnut, nut
nucă de cocos *f* coconut
nuclear *adj* nuclear
nud *adj* nude
nudism *n* nudism
nudist *m* nudist
nuditate *f* nudity
nul *adj* null
numai *adv* only, solely
număr *n* number
număr prim *adj* prime
nume *n* name
nume de familie *n* last name
numeros *adj* numerous
numi *v* appoint
numire *f* appointment
numitor *m* denominator
nuntă *f* wedding
nupţial *adj* bridal

O

oaie *f* sheep
oală *f* pot
oameni *m* folks
oarecum *adv* somewhat
oaspete *m* guest
oază *f* oasis
obez *adj* obese
obicei *n* habit
obiect *n* object, thing
obiecta *v* object
obiecţie *f* objection
obiectiv *n* objective
obişnui cu *v* accustom
obişnuit *adj* customary
obişnuit cu *adj* used to
oblic *adj* oblique
obliga *v* obligate
obligaţie *f* commitment
obligator *adj* binding
obligatoriu *adj* compulsory, obligatory
oboseală *f* fatigue
obosit *adj* tired, weary
obositor *adj* tiresome
obraz *m* cheek
obraznic *adj* insolent
obscen *adj* obscene, lewd
obscenitate *f* obscenity
obscur *adj* obscure
obscuritate *f* obscurity
obseda *v* obsess
observa *v* observe, notice
observaţie *f* observation
observator *n* observatory
obsesie *f* obsession
obstacol *n* obstacle
obţine *v* obtain
ocară *f* scolding
ocărî *v* chide, scold
ocazie *f* occasion
ocazional *adv* occasionally
ocean *n* ocean
ochelari *m* eyeglasses
ochi *m* eye
ocol *n* bypass, detour
ocoli *v* bypass
octombrie *m* October
ocult *adj* occult
ocupa *v* occupy
ocupa de *v* cater to
ocupant *m* occupant
ocupat *adj* busy
ocupaţie *f* occupation

odihnă *f* repose, rest
odihni *v* repose
odihnitor *adj* restful
odios *adj* odious
odisee *f* odyssey
odraslă *f* offspring
ofensa *v* offend
ofensă *f* offense
ofensiv *adj* offensive
oferi *v* offer
ofertă *f* offer, offering
oficia *v* officiate
oficial *adj* official
oficiu poştal *n* post office
ofiţer *m* officer
oftat *n* sigh
ogar *m* greyhound
oglindă *f* mirror
oglindi *v* reflect
Olanda *f* Holland
olandez *adj* Dutch
olimpiadă *f* olympics
om *m* man
omagiu *n* homage
omenire *f* mankind
omidă *f* caterpillar
omisiune *f* omission
omite *v* omit
omletă *f* omelette
omolog *m* counterpart
omorî *v* beef up
omucidere *f* homicide
ondulat *adj* curly, wavy
onoare *f* honor
opac *adj* opaque
opări *v* scald
operă *f* opera
operă de artă *f* artwork
operaţie *f* operation
opinie *f* opinion
opiu *n* opium
oportun *adj* opportune
oportunitate *f* opportunity
opoziţie *f* opposition
opri *v* halt, stop
oprire *f* stop
oprit *adj* standstill
opt *adj* eight
opta pentru *v* opt for
optic *adj* optical
optician *m* optician
optimism *n* optimism
optimist *adj* optimistic
opţional *adj* optional
opţiune *f* option
optsprezece *adj* eighteen

optzeci *adj* eighty
opulenţă *f* opulence
opune *v* antagonize, counter
opus *adj* opposite
oră *f* hour
oracol *n* oracle
orar *n* schedule
oraş *n* city, town
orb *adj* blind
orbeşte *adv* blindly
orbi *v* blind
orbire *f* blindness
orbită *f* orbit
orbitor *adj* dazzling
orchestră *f* orchestra
ordin *n* order
ordonat *adj* tidy
oreion *n* mumps
orez *n* rice
orfan *m* orphan
orfelinat *n* orphanage
organ *n* organ
organism *n* organism
organist *m* organist
organiza *v* organize
organizaţie *f* guild, organization
orgolios *adj* vain
oribil *adj* horrible
oricând *adv* whenever
orice *pro* anything
oricine *pro* anybody
oricum *pro* anyhow
orient *n* orient
oriental *adj* oriental
orientare *f* orientation
orientat *adj* oriented
original *adj* original
origine *f* origin
oriunde *c* wherever
orizont *n* horizon
orizontal *adj* horizontal
ornament *n* ornament
ornamental *adj* ornamental
oroare *f* horror
ortodox *adj* orthodox
orz *n* barley
os *n* bone
os zigomatic *n* cheekbone
ospăţ *n* feast
ospitalitate *f* hospitality
ostatec *m* hostage
ostentativ *adj* ostentatious
ostil *adj* hostile
ostilitate *f* hostility
oţel *n* steel
oţet *n* vinegar

otravă *f* poison
otrăvi *v* poison
otrăvire *f* poisoning
otrăvitor *adj* poisonous
ou *n* egg
oval *adj* oval
ovar *n* ovary
ovaţie *f* ovation
oxigen *n* oxygen

P

păcăleală *f* gimmick
păcăli *v* fool, cheat
păcat *n* sin
păcătos *adj* sinful
păcătui *v* sin
pace *f* peace
pachet *n* package
pacifica *v* pacify
pact *n* pact
păduche *m* louse
păduchi *m* lice
păduchios *adj* lousy
pădure *f* forest, wood
păgân *adj* pagan
păgân *m* heathen
pagină *f* page
pagubă *f* damage
pahar *n* glass
pai *n* straw
păianjen *m* spider
pâine *f* bread, loaf
paisprezece *adj* fourteen
pajişte *f* meadow
pălărie *f* hat
palat *n* palace
palid *adj* pale
palmă *f* palm, slap
pălmui *v* slap
palpabil *adj* palpable
pâlpâit *n* flare
pământ *n* earth, land
pamflet *n* pamphlet
pană *f* feather
până *pre* until
până acum *adv* hitherto
pancreas *n* pancreas
pandantiv *n* pendant
paner *n* basket
panglică *f* ribbon
panică *f* panic, scare
panoramă *f* panorama

pantă *f* slope
pantaloni *m* pants
pantaloni largi *m* slacks
pantaloni lungi *m* trousers
pântece *n* womb
panteră *f* panther
pantof *m* shoe
pânză *f* canvas
pânză de in *f* linen
Papa *m* Pope
papagal *m* parrot
papalitate *f* papacy
papetărie *f* stationery
papuc *m* slipper
păpuşă *f* doll
par *m* stake
păr *m* hair
pară *f* pear
parabolă *f* parable
paradă *f* parade
paradis *n* paradise
paradox *n* paradox
paragraf *n* paragraph
paralelă *f* parallel
paraliza *v* paralyze
paralizie *f* paralysis
parametri *m* parameters
paranoid *adj* paranoid
paranteză *f* parenthesis
părăsi *v* relinquish
părăsit *adj* derelict
paraşută *f* parachute
pârâu *n* creek, stream
parazit *m* parasite
parbriz *n* windshield
parc *n* park
parca *v* park
parcare *f* parking
parcelă *f* parcel, plot
pardesiu *n* overcoat
părea *v* seem
parfum *n* perfume
parfumat *adj* fragrant
pârghie *f* lever
paria *v* bet
părinţi *m* parents
paritate *f* parity
pariu *n* bet
pârjoli *v* broil
parlament *n* parliament
parohial *adj* parochial
parohie *f* parish
parolă *f* password
păros *adj* hairy
parte *f* part, side
partener *m* partner

P

parteneriat *n* partnership
parter *n* ground floor
parţial *adj* partial
parţial *adv* partially, partly
participa *v* participate
participare *f* participation
participiu *n* participle
particulă *f* particle
particular *adj* peculiar
partizan *m* partisan
pas *m* step, pace
pas cu pas *adv* step-by-step
pasager *m* passenger
pasaj *n* passage
pasaj subteran *n* underpass
paşaport *n* passport
pasăre *f* bird
păşi *v* stride
pasionat *adj* passionate
pasiune *f* hobby, passion
pasiv *adj* passive
paşnic *adj* law-abiding
pastă *f* paste
păstârnac *m* parsnip
Paşte *n* Easter
pastel *n* crayon
pasteuriza *v* pasteurize
păstor *m* shepherd
pastoral *adj* pastoral
păstra *v* preserve
păstrăv *m* trout
păşune *f* pasture
pat *n* bed
pat de copil *n* crib
pat de puşcă *n* butt
pat la şah *n* stalemate
pată *n* stain, blemish
păta *v* smear, stain
pătat *adj* tainted
patent *n* patent
patern *adj* fatherly
paternitate *f* fatherhood
patetic *adj* pathetic
păţi *v* undergo
patina *v* skate
patină *f* skate, ice skate
patiserie *f* pastry
pătrat *adj* square
pătrat *n* square
patriarh *m* patriarch
patrie *f* homeland
patrimoniu *n* patrimony
patriot *m* patriot
patriotic *adj* patriotic
patron *m* patron
patrona *v* patronize

patronaj *n* patronage
patru *adj* four
patrulă *f* patrol
pătrunde *v* permeate
pătrunde în *v* sink in
pătrunjel *m* parsley
patruzeci *adj* forty
patul morţii *n* deathbed
pătură *f* blanket
păun *m* peacock
pauză *f* recess
pavilion *n* pavilion
pază *f* guard, custody
păzi *v* watch
paznic *m* warden
pe *pre* on, per, upon
pe apă *adv* afloat
pe când *adv* as
pe când *c* whereas
pe cine *pro* whom
pe deasupra *adv* moreover
pe din două *adv* fifty-fifty
pe jumătate *adj* half
pe lângă *pre* besides
pe mine *pro* myself
pe nedrept *adv* unfairly
pe scurt *adv* briefly
pe ţărm *adv* ashore
pe termen lung *adj* long-term
pe vremuri *adv* formerly
pedagogie *f* pedagogy
pedală *f* pedal
pedant *adj* pedantic
pedeapsă *f* punishment
pedepsi *v* chastise, punish
peiorativ *adj* derogatory
peisaj *n* landscape
pelerin *m* pilgrim
pelerinaj *n* pilgrimage
pelican *m* pelican
peluză *f* lawn
pendulă *f* pendulum
penetra *v* penetrate
peni *m* penny
penicilină *f* penicillin
peninsulă *f* peninsula
penitenţă *f* penance
pensetă *f* tweezers
pensie *f* pension
pensulă *f* paintbrush
pentagon *n* pentagon
pentru *pre* for
pentru că *c* because
pentru o clipă *adv* momentarily
pepene galben *m* melon
pepene verde *m* watermelon

percepţie *f* perception
perciuni *m* sideburns
pereche *f* pair
peren *adj* perennial
perfect *adj* perfect
perfecţiune *f* perfection
perfora *v* perforate
perforare *f* perforation
pergament *n* parchment
peria *v* brush
pericol *n* danger
periculos *adj* dangerous
perie *f* brush
perie de cap *f* hairbrush
perimetru *n* perimeter
perioadă *f* period
perisabil *adj* perishable
perlă *f* pearl
permanent *adj* permanent
permisiune *f* permission
permite *v* allow, permit
pernă *f* cushion, pillow
persecuta *v* persecute
persevera *v* persevere
persista *v* persist, linger
persistent *adj* persistent
persistenţă *f* persistence
persoană *f* person
personal *adj* personal
personal *n* personnel
personalitate *f* personality
personifica *v* personify
perspectivă *f* perspective
perucă *f* wig
pervers *adj* pervert
perverti *v* pervert
pescar *m* fisherman
pescăruş *m* seagull
pesimism *n* pessimism
pesimist *adj* pessimistic
peste *pre* across, over
peşte *m* fish
peste bord *adv* overboard
peste noapte *adv* overnight
peşteră *f* cave
peşte-sabie *m* swordfish
pesticid *n* pesticide
petală *f* petal
petic *n* patch
petiţie *f* petition
petrece *v* revel
petrecere *f* party
pian *n* piano
pianist *m* pianist
piaţă *f* market
piatră *f* stone

piatră de râu *f* cobblestone
piatră funerară *f* tombstone
pică *f* spite
picant *adj* spicy
picătură *f* drip, drop
pici *m* brat
picior *n* leg
pictor *m* painter
pictură *f* painting
picura *v* drip, trickle
piedică *f* drawback
piele *f* leather, skin
pieptăna *v* comb
pieptene *m* comb
pierde *v* forfeit, lose
pierdere *f* loss
pierde-vară *m* drifter
pieri *v* perish
piersică *f* peach
pietate *f* piety
pieton *m* pedestrian
pietricică *f* pebble
pietrificat *adj* petrified
pietriş *n* gravel
pijama *f* pajamas
pilot *m* pilot
pilulă *f* pill
pin *m* pine
pinguin *m* penguin
pinten *m* spur
pionier *m* pioneer
pios *adj* pious, devout
piper *m* pepper
piramidă *f* pyramid
pirat *m* pirate
piraterie *f* piracy
pişcător *adj* stinging
piscină *f* pool
pisică *f* cat
pisicuţă *f* kitten
pistă *f* airstrip
pistol *n* gun, pistol
pistrui *m* freckle
pistruiat *adj* freckled
pitic *m* dwarf, midget
piton *m* python
pitoresc *adj* picturesque
piuneză *f* thumbtack
piure *n* puree
pivniţă *f* basement, cellar
placă *f* slate
plăcea *v* like
plăcere *f* pleasure
placid *adj* placid
plăcintă *f* pie
plăcut *adj* pleasant

plajă *f* beach
plămân *m* lung
plan *n* plan, scheme
planetă *f* planet
plânge *v* cry, weep
plângere *f* complaint
plânset *n* crying
planta *v* plant
plantă *f* plant
plănui *v* plan, plot
plăpând *adj* feeble
plapumă *f* quilt
plasă *f* mesh, net
plastic *n* plastic
plasture *m* plaster
plat *adj* flat
plată *f* payment, charge
plată completă *f* lump sum
plată în avans *f* down payment
platformă *f* platform
plăti *v* disburse, pay
plătibil *adj* payable
platină *f* platinum
platou *n* plateau
plauzibil *adj* plausible
pleca *v* depart, leave
plecare *f* departure
pledoarie *f* plea
pleoapă *f* eyelid
pliant *n* folder
pliant *adj* pliable
pliat *adj* pleated
plic *n* envelope
plicticos *adj* tedious
plictiseală *f* boredom
plictisi *v* bore
plictisit *adj* bored
plictisitor *adj* boring
plimba *v* hike, stroll
plimbare *f* walk, hike
plin *adj* replete, full
ploaie *f* rain
ploios *adj* rainy
plonja *v* plunge, dive
plonjon *n* plunge
ploua *v* rain
plumb *n* lead
plumbuit *adj* leaded
plural *n* plural
plută *f* raft
pluton *n* platoon
plutoniu *n* plutonium
pneumonie *f* pneumonia
poală *f* lap
poartă *f* gate
poate *adv* may-be, perhaps

pocăinţă *f* contrition
pocăit *adj* remorseful
pocni *v* clap, click
pocnitoare *f* firecracker
pod *n* bridge
podea *f* floor
podgorie *f* vineyard
poem *n* poem
poet *m* poet
poftă *f* lust
pofti *v* lust
pofti în casă *v* take in
pofticios *adj* lustful
pojar *n* measles
pol *m* pole
polar *adj* polar
polen *n* pollen
poligam *adj* polygamist
poligamie *f* polygamy
politeţe *f* politeness
politică *f* politics, policy
politician *m* politician
politicos *adj* polite
poliţie *f* police
poliţist *m* policeman
polonez *adj* Polish
Polonia *f* Poland
poluare *f* pollution
pomană *f* alms
pompa *v* pump
pompă *f* pump
pompier *m* fireman
pompozitate *f* pomposity
ponosit *adj* shabby
pontif *m* pontiff
popula *v* populate
popular *adj* popular
populariza *v* popularize
populaţie *f* population
por *m* pore
porc *m* pig
porc îngrăşat *m* hog
porc mistreţ *m* boar
porc spinos *m* porcupine
poreclă *f* nickname
poros *adj* porous
port *n* harbor, port
portabil *adj* portable
portar *m* goalkeeper
portchei *n* key ring
porţelan *n* porcelain
porţie *f* share
porţiune *f* portion
portocală *f* orange
portofel *n* wallet
portret *n* portrait

portretiza *v* portray
Portugalia *f* Portugal
portughez *adj* Portuguese
porumb *m* corn
porumbel *m* dove, pigeon
poruncitor *adj* mandatory
poseda *v* possess, own
posesie *f* possession
poşetă *f* handbag, purse
posibil *adj* possible
posibilitate *f* possibility
post *n* post
poştaş *m* mailman, postman
posterior *adj* backward
posteritate *f* posterity
potabil *adj* drinkable
potârniche *f* partridge
potenţial *adj* potential
potir *n* chalice
potoli *v* relive
potop *n* deluge
potrivi *v* conform, fit
potrivire *f* fit
potrivit *adj* suitable
potrivnic *adj* averse
povară *f* burden
poveste *f* tale, story
povesti *v* narrate
povestitor *m* teller
poză *f* pose
poziţie *f* position
pozitiv *adj* positive
prăbuşi *v* collapse
prăbuşire *f* collapse
practic *adj* practical
practica *v* practise
practică *f* practice
practicabil *adj* workable
pradă *f* loot, prey
prăda *v* pillage, loot
prădător *m* prowler
praf *n* dust
prăfuit *adj* dusty
prag *n* doorstep
pragmatic *adj* pragmatist
prăji *v* fry, toast
prăjină *f* boom
prăjitură *f* cake
prânz *n* lunch
prăpastie *f* precipice
preambul *n* preamble
precaut *adj* cautious, wary
precauţie *f* precaution
preceda *v* precede
precedent *adj* previous
precedent *n* precedent

precept *n* precept
precipita *v* precipitate
precis *adj* accurate
precizie *f* precision
precoce *adj* precocious
preconiza *v* envisage
preda *v* hand over
predare *f* delivery
predecesor *m* predecessor
predica *v* preach
predică *f* sermon
predicare *f* preaching
predicator *m* preacher
predilecţie *f* penchant, predilection
predispus *adj* predisposed
predomina *v* predominate
predominant *adj* prevalent
prefabrica *v* prefabricate
preface *v* masquerade
prefacere *f* upheaval
prefaţă *f* preface
prefera *v* prefer, choose
preferinţă *f* preference
prefix *n* prefix
pregăti *v* concoct
pregătire *f* readiness
pregătit *adj* ready
preistoric *adj* prehistoric
prejudecată *f* prejudice
prelegere *f* lecture
preliminar *adj* preliminary
prelua *v* take over
prelucra *v* process
preludiu *n* prelude
prelung *adj* lengthy
prelungi *v* prolong
prelungit *adj* protracted
prematur *adj* premature
premedita *v* premeditate
premeditare *f* premeditation
premier *adj* premier
premisă *f* premise
premiu *n* prize, award
premoniţie *f* premonition
preocupa *v* preoccupy
preocupare *f* preoccupation
preot *m* priest
preoteasă *f* priestess
preoţie *f* priesthood
prepara *v* prepare
preparare *f* preparation
prepeliţă *f* quail
prepoziţie *f* preposition
presa *v* press
presă *f* press
prescrie *v* prescribe

prescriere *f* prescription
prescurta *v* abridge
preşedinte *m* president
preşedinţie *f* presidency
presiune *f* pressure
prestigiu *n* prestige
presupoziţie *f* presupposition
presupune *v* suppose
presupunere *f* presumption
preţ *n* price
pretenţie *f* pretension
pretenţios *adj* demanding
pretinde *v* demand, claim, pretend
preţios *adj* precious
preţui *v* cherish
prevedea *v* foresee
prevenire *f* prevention
preventiv *adj* preventive
prevesti *v* foreshadow
prevestire *f* misgiving
previziune *f* foresight
prezent *adj* present
prezenta *v* present
prezenţă *f* presence
prezentare *f* presentation
prezice *v* foretell, predict
prezicere *f* prediction
prezida *v* chair
prieten *m* boyfriend
prietenă *f* girlfriend
prietenie *f* friendship
prietenos *adj* amicable
prim *adj* first
prim plan *n* foreground
primar *m* mayor
primărie *f* city hall, town hall
primat *n* primacy
primăvară *f* spring
primejdie *f* peril
primejdui *v* endanger
primi *v* receive, let in
primire *f* reception
primitiv *adj* primitive
prin *pre* through
prin forţă *adv* forcibly
principal *adj* principal
principiu *n* principle
prinde *v* catch
prins *adj* bound
prinţ *m* prince
prinţesă *f* princess
printre *pre* among
prioritate *f* priority
priponi *v* moor
prismă *f* prism
priva *v* deprive

privare *f* deprivation
privat *adj* deprived
priveliște *f* viewpoint
privi *v* glance, stare, look
privi în pământ *v* look down
privilegiu *n* privilege
privire *f* glance, glimpse, look
privitor *m* onlooker
prizioner *m* captive
prizonier *m* prisoner
proaspăt *adj* fresh
probabil *adj* probable
probabil *adv* likely
probabilitate *f* probability
problemă *f* problem
problematic *adj* problematic
procedură *f* procedure
procentaj *n* percentage
proces *n* process
proces verbal *n* record
procesiune *f* procession
proclama *v* proclaim
proclamare *f* proclamation
procrea *v* procreate
procura *v* procure
procuror *m* prosecutor
produce *v* produce
producție *f* output
productiv *adj* productive
produs *n* product
proeminent *adj* prominent
profan *adj* profane
profesie *f* profession, trade
profesional *adj* professional
profesor *m* professor
profet *m* prophet
profeție *f* prophecy
profil *n* profile
profit *n* profit
profita *v* benefit, profit
profitabil *adj* profitable
profund *adj* profound
prognoza *v* forecast
program *n* program
programa *v* schedule
programator *m* programmer
progres *n* progress
progresa *v* progress
progresiv *adj* progressive
proiect *n* project
proiecta *v* project
proiectil *n* missile
prolog *n* prologue
promenadă *f* promenade
promiscuu *adj* promiscuous
promisiune *f* promise

promiţător *adj* coming
promite *v* vow
promova *v* promote
promovare *f* promotion
prompt *adj* prompt
promulga *v* enforce
pronume *n* pronoun
pronunţa *v* pronounce
propaga *v* propagate
propagandă *f* propaganda
proporţie *f* proportion
proprietar *m* owner
proprietate *f* ownership
propriu *adj* own
propti *v* stay
propune *v* propose
propunere *f* proposal
proră *f* prow
prosop *n* towel
prosper *adj* prosperous
prospera *v* prosper
prosperitate *f* prosperity
prospeţime *f* freshness
prost *adj* fool, silly
prost îndrumat *adj* misguided
prostată *f* prostate
prostesc *adj* idiotic
prosti *v* goof
prostie *f* stupidity
protecţie *f* protection
protecţie solară *f* sunblock
proteină *f* protein
proteja *v* protect
protest *n* protest
protesta *v* complain
protocol *n* protocol
prototip *n* prototype
proveni *v* derive
proverb *n* proverb
providenţă *f* providence
provincie *f* province
provizii *f* supplies
provizoriu *adj* provisional
provoca *v* provoke
provocare *f* challenge
provocator *adj* challenging
proxim *adj* upcoming
proză *f* prose
prudent *adj* prudent
prudenţă *f* prudence
prună *f* plum
prună uscată *f* prune
pseudonim *n* pseudonym
psihiatrie *f* psychiatry
psihiatru *m* psychiatrist
psihologie *f* psychology

psihopat *m* psychopath
pubertate *f* puberty
public *adj* public
publica *v* publish
publicaţie *f* publication
publicitate *f* advertising
pudră *f* powder
puf *n* floss
pufăit *n* puff
pufăitor *adj* puffy
pui *m* chicken
pui de animal *m* cub
pui de somn *m* nap
pulpă *f* pulp
puls *n* pulse, throb
pulsa *v* pulsate, throb
pulveriza *v* spray, pulverize
pumn *m* fist
punci *n* punch
punct *n* dot
punct culminant *n* climax
punct de vedere *n* standpoint
punct dureros *n* sore
punctual *adj* punctual
pune *v* pose, put
pune botniţă *v* muzzle
pune de acord *v* pool
pune în grabă *v* shuffle
pune în joc *v* gage
pune în scenă *v* stage
pune la o parte *v* put aside
pune laolaltă *v* bundle
punte *f* deck
pupă *f* stern
pupitru *n* desk
pur *adj* pure
pur şi simplu *adv* simply
purgativ *n* purge
purgatoriu *n* purgatory
purice *m* flea
purifica *v* purify
purificare *f* purification
puril *adj* puerile
puritate *f* purity
puroi *n* pus
purpuriu *adj* purple
purta *v* behave
purta rău *v* misbehave
purta urât *v* mistreat
purtare *f* wear
purtare rea *f* misconduct
purtător *m* bearer
pururi *adv* forever
puşcaş *m* gunman
pustietate *f* desert
pustiu *adj* desolate

pustnic *m* hermit
pustulă *f* blister
putea *v* can
putere *f* power
puternic *adj* powerful
puţin *adj* little
puţin adânc *adj* shallow
puţini *adj* few
putred *adj* rotten
putregai *n* rot
putrezi *v* rot
putreziciune *f* decay

R

rabat *n* rebate
răbdare *f* patience
răbdător *adj* patient
rabin *m* rabbi
răbufnire *f* blast, surge
răceală *f* chill
rachetă *f* rocket, racket
răci *v* refrigerate
racire *f* coolness
răcitor *n* icebox
răcoritor *adj* refreshing
răcoros *adj* cool
rădăcină *f* root
radar *n* radar
râde *v* laugh
radiaţie *f* radiation
radiator *n* radiator
radical *adj* radical
radio *n* radio
radiografie *f* X-ray
rafală *f* gust
rafina *v* refine
rafinărie *f* refinery
rafinat *adj* genteel
raft *n* shelf
rafturi *n* shelves
râgâi *v* belch, burp
râgâială *f* belch, burp
răgaz *n* respite, leisure
răguşit *adj* hoarse
rahat *n* crap
rai *n* heaven
rămâne *v* remain, keep
rămăşiţă *f* remnant
rămăşiţe *f* wreckage
rambursa *v* reimburse
rambursare *f* refund
ramifica *v* branch out

ramificaţie *f* ramification
rampă *f* ramp
ramură *f* bough, branch
rană *f* injury, wound
ranchiună *f* rancor
rând *n* range, rank
rândui *v* rank
rang *n* grade
râpă *f* ravine, cliff
răpi *v* kidnap, abduct
rapid *adj* rapid, swift
răpire *f* abduction
răpit *adj* bereaved
raport *n* rapport, ratio
raportat la *adj* related
rar *adj* infrequent, rare
rar *adv* rarely
rareori *adv* seldom
râs *n* laugh, laughter
rasă *f* breed
răscoală *f* uprising
răscumpăra *v* redeem
răsfăţa *v* indulge, pamper
răsfoi *v* browse
rasism *n* racism
rasist *adj* racist
rasoli *v* botch
răspândi *v* disseminate
răspândit *adj* widespread
răspicat *adv* aloud
răsplată *f* reward
răsplăti *v* reward
răspunde *v* answer, reply, respond
răspuns *n* answer, reply
răsturna *v* overthrow, capsize
răsturnare *f* reversal
răsuci *v* twist, wring, intertwine
răsucire *f* twist
răsucit *adj* twisted
rată *f* installment
raţă *f* duck
rătăci *v* astray
rătăcit *adj* stray
raţie *f* ration
ratifica *v* ratify
ratificare *f* ratification
raţiona *v* reason
raţional *adj* rational
raţionaliza *v* ration
raţionament *n* reasoning
raţiune *f* reason
raton *m* raccoon
rău *n* evil, harm
rău *adj* malignant, bad
rău *adv* badly
rău de mare *adj* seasick

rău mirositor *adj* fetid
răutate *f* wickedness
răuvoitor *adj* malevolent
râvnă *f* ardor
râvni la *v* covet
rază *f* radius, ray
război *n* war
război de ţesut *n* loom
războinic *m* warrior
răzbuna *v* avenge, retaliate
răzbunare *f* revenge
răzbunător *adj* vindictive
razie *f* manhunt
răzvrăti *v* rebel
reacţie *f* reaction
reacţie inversă *f* feedback
reacţiona *v* react
reacţiune *f* backlash
readoptare *f* reenactment
real *adj* real
realege *v* reelect
realism *n* realism
realitate *f* reality
realiza *v* accomplish
realizabil *adj* attainable
realizare *f* attainment
realmente *adv* virtually
reapărea *v* reappear
rebel *m* rebel
rebeliune *f* rebellion
recăpăta *v* recover
recăsători *v* remarry
recâştiga *v* regain
rece *adj* chilly, cold
recensământ *n* census
recent *adj* recent
recepţioner *m* receptionist
receptiv *adj* receptive
rechema *v* recall
rechin *m* shark
recicla *v* recycle
recidivă *f* relapse
recif *n* reef
reciproc *adj* reciprocal
recita *v* recite
recital *n* recital
reclădi *v* rebuild
reclamant *m* plaintiff
recolta *v* harvest
recoltă *f* crop, harvest
recomanda *v* recommend
recomandabil *adj* advisable
recompensa *v* recompense
recompensă *f* recompense
reconsidera *v* reconsider
reconstrui *v* reconstruct

R

recrut *m* recruit
recruta *v* recruit
recrutare *f* draft
rect *n* rectum
rectifica *v* rectify
recunoaşte *v* acknowledge, recognize
recunoaştere *f* recognition
recunoscător *adj* grateful
recunoştinţă *f* gratitude
recupera *v* recuperate
recuperare *f* recovery
recurge *v* resort
recurgere *f* recourse
reda *v* restore
redacta *v* edit
reduce *v* reduce
reface *v* redo, remake
referendum *n* referendum
referi la *v* refer to
referinţă *f* reference
referitor la *pre* concerning
refinanţa *v* refinance
reflecţie *f* reflection
reflector *n* floodlight
reflexiv *adj* reflexive
reforma *v* reform
reformă *f* reform
refugiat *m* refugee
refugiu *n* refuge
refuz *n* refusal
refuza *v* refuse
regal *adj* regal, royal
regalitate *f* royalty
regat *n* kingdom, realm
rege *m* king
regenerare *f* regeneration
regent *m* regent
regim *n* regime
regiment *n* regiment
regină *f* queen
regional *adj* regional
registru *n* ledger
regiune *f* region
regiune rurală *f* countryside
regla *v* regulate
reglare *f* regulation
regret *n* regret, sorrow
regreta *v* regret, repent
regretabil *adj* regrettable
regulă *f* rule
regularitate *f* regularity
regulat *adv* regularly
reîmprospăta *v* refresh
reîncărca *v* recharge
reînnoi *v* renew
reînnoire *f* renewal

reintrare *f* reentry
relata *v* report
relatare *f* account, report
relaţie *f* relationship
relativ *adj* relative
relaxa *v* relax
relaxare *f* relaxation
relevant *adj* relevant
relicvă *f* relic
reliefa *v* set off
religie *f* religion
religios *adj* religious
relua *v* resume
reluare *f* resumption, replay
remarca *v* remark
remarcă *f* remark
remarcabil *adj* remarkable
remedia *v* remedy
remediu *n* remedy
remite *v* remit
remodela *v* remodel
remorca *v* tow
remorcă *f* trailer
remuşcare *f* remorse
ren *m* reindeer
renaştere *f* rebirth
renega *v* disown
renova *v* renovate
renovare *f* renovation
rentabil *adj* lucrative
renumit *adj* renowned
renunţa *v* give up
renunţa la *v* renounce
reorganiza *v* reorganize
repara *v* repair, mend
reparaţie *f* reparation
repartiza *v* assign
repartizare *f* allotment
repatria *v* repatriate
repede *adv* quickly
repeta *v* repeat
repetiţie *f* repetition
reporter *m* reporter
represalie *f* reprisal
reprezenta *v* represent
reprima *v* repress
reprimare *f* repression
reproduce *v* reproduce
reproducere *f* reproduction
reprodus *adj* resounding
reproş *n* reproach
reproşa *v* reproach
reptilă *f* reptile
republica *v* reprint
republică *f* republic
republicare *f* reprint

repudia *v* disclaim
reputat *adj* demeaning
reputaţie *f* reputation
resentiment *n* resentment
respect *n* respect
respecta *v* abide by, respect
respectiv *adj* respective
respectuos *adj* respectful
respingător *adj* repugnant
respinge *v* rebut, refute
respingere *f* repulse
respira *v* breathe
respiraţie *f* breathing
responsabil *adj* responsible
rest *n* remainder
restabili *v* rehabilitate
restaurant *n* restaurant
restaurare *f* restoration
restitui bani *v* pay back
restituire *f* restitution
restrânge *v* restrain
restricţie *f* restraint
resturi *n* leftovers
resursă *f* resource
resurse *f* funds
resuscita *v* resuscitate
reţea *f* network
reţetă *f* recipe
reteza *v* clip
reţine *v* withhold, retain
reţinere *f* retention, detention
retracta *v* recant, retract
retrage *v* retire, retreat, withdraw
retragere *f* recession, withdrawal
retransmite *v* relay
retras *adj* withdrawn
retroactiv *adj* retroactive
retrograda *v* demote
retuşa *v* touch up
reumatism *n* rheumatism
reumple *v* refill
reuniune *f* reunion
revedea *v* recap, review
revedere *f* review
revelaţie *f* revelation
revelator *adj* revealing
reveni *v* get back, rejoin
revenire *f* comeback
reverenţă *f* reverence
revers *n* reverse
reversibil *adj* reversible
revistă *f* magazine
revizie *f* revision
revizui *v* overhaul
revoca *v* revoke
revolta *v* revolt

revoltă *f* revolt
revoltător *adj* revolting
revolver *n* revolver
rezerva *v* reserve
rezervă *f* backup
rezervare *f* reservation
rezervor *n* reservoir
rezidenţă *f* residence
reziduu *n* residue
rezista *v* resist
rezistent *adj* tough
rezistenţă *f* resistance
rezolva *v* resolve, settle
rezonabil *adj* reasonable
rezultat *n* result
rezuma *v* summarize
rezumat *n* summary
ricoşa *v* rebound
ridica *v* raise, lift
ridicare *f* pickup, hoist
ridiche *f* radish
ridicol *adj* ridiculous
ridicol *n* ridicule
ridiculiza *v* ridicule
rigid *adj* rigid
rigoare *f* rigor
riguros *adv* harshly
rimă *f* rhyme
rinichi *m* kidney
rinocer *m* rhinoceros
ripostă *f* rebuff, snub
risc *n* risk
risca *v* risk, venture
riscant *adj* risky
risipă *f* waste
risipi *v* squander
risipitor *adj* wasteful
rit *n* rite
ritm *n* rhythm, rate
rival *m* rival
rivalitate *f* rivalry
roabă *f* wheelbarrow
roade *v* corrode
roată *f* wheel
rob *m* slave
robă *f* robe
robinet *n* faucet, tap
robust *adj* robust
rocă *f* rock
rochie *f* dress
rodie *f* pomegranate
rodnic *adj* fruitful
rogojină *f* mat
roi *n* swarm
rom *n* rum
roman *m* novel

romanicier *m* novelist
romantism *n* romance
rosătură *f* graze
roşeaţă *f* blush
roşi *v* blush
roşie *f* tomato
rosti *v* utter
rosti cu greu *v* stammer
roşu *adj* red
rota *v* rotate
rotaţie *f* rotation
rotulă *f* kneecap
rotund *adj* round, plump
rouă *f* dew
roz *adj* pink
rozător *n* rodent
rubin *n* ruby
rucsac *n* backpack
rudă *f* relative
rudimentar *adj* rudimentary
ruga *v* exhort, pray
rugăciune *f* prayer
rugător *adj* appealing
rugină *f* rust
rugini *v* rust
ruginit *adj* rusty
ruina *v* ruin
ruină *f* ruin
rula *v* roll
rupe *v* rupture, break, tear
rupe în două *v* rash
rupt *adj* broken
ruptură *f* rupture, break, tear
rural *adj* rural
rusesc *adj* Russian
Rusia *f* Russia
ruşina *v* shame
ruşinat *adj* ashamed
ruşine *f* shame
ruşinos *adj* shameful
rustic *adj* rustic
rută *f* route
rutină *f* routine

S

sabie *f* sword
sabota *v* sabotage
sabotaj *n* sabotage
sac *m* sack
sacrament *n* sacrament
sacrificiu *n* sacrifice
sacrilegiu *n* sacrilege

sacru *adj* sacred
sadic *m* sadist
safir *n* saphire
salariat *m* employee
salariu *n* salary, wage
salată *f* salad
salată verde *f* lettuce
sală *f* hall
sală de clasă *f* classroom
salcie *f* willow
salivă *f* saliva
salon de bal *n* ballroom
salt *n* leap
salutări *f* greetings
salva *v* rescue, save
salvamar *m* lifeguard
salvare *f* salvation
salvator *m* savior
sanctuar *n* sanctuary
sanda *f* sandal
sandviş *n* sandwich
sanie *f* sleigh
sarcasm *n* sarcasm
sarcastic *adj* sarcastic
sarcină *f* task
sardină *f* sardine
sare *f* salt
sat *n* village
satanic *adj* satanic
satâr *n* chopper
satelit *m* satellite
satiră *f* satire
satisface *v* satisfy
satisfacţie *f* satisfaction
satisfăcător *adj* satisfactory
satura *v* saturate
sau *c* or
savant *m* scientist
savoare *f* flavor
savura *v* enjoy, relish
săgeată *f* arrow
sălbatic *adj* savage, wild
sălbăticie *f* savagery
sălta *v* boost
sământă *f* seed
sănătate *f* health
sănătos *adj* healthy
săpa *v* mine, dig
săptămânal *adv* weekly
săptămână *f* week
sărac *adj* indigent
sărat *adj* salty
sărăcăcios *adv* poorly
sărăcie *f* poverty
sărăcime *f* poor
sărăcit *adj* impoverished

sărbătoare *f* holiday
sărbătorire *f* celebration
sări *v* jump, leap
sări peste *v* trip
săritură *f* skip, jump
sărut *n* kiss
săruta *v* kiss
sătean *m* villager
sătul *adj* fed up
sâmbătă *f* Saturday
sân *m* bosom, breast
sânge *n* blood
sângera *v* bleed
sângerare *f* bleeding
sângeros *adj* bloody
sârmă *f* wire
scabros *adv* grossly
scafandru *m* diver
scalp *n* scalp
scandal *n* scandal
scandalagiu *adj* rowdy
scandaliza *v* scandalize
scandalos *adj* outrageous
scară *f* ladder
scară mobilă *f* stepladder
scară rulantă *f* escalator
scaun *n* chair, stool
scădea *v* decrease, deduct
scădere *f* subtraction
scăpa *v* drop, miss
scăpa de *v* get off
scăpare *f* miss
scâncet *v* whine
scânteia *v* sparkle
scânteie *f* spark
scârţăit *adj* squeaky
scârţâi *v* creak
scârţâit *n* creak
scenariu *n* scenario, script
scenă *f* stage, scene
sceptic *adj* skeptic
schelărie *f* scaffolding
schelet *n* skeleton
schia *v* ski
schilodire *f* mayhem
schimb *n* swap, shift
schimba *v* chang, swape
schimbare *f* conversion
schimbător *adj* fickle
schiţa *v* outline, sketch
schiţat *adj* sketchy
schiţă *f* sketch
sclavie *f* slavery
scoate *v* eject
scobit *adj* hollow
scobitoare *f* toothpick

scobitură *f* groove
scofâlcit *adj* sunken
scoică *f* clam
scop *n* purpose
scor *n* score
scorpion *m* scorpion
scorţişoară *f* cinnamon
scorţos *adj* crusty
scotoci *v* ransack
scrie *v* write
scriitor *m* writer
scrimă *f* fencing
scripcă *f* fiddle
scripete *m* pulley
scris *adj* written
scris *n* writing
scrumieră *f* ashtray
scrupul *n* scruples
scrupulos *adj* scrupulous
scrutare *f* scrutiny
scufunda *v* go under, sink
scufundare *f* diving
scuipa *v* spit
sculptor *m* sculptor
sculptură *f* sculpture
scump *adj* expensive
scurge *v* elapse, leak
scurgere *f* leakage
scurt *adj* brief, short
scurta *v* shorten
scurtătură *f* shortcut
scut *n* shield
scutec *n* diaper
scuter *n* scooter
scuti *v* absolve
scutire *f* exemption
scutit *adj* exempt
scuza *v* excuse, apologize
scuză *f* apology
se *pre* oneself
seară *f* evening
secară *f* rye
secera *v* reap
seceră *f* sickle
secetă *f* drought
secol *n* century
secret *n* secret
secretar *m* secretary
sectă *f* sect
sector *n* sector
secţiune *f* section
secundar *adj* secondary
secundă *f* second
securitate *f* security
seda *v* sedate
seduce *v* seduce

seducţie *f* seduction
segment *n* segment
segregaţie *f* segregation
selecta *v* select
selecţie *f* selection
semăna *v* sow
semăna cu *v* resemble
semestru *n* semester
semeţ *adj* aloof, haughty
seminar *n* seminary
semn *n* mark, token, sign
semn rău *n* portent
semnal *n* signal
semnătură *f* signature
senat *n* senate
senator *m* senator
senil *adj* senile
senin *adj* cloudless
seninătate *f* serenity
senior *adj* senior
sensibil *adj* sensible, sensitive
sentiment *n* feeling, sentiment
sentimental *adj* sentimental
sentimente *n* feelings
sentinelă *f* sentry
sentinţă *f* sentence
senzaţie *f* sensation
senzual *adj* sensual
separa *v* separate, part, segregate
separare *f* separation
separat *adj* separate
separat *adv* asunder
separaţie *f* severance
septembrie *m* September
ser *n* serum
seră *f* greenhouse
serenadă *f* serenade
sergent *m* sergeant
serie *f* series
seringă *f* syringe
serios *adj* serious
seriozitate *f* seriousness
sertar *n* drawer
servi *v* serve, minister
serviciu *n* service
servietă *f* briefcase
servitor *m* servant
sesiune *f* session
sevă *f* sap
sever *adj* stern, strict
severitate *f* severity
sex *n* sex
sexualitate *f* sexuality
sezonier *adj* seasonal
sfat *n* advice
sfărâma *v* smash, shatter

sfătui *v* counsel, advise
sfătuitor *m* counselor
sfânt *adj* holy, saint
sfârşi *v* end, end up, die out
sfârşit *n* ending, end
sfeclă *f* beet
sferă *f* sphere
sfert *n* quarter
sfeşnic *n* candlestick
sfida *v* defy
sfidare *f* defiance
sfidător *adj* defiant
sfinţenie *f* holiness
sfinţi *v* sanctify
sfoară *f* string
sforăi *v* snore
sforăit *n* snore
sfredel *n* drill
sfredeli *v* drill
sicriu *n* casket, coffin
sifilis *n* syphilis
sigila *v* seal
sigur *adj* secure, safe
siguranţă *f* safety
silabă *f* syllable
silabisi *v* spell
silă *f* loathing
sili *v* coerce
silinţă *f* diligence
silitor *adj* diligent
siluetă *f* silhouette
simbol *n* symbol
simbolic *adj* symbolic
simetrie *f* symmetry
simfonie *f* symphony
similar *adj* alike, similar
simpatie *f* sympathy
simpatiza *v* sympathize
simplifica *v* simplify
simplitate *f* simplicity
simplu *adj* bare, simple
simptom *n* symptom
simţ *n* sense
simţi *v* feel, sense
simula *v* simulate, feign
simultan *adj* simultaneous
sinagogă *f* synagogue
sincer *adj* frank, sincere
sinceritate *f* sincerity
sincroniza *v* synchronize
singular *adj* singular
singur *adj* alone, single
singur *m* single
singuratic *adj* secluded
singuratic *adv* lonely
singurătate *f* loneliness

sinod *n* synod
sinonim *n* synonym
sinstru *adj* sinister
sinteză *f* synthesis
sinucidere *f* suicide
sirenă *f* mermaid, siren
sirop *n* syrup
sistem *n* system
sistem de ţevi *n* pipeline
sistematic *adj* systematic
situat *adj* situated
situaţie *f* situation
situaţie grea *f* predicament
slab *adj* skinny, weak
slăbi *v* impair; loosen weaken
slăbiciune *f* weakness
slănină *f* bacon
slogan *n* catchword
slujitor *m* attendant
smarald *n* emerald
smochin *m* fig
smucitură *f* jerk
smulge *v* pluck
smulgere *f* wrench
snop *m* bundle
soacră *f* mother-in-law
soare *m* sun
soartă *f* fate
soartă rea *f* doom
sobă *f* heater, stove
sobru *adj* lowkey
sociabil *adj* sociable
socialism *n* socialism
socialist *adj* socialist
socializa *v* socialize
societate *f* society
socoteală *f* count
socoti *v* count; reckon
socru *m* father-in-law
soios *adj* sleazy
sol *m* soil
solar *adj* solar
soldat *m* soldier
solemn *adj* solemn
solicita *v* apply for, solicit
solid *adj* solid
solidaritate *f* solidarity
solitar *adj* solitary
solitar *m* loner
solubil *adj* soluble
soluţie *f* solution, clue
solvabil *adj* solvent
somieră *f* mattress
somn *n* sleep
somon *m* salmon
somptuos *adj* sumptuous

sonda *v* probe
sonerie *f* doorbell
soră *f* sister
soră vitregă *f* stepsister
sorbi *v* guzzle, sip
sorbitură *f* sip
sordid *adj* squalid
sorta *v* sort out
sortiment *n* assortment
sos *n* gravy, sauce
sosi *v* arrive
sosieră *f* saucepan
sosire *f* arrival
soţ *m* husband
soţie *f* spouse, wife
soţii *f* wives
sovietic *adj* soviet
spaimă *f* dismay, fright
Spania *f* Spain
spaniol *adj* Spanish
spaniol *m* Spaniard
sparanghel *m* asparagus
spargere *f* burglary
spasm *n* spasm
spate *n* back, rear
spaţios *adj* roomy
spaţiu *n* space
spăla *v* bathe, wash
spăla creierul *v* brainwash
spălătorie *f* laundry
spărgător *m* burglar
spărtură *f* chasm, rift
spânzutătoare *f* gallows
special *adj* special
specialitate *f* specialty
specializa *v* specialize
specializa în *v* major in
specie *f* species
specific *adj* specific
specimen *n* specimen
spectacol *n* spectacle
spectator *m* bystander
specula *v* speculate
speculaţie *f* speculation
speranţă *f* expectation
speria *v* scare, frighten
speriat *adj* afraid
sperjur *n* perjury
spermă *f* sperm
spicher *m* broadcaster
spin *m* thorn
spinteca *v* rip
spion *m* spy
spiona *v* spy
spionaj *n* espionage
spirit *n* spirit

S

spiritual *adj* spiritual
spital *n* hospital
spitaliza *v* hospitalize
splendid *adj* splendid
splendoare *f* splendor
sponsor *m* sponsor
spontan *adj* spontaneous
spontaneitate *f* spontaneity
spor de salariu *n* raise
sporadic *adj* sporadic
spori *v* enhance
sporire *f* boost, upturn
sport *n* sport
sportiv *m* sportman
spovedanie *f* confessional
sprânceană *f* eyebrow
spre est *adv* eastward
spre interior *adv* inwards
sprijin *n* backing
sprijini *v* support, bolster
spumă *f* foam
spumă de săpun *f* lather
spune *v* say, tell
spune oftând *v* sigh
spurca *v* defile
sta ascuns *v* lurk
sta culcat *v* lie
sta în picioare *v* stand
sta jos *v* sit
sta la pândă *v* prowl
sta la soare *v* bask
stabil *adj* stable
stabili *v* establish
stabilitate *f* stability
stafidă *f* raisin
stagna *v* stagnate
stagnant *adj* stagnant
stagnare *f* stagnation
standardiza *v* standardize
stare *f* state
start *n* start
stat de plată *n* payslip
statistică *f* statistic
statuie *f* statue
statut *n* status
staţie *f* station
staţionar *adj* stationary
stăpân *m* master
stăpâna casei *f* housewife
stăpână *f* mistress
stăpâni *v* master, rule
stăpânire *f* mastery
stăpânit *adj* pent-up
stăpânit de *adj* addicted
stătut *adj* stale
stăvilar *n* dam

stăvili *v* stem
stâlp *m* pile, pillar
stângaci *adj* clumsy
stângăcie *f* clumsiness
stârni *v* incite, rouse
stea *f* star
steag *n* banner, flag
stejar *m* oak
stenografie *f* shorthand
stepă *f* prairie
steril *adj* barren, sterile
steriliza *v* sterilize
stewardesă *f* stewardess
sticlă *f* bottle
sticlărie *f* glassware
stil *n* style
stil de viaţă *n* lifestyle
stilou *n* pen
stima *v* esteem
stimula *v* stimulate
stimulent *n* incentive
stinge *v* extinguish
stins *adj* extinct
stipendia *v* subsidize
stipula *v* stipulate
stoarce *v* extort, mangle
stoca *v* stock
stoic *adj* stoic
stomac *n* stomach
stop cardiac *n* cardiac arrest
stradă *f* street
strană *f* pew
strangula *v* strangle
straniu *adj* eerie, queer
straşnic *adj* terrific
strat *n* layer
strategie *f* strategy
străbate *v* roam, walk
strădanie *f* endeavor
strădui *v* endeavor, strive
străin *m* stranger, foreigner
străluci *v* shine, glow
strălucire *f* brightness
strălucitor *adj* bright, shiny
strămoş *m* ancestor
strănut *n* sneeze
strănuta *v* sneeze
străpunge *v* pierce
strâmb *adj* crooked
strâmpt *adj* cramped
strâmtoare *f* gorge, strait
strânge *v* shrink, squeeze, clench
strângere *f* rally
strâns *adj* fast
strânsoare *f* grasp
strecura *v* slip

strecurătoare *f* strainer
stres *n* stress
stresant *adj* stressful
strica *v* break down, spoil, damage
stricat *adj* cranky
stricăciune *f* breakdown
stricător *adj* damaging
strict *adj* stringent
strictețe *f* austerity
strident *adj* shattering
stridie *f* oyster
striga *v* call out, shout
strigare *f* shouting
strigăt *n* shout
stropi *v* splash
structură *f* structure
strugure *m* grape
struț *m* ostrich
student *m* student
studia *v* study
stuf *n* reed
stup *m* beehive
stupefiant *n* dope
stupid *adj* stupid
sub *pre* below, under
subetalon *adj* substandard
subiect *n* subject
sublim *adj* sublime
sublinia *v* emphasize
subscrie *v* subscribe
subscripție *f* subscription
subsidiu *n* subsidy
substantiv *n* noun
substanță *f* substance
substanțial *adj* substantial
subteran *adj* underground
subtil *adj* subtle
subtitlu *n* subtitle
subția cu apă *v* water down
subțire *adj* flimsy, tenuous
subțirel *adj* slim
suburbie *f* suburb
suburbii *f* outskirts
suc *n* juice
succes *n* success
succesiune *f* sequence
succesor *m* successor
suci *v* curl
suculent *adj* succulent
sud *n* south
suda *v* weld
sud-est *n* southeast
sudic *adj* southern
sudor *m* welder
sud-vest *n* southwest
suedez *adj* Sweedish

Suedia *f* Sweden
suferi *v* suffer
suferi de *v* suffer from
suferinţă *f* suffering
suficient *adj* sufficient
sufla *v* blow
suflet *n* soul
sufoca *v* suffocate
sufocant *adj* stifling
sufragerie *f* dining room
sugaci *adj* sucker
suge *v* suck
sugera *v* suggest, hint
sugestie *f* suggestion
sugestiv *adj* suggestive
sughiţ *n* hiccup
sul de hârtie *n* scroll
sulf *n* sulphur
suliţă *f* spear, dart
sumariza *v* sum up
sumă *f* sum
sumbru *adj* somber
suna *v* ring
suna din *v* sound
sunet *n* sound
supă *f* soup, broth
supăra *v* enrage
supărare *f* tantrum
supărat *adj* sorry, cross, angry
supărător *adj* troublesome
superb *adj* superb
superior *adj* superior
superioritate *f* superiority
supermarket *n* supermarket
superstiţie *f* superstition
suplimentar *adj* additional
suplu *adj* supple
suport *n* stand
suporta *v* brace for
suportabil *adj* bearable
supraaprecia *v* overestimate
supradoză *f* overdose
supraestima *v* overrate
suprafaţă *f* surface, area
supraîncărca *v* overcharge
supraîncărcare *f* surcharge
suprapune *v* overlap
supraputere *f* superpower
supraveghea *v* supervise
supraveghere *f* surveillance
supravieţui *v* survive
supravieţuire *f* survival
supravieţuitor *m* survivor
suprem *adj* paramount
supremaţie *f* supremacy
supune *v* comply, obey, subdue, submit

supunere *f* allegiance
supus *adj* submissive, meek
surd *adj* deaf
surghiunit *adj* outcast
surplus *n* surplus
surprinde *v* surprise
surprins *adj* unaware
surpriză *f* surprise
sursă *f* source
surzenie *f* deafness
sus pe scări *adv* upstairs
susceptibil *adj* susceptible
suspect *adj* fishy
suspect *m* suspect
suspecta *v* distrust, suspect
suspenda *v* suspend
suspendare *f* suspension
suspicios *adj* suspicious
suspiciune *f* suspicion
suspin *n* sob
sustragere *f* evasion
susţinător *m* supporter
susţine *v* uphold, sustain
susţinere *f* sustenance
sutană *f* cassock
sută *adj* hundred
sutien *n* bra
suvenir *n* souvenir
suveran *adj* sovereign
suveranitate *f* sovereignty

Ş

şa *f* saddle
şacal *m* jackal
şah *n* chess
şaisprezece *adj* sixteen
şaizeci *adj* sixty
şalupă *f* barge
şansă *f* chance, hazard
şanse *f* odds
şantaj *n* blackmail
şantaja *v* blackmail
şantier naval *n* shipyard
şanţ *n* ditch
şapcă *f* cap
şapte *adj* seven
al şaptelea *adj* seventh
şaptesprezece *adj* seventeen
şaptezeci *adj* seventy
şaradă *f* charade
şarm *n* charm
şarpe *m* serpent, snake

şase *adj* six
al şaselea *adj* sixth
şchiop *adj* lame
şchiopăta *v* limp
şchipătat *n* limp
şcoală *f* school
şedere *f* sitting, stay
şef *m* boss, chief
şemineu *n* fireplace
şeptel *n* livestock
şerpuitor *adj* winding
şerveţel *n* napkin
şi *c* and
şir *n* row
şiret *adj* foxy
şmecherie *f* trick
şoaptă *f* whisper
şoarece *m* mouse
şoareci *m* mice
şobolan *m* rat
şoc *n* shock
şoca *v* shock, stun
şocant *adj* shocking
şofer *m* driver
şoim *m* hawk
şold *n* hip
şomaj *n* unemployment
şomer *adj* unemployed
şopârlă *f* lizard
şopti *v* whisper, murmur
şort *n* shorts
şosetă *f* sock
şovăi *v* waver, vacillate
şrapnel *n* shrapnel
ştampila *v* stamp
ştampilă *f* stamp
ştanţa *v* emboss
şterge *v* delete, erase
şterpeli *v* pilfer
ştiinţă *f* science
ştiinţific *adj* scientific
ştiri *f* news
şubred *adj* shaky
şuncă *f* ham
şura de fân *f* haystack
şură *f* barn
şurub *n* screw
şurubelniţă *f* screwdriver

T

tabără *f* camp
tablă *f* chalkboard
tabletă *f* tablet
tablou *n* picture
tacâmuri *n* cutlery
tachina *v* tease
tact *n* tact
tactic *adj* tactical
tactică *f* tactics
taină *f* secrecy
talent *n* talent
talie *f* waist
talpă *f* sole
tandreţe *f* tenderness
tandru *adj* fond
tangentă *f* tangent
tapet *n* tapestry
tapisa *v* cushion
tapiţerie *f* upholstery
tarantulă *f* tarantula
tare *adj* hardy, rocky
tare *adv* aloud
targă *f* stretcher
tarif *n* tariff, fare
tarif poştal *n* postage
tartă *f* tart
tartru *n* tartar
tată *m* father
tati *m* dad
taur *m* bull
tavan *n* ceiling
tavă *f* tray
taxă *f* fee, tax,
taxă şcolară *f* tuition
taxe *f* dues
taxi *n* cab
tăcere *f* hush
tăcut *adj* silent
tăia *v* chop, cut, slit
tăia copaci *v* log
tăia felii *v* slash, slice
tăietură *f* clipping, cut
tăinui *v* connive
tămâie *f* incense
al tău *pro* yours
tău *adj* your
tâmplar *m* carpenter
tâmplărie *f* carpentry
tânăr *adj* junior, young
tânji *v* crave, yearn
târg *n* fair
târî *v* crawl
târziu *adv* late

teanc *n* stack
teatru *n* theater
tehnic *adj* technical
tehnică *f* technique
tehnician *m* technician
tehnologie *f* technology
tei *m* lime
tejghea *f* counter
telefon *n* telephone
telefona *v* phone
telegramă *f* telegram
telepatie *f* telepathy
telescop *n* telescope
televiza *v* televise
televiziune *f* television
temă *f* homework; theme, topic
temător *adj* apprehensive
temnicer *m* jailer
temniţă *f* dungeon, jail
tempera *v* dampen
temperament *n* temper
temperatură *f* temperature
templu *n* temple
temporar *adj* temporary
ten *n* complexion
tenacitate *f* tenacity
tencuială *f* mortar
tendinţă *f* tendency
tenis *n* tennis
tenor *m* tenor
tensiune *f* tension
tentacul *n* tentacle
teolog *m* theologian
teologie *f* theology
teorie *f* theory
terapie *f* therapy
terasă *f* terrace
terciui *v* squash, mash
teren *n* terrain, ground
terestru *adj* terrestrial
teribil *adj* awful
teritoriu *n* territory
termen *n* term
termina *v* complete
terminologie *f* terminology
termită *f* termite
termometru *n* thermometer
termostat *n* thermostat
teroare *f* terror
terorism *n* terrorism
terorist *m* terrorist
teroriza *v* terrorize
test *n* test
testa *v* test
testament *n* testament
text *n* text

text de cântec *n* lyrics
teză *f* thesis
ticălos *adj* evil
ticălos *m* villain, rascal
ticăloşie *f* mischief
tifon *n* gauze
tigaie *f* frying pan
tigru *m* tiger
tihnă *f* ease
tihnit *adj* uneventful
timid *adj* shy, bashful
timiditate *f* shyness
timp *n* time
tineresc *adj* youthful
tinereţe *f* youth
tinichea *f* tin
tip *n* type, guy
tipări *v* print
tipăritură *f* print
tipic *adj* typical
tiran *m* despot, tyrant
tiranie *f* tyranny
tiroidă *f* thyroid
titlu *n* heading, title
tiv *n* hem
toaletă *f* rest room
toamnă *f* autumn
toast *n* toast
toată lumea *pro* everybody
toată viaţa *adj* lifetime
tobă *f* drum
tobogan *n* chute
toca *v* mince
tocană *f* stew
tocătură *f* mincemeat
tocit *adj* blunt, pointless
tocmeală *f* bargain
tocmi *v* bargain, haggle
tolera *v* tolerate
tolerabil *adj* tolerable
toleranţă *f* tolerance
tombolă *f* raffle
ton *m* tuna, tone
ton la telefon *n* dial tone
tonă *f* ton
tonic *n* tonic
topi *v* melt, thaw
topitorie *f* foundry
topor *n* ax
toptan *n* wholesale
toreador *m* bull fighter
torent *n* torrent
torid *adj* torrid
tors *n* torso
tortura *v* agonize, torture
tortură *f* torture

torţă *f* torch
tot *adj* all
tot *pro* everything
total *adj* total, entire
totalitar *adj* totalitarian
totalitate *f* totality
totaliza *v* amount to
totuşi *c* however, yet
totuşi *adv* nevertheless
tovarăş *m* comrade, pal
tovărăşie *f* fellowship
toxic *adj* toxic
toxină *f* toxin
trabuc *n* cigar
tractor *n* tractor
tracţiune *f* traction
tradiţie *f* tradition
traducător *m* translator
traduce *v* translate
trafic *n* traffic
trafica *v* traffic
trage *v* haul, drag, pull
tragedie *f* tragedy
tragere *f* draw
tragic *adj* tragic
trai *n* livelihood
traiectorie *f* trajectory
trambulină *f* springboard
tramvai *n* streetcar, tram
trandafir *m* rose
trandafiriu *adj* rosy
transă *f* trance
transcrie *v* transcribe
transfer *n* transfer
transfera *v* transfer
transforma *v* transform
transformare *f* transformation
transfuzie *f* transfusion
transmite *v* transmit
transparent *adj* transparent
transpira *v* sweat
transpiraţie *f* sweat
transplanta *v* transplant
transporta *v* transport
tranşee *f* trench
tranzacţie *f* transaction
tranzacţii *f* dealings
tranzitare *f* transit
tranziţie *f* transition
trasa *v* trace
trata *v* treat
trata cu *v* deal
tratament *n* treatment
tratat *n* treaty
trataţie *f* treat
traumatic *adj* traumatic

traumatiza *v* traumatize
traversa *v* cross, span
traversare *f* crossing
trăda *v* betray
trădare *f* betrayal
trădător *m* traitor
trăgaci *n* trigger
trăi *v* live
trăsător *adj* treacherous
trăsătură *f* feature, trait
trăsură *f* carriage
trândav *adj* idle
trândăveală *f* lounge
trânti *v* flunk, slam
treabă *f* chore, job
treaptă *f* stair
treaz *adj* awake, sober
trebui *v* need, must
trebui să *v* have to
trecător *adj* transient
trece *v* pass
trece dincolo *v* get over
trece pe la *v* come over
trece peste *v* skip
trece prin *v* go through
trecere *f* pass
trecut *adj* past
trei *adj* three
treiera *v* thresh
al treilea *adj* third
treisprezece *adj* thirteen
treizeci *adj* thirty
tremur *n* tremor, shudder
tremura *v* tremble, shudder
tren *n* train
trepied *n* tripod
treptat *adv* little by little
trezi *v* awake, wake up, arouse
trezire *f* awakening
trezorier *m* treasurer
trib *n* tribe
tribunal *n* courthouse
tribună oficială *f* grandstand
tribut *n* tribute
trimestrial *adj* quarterly
trimestru *n* trimester
trimis *m* envoy
trimite *v* send
triplu *adj* triple
trist *adj* sad, dejected
tristeţe *f* sadness
triumf *n* triumph
triumfa *v* prevail
triumfal *adj* triumphant
triumfător *adj* jubilant
triunghi *n* triangle

trofeu *n* trophy
tromboză *f* thrombosis
trompetă *f* trumpet
tron *n* throne
tropic *n* tropic
tropical *adj* tropical
trosnet *n* crash
trotuar *n* pavement, sidewalk
truc *n* ploy, ruse
trudi *v* grind
truditor *m* sweater
trunchi *n* trunk
trupă *f* troop
trupesc *adj* bodily
tu *pro* you
tu însuţi *pro* yourself
tuberculoză *f* tuberculosis
tufiş *n* bush
tulbura *v* disturb, perturb
tulburare *f* commotion
tulburat *adj* worrisome
tulburător *adj* disturbing
tulpină *f* stalk, stem
tumoare *f* tumor
tumult *n* tumult, tumult
tumultuos *adj* tumultuous
tun *n* cannon
tunde oile *v* shear
tunel *n* tunnel
tunet *n* thunder
tunică *f* tunic
tunsoare *f* haircut
tur *n* tour
turbare *f* rabies
turbină *f* turbine
turbulenţă *f* turbulence
turc *adj* Turk
Turcia *f* Turkey
turism *n* tourism
turist *m* tourist
turmă *f* flock
turn *n* tower
turna *v* pour, hail
turneu *n* tournament
turnuleţ *n* turret
turti *v* flatten
tuse *f* cough
tuşi *v* cough
tutun *n* tobacco

Ţ

ţap ispăşitor *m* scapegoat
ţar *m* czar
ţară *f* country
ţăran *m* countryman
ţărână *f* dirt
ţărm *n* shore
ţărmul mării *n* seashore
ţâfnos *adj* grumpy
ţânţar *m* mosquito
ţeapăn *adj* stiff, stark
ţeavă *f* pipe
ţeciorapi *v* darn
ţelină *f* celery
ţepos *adj* thorny
ţesătură *f* fabric, texture
ţese *v* weave
ţesut *n* tissue
ţigan *m* gypsy
ţigară *f* cigarette
ţiglă *f* tile
ţine *v* hold, hold out
ţine de *v* hang on
ţine în frâu *v* curb
ţine minte *v* remember
ţintaş *m* marksman
ţintă *f* target, goal
ţinti *v* aim
ţinută *f* poise
ţipa *v* shriek, yell
ţipa sinistru *v* scream
ţipăt *n* scream, shriek
ţipător *adj* flamboyant
ţiţei *n* petroleum

ucenic *m* apprentice
ucide *v* slay
ucidere *f* killing
ud leoarcă *adj* soggy
uda *v* water, soak
uita *v* forget
uita prin *v* look through
uitare *f* oblivion
ulcer *n* ulcer
ulcior *n* jug
ulei *n* oil
uliţă *f* lane
ulm *m* elm
ulterior *adj* subsequent

ultim *adj* last, ultimate
ultimatum *n* ultimatum
ultrasunet *n* ultrasound
ului *v* amaze
uluire *f* amazement
uluitor *adj* amazing
uman *adj* human
umanistică *f* humanities
umăr *n* shoulder
umbră *f* shadow, shade
umbrelă *f* umbrella
umbros *adj* shady
umed *adj* damp, humid
umeraş *n* hanger
umezeală *f* moisture
umezi *v* moisten
umfla *v* bloat, inflate, swell
umflat *adj* bloated, swollen
umflătură *f* bulge, swelling
umiditate *f* humidity
umil *adj* humble
umili *v* humiliate
umilit *adj* downtrodden
umor *n* humor
umple *v* replenish
umplere *f* filling
umplutură *f* stuffing
un *a* an, a
un pumn *m* handful
unanimitate *f* unanimity
unchi *m* uncle
uncie *f* ounce
unde *adv* where
unealtă *f* utensil, tool
uneori *adv* sometimes
unformitate *f* uniformity
unge *v* anoint, grease
unghi *n* angle
unghie *f* fingernail
uni *v* unite, link
unic *adj* unique
unifica *v* unify
unificare *f* unification
uniformă *f* uniform
unilateral *adj* unilateral
unitate *f* unit, unity
uniune *f* union
univers *n* universe
universal *adj* universal
universitate *f* university
unsprezece *adj* eleven
unsuros *adj* greasy
unt *n* butter
untură *f* lard, grease
unul *adj* one
ură *f* hatred

ura bun venit *v* welcome
urâcios *adj* hateful
uragan *n* hurricane
urangutan *m* orangutan
urât *adj* ugly
urâţenie *f* ugliness
urban *adj* urban
urca *v* climb, run up, ascend
ureche *f* ear
urgent *adj* urgent
urgenţă *f* urgency
urî *v* abhor, hate
uriaş *m* giant, huge
urina *v* urinate
urină *f* urine
urla *v* howl, roar
urlet *n* howl, roar
urma *v* follow, pursue
urmă *f* track, trail
urmare *f* corollary
urmări *v* stalk, track
urmărire *f* pursuit
următorul *adj* next
urnă *f* urn
urs *m* bear
uşă *f* door
usca *v* dry
uscat *adj* dried, dry
uscător *n* dryer
uşier *m* bailiff
uşor *adv* easily, slightly
uşor *adj* easy, light
usturoi *m* garlic
uşura *v* relieve, ease
uşurare *f* relief
uşurel *adv* softly
uter *n* uterus
util *adj* useful
utilitate *f* usefulness
utiliza *v* utilize
utilizare *f* usage
utilizator *m* user
uza *v* wear down
uzurpa *v* usurp

vacă *f* cow
vacanţă *f* vacation
văcar *m* cowboy
vaccin *n* vaccine
vaccina *v* vaccinate
văduv *m* widower

văduvă *f* widow
vag *adj* fuzzy, vague
vagabond *m* bum, vagrant
vagabonda *v* hang around
vagon *n* wagon
val *n* wave
văl *n* veil
val mic *n* ripple
valabil *adj* valid
valabilitate *f* validity
vale *f* valley
valida *v* validate
valiză *f* suitcase
valoare *f* value
valoros *adj* valuable
vals *n* walţ
valvă *f* valve
vamă *f* customs
vampir *m* vampire
vâna *v* hunt
vânătoare *f* hunting
vânător *m* hunter
vandal *m* vandal
vandalism *n* vandalism
vandaliza *v* vandalize
vândut *adj* sold-out
vanitate *f* vanity
vânt *n* wind
vântos *adj* windy
vânzare *f* sale
vânzător *m* seller
văr *m* cousin
vară *f* summer
vârf *n* summit, top, peak
vârf de deal *n* hilltop
varia *v* vary
variabil *adj* variable
variat *adj* varied
varietate *f* variety
variolă *f* smallpox
vărsa *v* spill, shed
vărsare *f* spill
vărsat de vânt *n* chicken pox
vărsătură *f* vomit
vârstă *f* age
varză *f* cabbage
vas *n* vessel, ship
vâslă *f* oar
vâsli *v* paddle, row
vast *adj* vast
vatră *f* hearth
vază *f* vase
vechi *adj* old
vecin *m* neighbor
vecinătate *f* vicinity
vedea *v* see

vedere *f* vision, sight, eyesight
vegetarian *m* vegetarian
vegetaţie *f* vegetation
veghe *f* vigil
vehicul *n* vehicle
venă *f* vein
venera *v* venerate
veneraţie *f* worship
veni *v* come
venin *n* venom
venire *f* coming
venit *n* income, revenue
ventila *v* ventilate
ventilaţie *f* ventilation
verandă *f* porch
verb *n* verb
verbal *adv* orally
verde *adj* green
verdict *n* verdict
vergea *f* rod
verifica *v* verify
verificare *f* verification
verigă *f* link
veritabil *adj* genuine
vernisa *v* varnish
vers *n* verse
versat *adj* versed
versiune *f* version
vertebră *f* vertebra
vesel *adj* merry, joyful
vesel *adv* joyfully
veşmânt *n* guise
veşminte *n* apparel
vest *n* west
vestă *f* vest
veşteji *v* wither
vesti *v* herald
vestiar *n* locker room
vestic *adj* western
vestigiu *n* vestige
vestitor *m* announcer
veteran *m* veteran
veterinar *m* veterinarian
veveriţă *f* squirrel
vezica biliară *f* gall bladder
viaduct *n* viaduct
viaţă *f* life
vibra *v* vibrate
vibrant *adj* vibrant
vibraţie *f* vibration
vicar *m* dean
vicios *adj* vicious
viciu *n* vice
viclean *adj* wily, cunning
viclenie *f* guile, craft
victimă *f* victim

victorie *f* victory
victorios *adj* successful
vidră *f* otter
vierme *m* worm
viespe *f* wasp
vigilenţă *f* awareness
viguros *adj* sturdy
viitor *n* future
vin *n* wine
vin de Xeres *n* sherry
vină *f* blame, guilt
vinde *v* sell
vindeca *v* cure, heal
vindecabil *adj* curable
vindecare *f* cure
vindecător *m* healer
vineri *f* Friday
vinovat *adj* guilty
vioară *f* violin
vioi *adj* vivid, lively
viol *n* rape
viola *v* rape, violate
violator *m* rapist
violent *adj* violent, fierce
violenţă *f* violence
violet *n* violet
violonist *m* violinist
viperă *f* viper
vira *v* veer
virginitate *f* virginity
virgulă *f* comma
viril *adj* virile
virilitate *f* virility
virtuos *adj* virtuous
virtute *f* virtue
virus *m* virus
vis *n* dream
visa *v* dream
viscol *n* blizzard
viţă de vie *f* grapevine
vital *adj* vital
vitalitate *f* vitality
vitamină *f* vitamin
vite *f* cattle
viteaz *adj* valiant
vitejeşte *adv* bravely
vitejie *f* fortitude
viţel *m* calf
viteză *f* speed, velocity
viu *adj* alive, live
vivace *adj* vivacious
vizavi de *pre* across
vizibil *adj* visible
vizibilitate *f* visibility
vizita *v* visit
vizită *f* visit

vizitator *m* visitor
vizual *adj* visual
vizualiza *v* visualize
vizuină *f* burrow, den
vocabular *n* vocabulary
vocală *f* vowel
vocaţie *f* vocation
voce *f* voice
vogă *f* vogue
voinic *adj* husky
voinţă *f* will
volatil *adj* volatile
volei *n* volleyball
voltaj *n* voltage
volum *n* volume
voluminos *adj* bulky
voluntar *m* volunteer
vomita *v* throw up
vopsea *f* dye, paint
vopsi *v* paint, dye
vorbe *f* hearsay
vorbi *v* speak
vorbi urât *v* lash out
vorbitor *m* speaker
vot *n* vote
vota *v* vote
votare *f* voting
vrabie *f* sparrow
vrajbă *f* feud
vrăji *v* bewitch
vrăjitoare *f* witch
vrăjitor *m* wizard
vrăjitorie *f* witchcraft
vreme *f* weather
vremuri *f* times
vulcan *m* volcano
vulgar *adj* vulgar
vulgaritate *f* vulgarity
vulnerabil *adj* vulnerable
vulpe *f* fox
vultur *m* vulture

watt *m* watt
web site *n* web site
weekend *n* weekend

Z

zăbovi *v* loiter
zadarnic *adv* vainly
zădărnici *v* baffle
zădărnicie *f* futility
zahăr *n* sugar
zâmbet *n* smile
zâmbi *v* smile
zână *f* fairy
zăpăci *v* bewilder
zăpăcit *adj* dazed
zăpadă *f* snow
zaruri *n* dice
zăvor *n* bolt, latch
zăvorî *v* bolt
zbârcitură *f* wrinkle
zbate *v* struggle
zbenguială *f* prank
zbor *n* fly, flight
zbura *v* fly
zburător *m* flier
zdreanţă *f* shred
zdrobi *v* crush, crash
zdrobit *adj* crushing
zdruncina *v* jolt, jerk
zdruncinătură *f* jolt
zebră *f* zebra
zece *adj* ten
zecimal *adj* decimal
zecime *f* tenth
zeiţă *f* goddess
zeitate *f* deity
zel *n* zeal, zest
zelos *adj* zealous
zemos *adj* juicy
zero *n* zero
zestre *f* dowry
zgârcit *m* miser
zgâria *v* claw, scratch
zgârie-nori *m* skyscraper
zgârietură *f* scratch
zgomot *n* noise
zgomotos *adj* noisy
zgomotos *adv* noisily
zgudui *v* convulse
zguduit *adj* shaken
zi *f* day
zi de lucru *adj* weekday
zi de naştere *f* birthday
ziar *n* newspaper
zicală *f* saying
zid *n* wall
zidar *m* bricklayer, mason
zilnic *adj* everyday

zilnic *adv* daily

zimţ *m* dent

zinc *n* zinc

zmeu *n* kite

zmeură *f* raspberry

zonă *f* zone

zoologie *f* zoology

zori *m* dawn

zornăi *v* rattle

zumzăi *v* hum

zvârcoli *v* writhe

zvelt *adj* slender

zvon *n* rumor

Word to Word® Bilingual Dictionary Series

Language - Item #
ISBN #

Albanian - 500X
ISBN - 978-0-933146-49-5

Amharic - 820X
ISBN - 978-0-933146-59-4

Arabic - 650X
ISBN - 978-0-933146-41-9

Bengali - 700X
ISBN - 978-0-933146-30-3

Burmese - 705X
ISBN - 978-0-933146-50-1

Cambodian - 710X
ISBN - 978-0-933146-40-2

Chinese - 715X
ISBN - 978-0-933146-22-8

Czech - 520X
ISBN - 978-0-933146-62-4

Farsi - 660X
ISBN - 978-0-933146-33-4

French - 530X
ISBN - 978-0-933146-36-5

German - 535X
ISBN - 978-0-933146-93-8

Greek - 540X
ISBN - 978-0-933146-60-0

Gujarati - 720X
ISBN - 978-0-933146-98-3

Haitian-Creole - 545X
ISBN - 978-0-933146-23-5

Hebrew - 665X
ISBN - 978-0-933146-58-7

Hindi - 725X
ISBN - 978-0-933146-31-0

Hmong - 728X
ISBN - 978-0-933146-31-0

Italian - 555X
ISBN - 978-0-933146-51-8

Japanese - 730X
ISBN - 978-0-933146-42-6

Korean - 735X
ISBN - 978-0-933146-97-6

Lao - 740X
ISBN - 978-0-933146-54-9

Nepali - 755X
ISBN - 978-0-933146-61-7

Pashto - 760X
ISBN - 978-0-933146-34-1

Polish - 575X
ISBN - 978-0-933146-64-8

Portuguese - 580X
ISBN - 978-0-933146-94-5

Punjabi - 765X
ISBN - 978-0-933146-32-7

Romanian - 585X
ISBN - 978-0-933146-91-4

Russian - 590X
ISBN - 978-0-933146-92-1

Somali - 830X
ISBN- 978-0-933146-52-5

Spanish - 600X
ISBN - 978-0-933146-99-0

Swahili - 835X
ISBN - 978-0-933146-55-6

Tagalog - 770X
ISBN - 978-0-933146-37-2

Thai - 780X
ISBN - 978-0-933146-35-8

Turkish - 615X
ISBN - 978-0-933146-95-2

Ukrainian - 620X
ISBN - 978-0-933146-25-9

Urdu - 790X
ISBN - 978-0-933146-39-6

Vietnamese - 795X
ISBN - 978-0-933146-96-9

All languages are two-way:
English-Language / Language-English.
More languages in planning and production.

Order Information

To order our Word to Word® bilingual dictionaries or any other products from Bilingual Dictionaries, Inc., please contact us at (951) 296-2445 or visit us at **www.BilingualDictionaries.com**. Visit our website to download our current catalog/order form, view our products, and find information regarding Bilingual Dictionaries, Inc.

PO Box 1154 • Murrieta, CA 92564 • Tel: (951) 296-2445 • Fax: (951) 296-9911
www.BilingualDictionaries.com

Special Dedication & Thanks

Bilingual Dicitonaries, Inc. would like to thank all the teachers from various districts accross the country for their useful input and great suggestions in creating a Word to Word® standard. We encourage all students and teachers using our bilingual learning materials to give us feedback. Please send your questions or comments via email to **support@bilingualdictionaries.**